Unwin Education Books: 22

PRINCIPLES OF CLASSROOM LEARNING AND PERCEPTION

Unwin Education Books

Series Editor: Ivor Morrish, BD, BA, Dip. Ed. (London), BA (Bristol)

Unwin Education Books: 22
Series Editor: Ivor Morrish

Principles of Classroom Learning and Perception

RICHARD J. MUELLER
Northern Illinois University, De Kalb, Illinois

London
GEORGE ALLEN & UNWIN LTD
RUSKIN HOUSE · MUSEUM STREET

8981

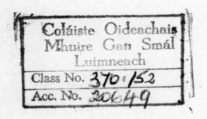
Printed in Great Britain
by REDWOOD BURN LIMITED
Trowbridge & Esher

For my daughter, Christine

Contents

Preface

WRITING A BOOK on the process of learning in the classroom poses a serious problem of selection. The field of educational psychology is vast; whole professional careers and entire books have been devoted to the study of specific areas of human behavior, as well as to the less behavior-oriented fields of educational measurement and statistics. I have attempted to approach the selection task from the point of view of the beginning teacher, teacher aide, or student teacher, who will eventually interact with elementary- or secondary-school-age youth in the classroom.

Although I hope that what the reader derives from this book will be directly useful in the classroom, it must be strongly emphasized that much of psychology—both behaviorist and perceptual—can at best only *explain* behavior. Explanations are not necessarily reality, nor can they be counted on to predict the future accurately. Often in the past, my former undergraduate students have returned to visit me and complained, "It wasn't at all what I had expected; kids are unpredictable—you never know what's going to happen next!" These students knew their subject matter very thoroughly; they naturally hoped that their erudition and eloquence would excite and amaze their pupils and that their newly acquired knowledge of psychology would solve their problems of classroom guidance. All too frequently, it didn't turn out that way. What they didn't want to remember from their beginning course in educational psychology was that behavior is complex. We simply do not know enough about the fundamental nature of the child.

Nevertheless, I believe that this text provides a first step. The teacher

x

who functions as a "behaviorist" (facilitator) in some situations and as a "perceptualist" in others has a fair chance to become effective in understanding and guiding children. Without *both* learning principles and some degree of perceptual awareness—plus a little common sense —the teacher may have little to offer regarding the reasons for a child's actions in the classroom except "The devil made him do it."

This text focuses on three major concerns. Part I, "The Process of Learning," is addressed to the principles of learning, language, and cognitive development as a basis for the more specific practices of the classroom.

Part II, "Psychology and the Child," considers three important sources of individual differences: perceptual processes, mental functioning, and personal adjustment. Each of these is a significant aspect of learning in the classroom.

Part III, "Factors in Classroom Learning," is devoted to the teaching-learning process itself—motivational problems, planning and managing instruction, performance assessment, and dealing with one of the schools' most serious problems, the culturally deprived or disadvantaged child.

This is not a "methods" book on how to teach school. Its purpose is primarily to supply introductory theoretical material (with some informal classroom applications), to be used along with seminars, small-group work, individualized assignments, and clinical or participatory experiences in schools.

But I have attempted to add "something else" to this text—namely, the point of view that teaching children can be exciting and challenging. In any field, any introductory text that is worth its salt should not only inform and educate but also "hook" the reader. It is my hope that this book will inspire talented young people to make a strong career commitment to the profession of teaching.

RICHARD J. MUELLER

De Kalb, Illinois
January, 1974

Acknowledgements

A NUMBER OF my colleagues at Northern Illinois University made valuable contributions to this book, and I wish to extend grateful appreciation to them. Jerry Johns provided substantial help and advice on Chapter 4. Leonard Kise prepared the material on Jean Piaget on which Chapter 3 is based, explaining a very complex subject in a way that will have meaning for prospective teachers. Tom Roberts provided both ideas and content for the section on humanistic psychology in the final chapter. My thanks go to many others in the College of Education for suggestions and advice, as well as for the use of their reference materials.

A special word of appreciation is due to Don Ary and Charlie McCormick for their considerable help throughout the manuscript—especially with Chapter 10, on performance assessment—and in the preparation of the test manual.

I want to express heartfelt appreciation to Praeger editor Gladys Topkis for her skill and wise counsel throughout the odyssey of this writing. I have learned the value of a good editor.

Finally, I want to mention the names of two individuals to which the genesis of this book can be traced. Dr. James B. Stroud, Professor Emeritus of the University of Iowa, provided a most important first career step toward the field of educational psychology and research. Above all, to my doctoral advisor, Dr. L. A. Van Dyke, recently retired Associate Dean of the University of Iowa College of Education, I acknowledge a great debt of gratitude for the professional leadership and personal support he has given me since my first association with him as a graduate student at the University of Iowa. From him to me, as well as to many others, has flowed a great personal commitment to the field of education.

Editor's Note

THIS American text has been left virtually unchanged since it is felt that most English students, in the course of their reading, will come into contact with a large number of American books and will be familiar with both American spelling and expression. The reader should note, however, that throughout this work the term 'public school' connotes 'state school' and not some form of private school; in addition, American educators talk about 'math' where we use the abbreviation 'maths'.

No attempt has been made to translate terms such as 'elementary', 'senior high', 'sophomore', and so on, into the nomenclature of the English educational system. Instead, this brief note is followed by a simple diagram adapted from one published by the American Information Bureau. This diagram shows, as accurately as any such diagram can, the differences between the American and the English systems of education. This should be of use as a reference point throughout the reading of the book; but it will also be of interest from the point of view of the student involved in comparative and cross-cultural study.

The author's original references have been retained throughout, although it is recognized that many of the books and articles referred to will not be readily available to the English student. A section has, however, been added at the end of the book providing special bibliographies to supplement the references in each chapter. In most cases these books are to be found in academic libraries in this country.

IVOR MORRISH

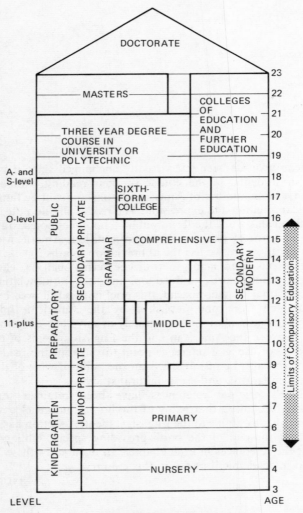

ENGLISH SYSTEM OF EDUCATION

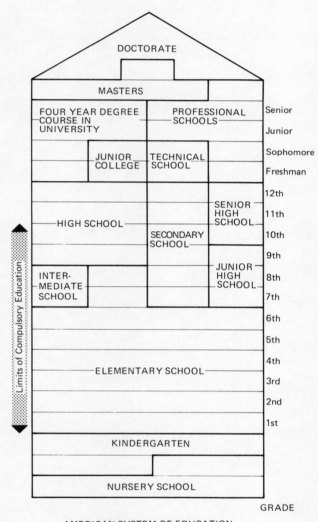

AMERICAN SYSTEM OF EDUCATION

Within the diagram:

DOCTORATE

MASTERS

FOUR YEAR DEGREE COURSE IN UNIVERSITY — PROFESSIONAL SCHOOLS — Senior / Junior

JUNIOR COLLEGE — TECHNICAL SCHOOL — Sophomore / Freshman

HIGH SCHOOL — SECONDARY SCHOOL — SENIOR HIGH SCHOOL — 12th / 11th / 10th

INTER-MEDIATE SCHOOL — JUNIOR HIGH SCHOOL — 9th / 8th / 7th

ELEMENTARY SCHOOL — 6th / 5th / 4th / 3rd / 2nd / 1st

KINDERGARTEN

NURSERY SCHOOL

Limits of Compulsory Education

GRADE

PART 1

The Process of Learning

CHAPTER ONE

The Scope of Educational Psychology

MAN LEARNS BEST what he most urgently needs and wants to know. He also learns best what he feels good about. There is little doubt that the future welfare of our nation and perhaps even its survival as a nation and as a world leader will depend on how successfully our schools teach young people to profit from what man has learned about himself and his planet and to generate new ways of solving both old and new problems.

The objective of educational psychology is to discover, explain, and apply knowledge to the educative process. But, before we can design and implement an effective educational program for the child, we must understand how he thinks and acts and feels. This is a formidable mission, for nothing is more complex than the behavior of a human being. Yet, ironically, so important a concern as the nature of a child was not considered a scientific subject worth studying until the late nineteenth century. Of all the applications of the scientific method of inquiry, the study of man's psychological nature has been among the last to develop.

THE ORIGINS OF EDUCATIONAL PSYCHOLOGY

Educational psychology began during the latter half of the nineteenth century as a part of the expanding field of psychology itself. Such individuals as E. L. Thorndike studied the learning and retention of school subjects, in the hope of building a body of theory that would describe the basic learning processes. From this, they believed, would flow the power to predict and ultimately control or change human learning in the direction of positive goals. The difficulties of achieving this goal were readily apparent. An eminent educator, William James, expressed the view of many of his time: Teaching will always remain more an art than a science. Nevertheless, the study of educational psychology began to grow.

Except for the work of Thorndike, who formulated several laws of learning that have stood well the test of time, psychology in those early days was limited in both theory and scientific method. Much research dealt with reflex actions and other basic aspects of physical behavior. Some of the early efforts at theory building drew on ideas originally advanced by Aristotle, which later served as a foundation for modern experimental psychology. Another source, the new field of psychoanalysis, led by the Viennese physician Sigmund Freud, gave us a dynamic view of human thought and behavior while it explored the problems of psychosis and neurosis. Eventually, psychoanalytic theory contributed to educational psychology by casting new and penetrating light on the nature of the child's internal forces, the role of fear in learning, and the diagnosis and control of deviant behavior.

THE PREDICTION OF HUMAN BEHAVIOR

Most of those in the mainstream of educational psychology have believed that the key to learning and behavior lies in the research methods and tools of the physical sciences. Science has enabled man to predict, control, and offer increasingly accurate explanations of the world around him. Without prediction there can be no control, and without prediction and the possibility of control, explanation is meaningless. Obviously, the better our explanations or theories, the more sensitive our predictions will become and the greater will be our ability to bring about constructive change. The methods of science require that behavioral as well as physical scientists be objective in their pursuit of knowledge.

The behavioral scientist begins the process of developing theories by making first-hand observations, studying achievement-test results or responses made to items on a questionnaire, or examining the results of any other way of measuring human or animal behavior. How the investigator feels or believes is not acceptable scientific evidence. Nor can conclusions reached by logic alone be accepted as scientific truth. A person who believes that all tall people are born leaders because he has seen many people in leadership positions who are tall is basing his conclusions on inadequate observation and logic. Beliefs such as "gifted children are usually weak and underdeveloped physically" or "high-strung people are more sensitive and artistic by nature" are oversimplifications rejected by scientists because they do not square with evidence from the scientific study of behavior.

Scientific investigation is a combination of theory, shrewd guesswork, and painstaking, thorough gathering of data. Usually, the more the scientist knows about the subject at hand, the more accurate is his guesswork, or hypotheses. Most theories are a refinement of theories that preceded them, so that the development of a body of scientific knowledge is really the process of developing better and better research questions. As long as a hypothesis does not have 100 per cent predictive value, it remains a hypothesis. When it has been so thoroughly supported by evidence that it *always* turns out as predicted, then it is no longer a theory but a law. Newton's original theory of gravity is now a law because it yields perfect prediction. When a celestial body appears to resist gravitational force, the explanation is sought elsewhere than in the possibility of a breakdown in the theory itself. To cite an example from psychology, as we will see later in this text, the so-called reinforcement principle is no longer a hypothesis, because its basic validity is no longer questioned. What *is* under investigation is the dynamics of reinforcement phenomena—how they function. Furthermore, although the principle itself is supported by substantial research, it frequently fails to predict behavior in real-life situations—in other words, it does not always work. Nevertheless, as with gravity, the reason is sought elsewhere, because so many complex factors operate in human behavior that any one factor or combination of factors can nullify the effects of a principle of behavior such as reinforcement.

INFORMAL LEARNING

A primitive society has little need for an educational psychologist. Everything the child must learn is reinforced by social sanction. Life in a primitive society is much more homogeneous and closely knit than life in a civilized community. What one child must learn, all must learn. Learning is informal and tied in with daily tribal life. The child is expected to learn (1) the skills of food gathering, hunting, and fishing and (2) the religious customs and beliefs of the tribe. To the child in such a society, it is quite obvious that both areas of subject matter must be mastered if he wants to join the adult world. Failure to do so will result in starvation, exclusion from tribal activities, or both. The child is motivated to learn the curriculum of his society because he is rewarded for doing so, and the reasons for performing the activities are *intrinsic* to the activities, not extraneous to them.

Our society, by contrast, makes much greater demands on the child. There is much more to learn, and the child is expected to take longer to learn it. Furthermore, the American child in elementary school is not so clearly aware of the survival value of what he learns. For example, he is exhorted by his parents to learn to read, and his teacher tells him how his life will be enriched by reading, but from his frame of reference there is little direct connection between reading and meeting his primary needs. Even the "tribal customs" of an American family do not appear to be a compelling reason for learning to read. After all, plenty of people appear to get along quite well with very little reading. In modern society, the child must accept the value of reading largely on faith.

As Margaret Mead (1943, p. 634) has stated:

> There are several striking differences between our concept of education today and that of any contemporary society, but perhaps the most important one is the shift from the need for an individual to learn something that everyone agrees he would wish to know to the will of some individual to teach something which it is not agreed that anyone has any desire to know.

Our society is diverse. Variable home environments, parental values, life-styles, and other culturally related forces influence the motivation of children—but not uniformly. In addition, the relationship of formal schooling to life usually becomes apparent quite late in the educational process. Even many high-school students have difficulty making a connection between what they study in school and what appear to them to be the demands of daily life, and this contributes to large differences in attitudes toward school. Partly as a result, the outcomes of our educational system become ever more variable, even though schools are moving closer to providing equal educational opportunities for all children. In the first week of first grade, every child is confronted with about the same curriculum, but the products that finally emerge at the end of the process some twelve years later range from near illiterates to highly sophisticated National Merit Scholarship winners.

To be sure, there are instances of strong motivation and much informal learning in the home, on the playground, and even in school. I doubt that anyone has ever found it necessary to study the motivational problems involved in getting kids to turn out for baseball in the spring.

The home, too, is a motivational source because the reward and punishment system is so closely tied to the personal needs of the child.

But the school poses a special problem. Education serves not merely to preserve and perpetuate the cultural heritage but also to advance it, to raise the cultural level of society by leading the child to new skills and understandings—much of which the child is not ready for in the sense that he actively seeks them. Can our schools continue to use the pressures of competition to get children to study and still provide the conditions that lead to a spontaneous desire to learn?

The teacher today is faced with two emerging conditions: the explosion of knowledge, and the growing size and complexity of the classroom scene. There has been a fantastic growth of subject matter in all fields, and new fields are introduced almost every year. The teacher must deal with an awesome accumulation of information, much of which is labeled "crucial" for survival. Furthermore, basic skills, such as reading and study techniques, are now a requirement for everyone regardless of economic or cultural level. We need especially to discover how to make the learning of basic skills more efficient and less time-consuming, so that more teacher effort can be devoted to promoting self-directed learning by students.

In addition, there is a growing concern for treating each member of our society as an individual—not as a faceless unit within a mass of people. Government, institutions, military groups, communities, clubs, and schools have always been forced to deal with people in groups—whether the individuals involved liked it or not. When there were fewer people on this planet and life was much simpler, there was a more personal sea of humanity in which to swim. In fact, for most people, the world was not much larger than a pond. Today, the individual has to contend with an ever larger urban mass, and he can very easily begin to lose sight of himself as a distinctive human being. Many in our society have reacted to this situation by developing diverse life-styles, characterized largely by affective responses to environmental forces. The primary objective of these life-styles seems to be to put greater emphasis on the individual and what he himself believes is best for him. Because schools have usually prescribed what is best for young people in terms of the requirements of society, self-determined behavior patterns inevitably come into conflict with traditional school practices. In the past, schools relegated social and emotional development largely to extracurricular programs, but now there appears to be a growing interest in allowing more personal involvement and values in the classroom itself.

It is the task of the teacher to understand and perhaps to help reconcile the personal, emotional needs of the individual child and the expanding educational requirements and depersonalizing social forces. This will require answers to many new questions. For example, to what extent is freedom compatible with learning? When is it better to learn something on one's own terms, spontaneously, than to do so by traditional, teacher-centered methods of instruction? At what age can a child begin to take active responsibility for his own learning in school? When is he mature enough to make really important choices? These are some of the questions that are being asked by many leaders in education and other elements of society. The study of educational psychology may bring prospective teachers and school administrators to a more analytical understanding of these new and dynamic concerns, and perhaps help to mediate them.

THE TEACHER AS BEHAVIORIST

The traditional role of the teacher has been as a conveyor of academic subject matter and an instructor in basic skills. But the subject-matter requirements for a teaching certificate have increased tremendously since the nineteenth century. Then, the typical public-school teacher was likely to have the equivalent of a high-school education. Today, four or more years of university course work are required. Of these, a few professional education courses and a stint of student teaching are all that is mandated to prepare teachers for classroom responsibilities. Yet, both the teacher's role and the conditions of learning are in a state of ferment. New resources for learning are becoming available, many of which are designed for the student's individual use. Students are being grouped in different ways as schools adopt team teaching, individually prescribed instruction, and automated, or programmed, learning. New buildings and facilities are being constructed that include television, electronic learning laboratories, computer systems, and dial-access information and problem-solving systems. Many teachers have an ever expanding array of alternatives from which to choose the learning activities, resources, and spaces required to accomplish defined learning outcomes.

Instead of being an information giver, the teacher is becoming a facilitator of learning. As a consequence, many schools—both elementary and secondary—are beginning to base their teaching on an instructional design model that identifies and arranges all the components of the instructional program, from objectives through performance assessment. Although this is usually referred to as a systematic approach, it is also a behavioral approach, because it focuses on observable, measurable learning outcomes.

In order for a total instructional design system to work, the characteristics of the learner must be identified—especially those that affect his capacity and willingness to learn. In order to achieve this, the teacher-facilitator of learning should know something about (1) the principles of human growth and development, (2) the principles and practices of learning, and (3) the principles of measurement and evaluation of abilities and achievement. Most of these principles are drawn from the field of general psychology, but other fields contribute as well. The teacher needs to know something of the social forces in the community through the study of sociology. The fields of physiology and genetics provide insight into inherited characteristics and the pattern of a child's physical growth and development. Psychiatry and the principles of mental health offer the teacher a theoretical basis as well as valuable clinical procedures in working with children in the emotional realm. In fact, any field that studies aspects of human behavior has something to contribute to the teacher's role as a facilitator of learning.

Behaviorist psychologists especially have built up an extensive and complex body of theory and research that provides an objective and scientifically verifiable description of much of human development and learning. In general, behaviorist psychology provides (1) a language and vocabulary for the study of behavior, (2) a scientific method of inquiry into questions relating to learning and behavior, (3) a body of generalizations and principles of behavior that serve as research hypotheses, and (4) various instruments and techniques for the measurement of human characteristics, skills, and abilities.

THE TEACHER AS PERCEPTUALIST

If we associate science with an objective, somewhat cold and impersonal approach to the attainment of knowledge, then behaviorism is essentially scientific in nature. But there are many who believe that the mind and consciousness of man are neglected in such a scientific and external approach.

"Perceptualism," as used in this book, refers to the analysis of behavior on the basis of the premise that the child's attitudes and actions are largely manifestations of innate perceptual and cognitive processes. The perceptualist views the child in the classroom as the source of acts that the child is essentially free to choose in each situation. The child is controlled by his own consciousness. According to the perceptualist, the most appropriate methodology for the study of the child, therefore, begins with a look at the child's own inner world of experience.

The value of perceptualism lies in its attempt to get "under the skin" of the individual child—to understand what causes him to act and why he perceives people and events around him as he does. Every new teacher quickly notices how unpredictable and irrational youth can be. Children easily evade our neat preconceptions of what they will do next, and the application of behaviorist principles of learning may or may not result in the expected outcomes. Furthermore, to regard the child scientifically as a "behaving organism" does not do him total justice; each child is also a thinking, feeling human being with individual characteristics, needs, experiences, and aspirations.

In fact, research evidence indicates that the best teachers tend to be sensitive to the needs, feelings, and perceptions of children, in addition to being knowledgeable and skillful in using teaching techniques (Biddle and Ellena, 1964; Amidon and Flanders, 1963). One way to achieve this sensitivity is for the teacher to become an active, continuous inquirer into the effectiveness of his own procedures. The professional, career-committed teacher always questions his own teaching methods and makes continual efforts toward self-improvement. As Coladarci (1965, p. 490) puts it:

> Our schools cannot keep up with the life they are supposed to sustain and improve unless teachers, pupils, supervisors, administrators, and school patrons continuously examine what they are doing. Singly and in groups, they must use their imagination creatively and constructively to identify the practices that must be changed to meet the needs and demands of modern life, courageously to try out those practices that give better promise, and methodically and systematically gather evidence to test their worth.

Another, related objective of the teacher should be to develop his own "style" of teaching. It is a mistake to expect all beginning teachers to prepare for the identical teaching role. There are teachers who are effective with a strict, no-nonsense approach and others whose effectiveness results from a highly personal and informal teaching style. But, regardless of style, every teacher possesses personal characteristics, knowledge, and skills that are uniquely his own. He uses these qualities to reach his students more effectively. Thus, we may define the effective teacher formally as *a unique human being who has learned to use himself effectively and efficiently to carry out his own and society's pur-*

poses in the education of others (Combs, 1967, 1972). To accomplish this, the teacher must accept the fact that the child's inner state of consciousness, his accumulation of feelings and attitudes—the personal, hidden "agenda" that he brings to every class—are significant factors that must be taken into account if learning is to be facilitated.

The point of view of this book is that the teacher should function as a *facilitator* of learning whenever feasible, along the lines of behaviorist principles, and that learning is best facilitated when the teacher is aware of and responsive to each child's perceptions of the learning assignment. To help the prospective teacher perform the role of facilitator, this book will expose him to those basic learning principles of behaviorism that appear to have the closest relationship to the classroom. Perceptual theory will be used to sensitize the prospective teacher to the *personal* world of the child.

REFERENCES

AMIDON, E. J., and N. FLANDERS. 1963. *The role of the teacher in the classroom*. Minneapolis: Pauls Amidon & Associates, 56–62.

BIDDLE, B. J., and W. J. ELLENA (eds.). 1964. *Contemporary research on teacher effectiveness*. New York: Holt, Rinehart & Winston.

COLADARCI, A. P. 1965. Relevancy of educational psychology. *Educational Leadership*, 13, 489–92.

COMBS, A. W. 1967. *The professional education of teachers*. Boston: Allyn & Bacon.

———. 1972. Some basic concepts for teacher education. *Journal of Teacher Education*, 23(3), 286–90.

MEAD, M. 1943. Our educational emphases in primitive perspective. *American Journal of Sociology*, 48, 633–39.

CHAPTER TWO

Behaviorism in the Classroom

LEARNING is something we do almost every moment of the day as we assimilate and adapt to the environmental influences around us. Learning takes place in a wide variety of situations and at all levels of animal life—from the conditioned reflexes of lower animals to the complex thinking processes of man.

Early evidence of learning among very low forms of life was reported by Day and Bentley (1911), who found that paramecia can, after repeated trials, reduce the time required for them to turn around in a capillary tube. More recent investigations show that the planarium, a simple flatworm, can be conditioned to respond to a stimulus of strong light (Thompson and McConnell, 1955). Although lower forms of life can learn, their learning is limited and slow. By comparison, the human child learns quite rapidly, although he requires a long period of infancy before he reaches the level of maturity necessary for independent survival.

The most popular definition of learning among behaviorist psychologists is that it is a change of behavior. Or, as Cronbach (1963, p. 71) stated, learning is shown by a change of behavior as a result of experience.

What is meant by "change of behavior"? If someone begins to react to a stimulus in an observably different way and continues this changed reaction over a period of time, he has learned something. From the standpoint of psychology, any change of behavior is considered an indication that something has been learned, whether or not the new behavior is desirable or useful. *Educational* psychology, however, focuses largely on changes of behavior that are positive and desirable—usually within the context of school objectives.

EARLY BEHAVIORISM: ASSOCIATIONISM

For nearly a half century, the learning theories of one man dominated all others in America. In his book *Animal Intelligence* (1911), Edward L. Thorndike announced that the basis of learning was the association between sense impressions and impulses to action. This association came to be known as a "bond," or "connection." In Thorndike's view, learning was the strengthening or weakening of these bonds. As he described it, learning was largely a matter of habit formation.

Thorndike identified the most characteristic form of learning for both lower animals and man as trial-and-error learning. The learner is confronted by a problem situation—frequently escape from a problem box. After trying a number of possible solutions, he hits on the right one and is rewarded by escape or by food. A trial is defined by the length of time (or number of errors) it takes the subject to attain the right solution. The important element involved is *motivational arousal*. The learner has to gain something from what he does.

> . . . practice without zeal—with equal comfort at success and failure— does *not* make perfect, and the nervous system grows away from the modes in which it is exercised with *resulting discomfort*. When the law of effect is omitted—when habit-formation is reduced to the supposed effect of mere repetition—two results are almost certain. By the resulting theory, little in human behavior can be explained by the law of habit; and by the resulting practice, unproductive or extremely wasteful forms of drill are encouraged. [Thorndike, 1913, p. 22.]

Thorndike believed that learning was largely a matter of "stamping in" correct responses and "stamping out" incorrect responses as a result of, respectively, rewarding or annoying consequences. Thus, he postulated the *Law of Effect*, which held that the learner would tend to repeat, and therefore learn, those responses which are followed by satisfying consequences and that adverse aftereffects (punishment) or the absence of aftereffects would lessen the tendency for the individual to repeat behavior.

Although Thorndike originally assumed that reward and punishment work in "equal and opposite" ways, he later concluded that punishment was relatively ineffective. As we shall see, research on this subject has shown that punishment, in fact, has variable effects. For example, punishment produces a temporary suppression of activity in rats; but, after punishment is terminated, punished animals require *more* trials to extinguish their behavior than those that have not been punished.

Thorndike's experiments with animals had a profound influence upon his theories of how people learn. Because he considered the essential nature of animal learning to be associationist, he tended to believe that animals lacked a capacity for ideas. With humans, too, Thorndike tended to minimize the ideational functions. Although his theories regarding learning no longer occupy the center of the field of psychology, and although some of the teaching practices to which he lent support —for example, strong emphasis on drill—are now considered obsolete, nevertheless the influence of Thorndike's associationism is still present in both theoretical formulations and classroom practices.

CLASSICAL CONDITIONING AND RESPONDENT BEHAVIOR

Not all human behavior is a result of conscious learning. If a person touches a hot stove, he is likely to withdraw his hand hastily. Food placed in the mouth produces the response of salivation. These are unlearned responses, but under some circumstances we might respond in the same way to a different set of stimuli. A sharply spoken "Hot!" produces a quick withdrawal of the hand, even though the command in itself is not painful or dangerous. At the end of a long day of teaching active adolescents in the classroom, just hearing the words "broiled steak" or "dry martini" may cause the teacher to salivate a little. In other words, when one event evokes a particular response and that event happens often in the presence of another event, or stimulus, then the second stimulus alone will come to elicit the same response. This is called *classical conditioning*.

Conditioning as a psychological principle originated in the work of Ivan Pavlov (1849–1936), a Russian physiologist. Pavlov was interested in the functioning of the digestive organs—among other things, in the causes of the flow of saliva into the mouth. This response is the result of activity of the salivary glands, and it is mediated by the autonomic nervous system. Pavlov discovered that, when a bell was sounded at the same time as a hungry dog was confronted with food, eventually, after many repetitions, the sound of the bell alone caused the dog to salivate. The food was the *unconditioned stimulus*, and salivation was the *un-*

conditioned response. Ultimately, the bell—the *conditioned stimulus*—directly elicited a *conditioned response*—salivation.

An important effect in classical conditioning, and one that is of great significance in understanding how young people develop attitudes and values, is *stimulus generalization*. This occurs when a conditioned response is elicited by a stimulus that resembles the original stimulus but is not identical to it. Thus, a response previously made to one stimulus will now be made to a different stimulus. In other instances, the old stimulus will come to elicit a different response. These deceptively simple changes have implications of major importance for the understanding of learning in the classroom; to the extent that a response can be shifted from one stimulus to another, behavior can be changed.

"Stimulus-response contiguity" constitutes a fair description of much of classroom practice. For example, teachers often write words on the board and then ask pupils first to say each word aloud and then to spell it aloud. The assumption is that saying the word aloud eventually will be a sufficient stimulus to produce the correct spelling at appropriate times. Much foreign-language instruction involves this practice—associating the sound of a word with the proper spelling or naming a number of objects and later asking the child to state the names of the objects as they are placed before him.

Some psychologists maintain that a good deal of human behavior can be explained in terms of classical conditioning. Staats and Staats (1957), for example, have demonstrated that nonsense syllables, if learned in association with words that already possess a pleasant or an unpleasant connotation, acquire the emotional significance of those words. Frequently, we call a child "bad" or "lazy" while punishing him, or "good" while rewarding him. The child in this way not only receives punishment or reward but may also learn the meaning of the words that accompany these actions.

Most attitudes are learned by classical conditioning, or contiguity. While children are attaining a given level of achievement in a skill or academic subject, they are also acquiring—through conditioning—a set of attitudes toward what they are studying. Too much emphasis on the former can result in a negative outcome in the latter; the two outcomes have to be in balance. For example, a math teacher might be willing to accept a lower level of accuracy or punctuality from a particular child in order to make the math sessions a little less tense and more enjoyable for him. Many experts—Arthur Combs, for example—say that a child's feelings about a subject may have a more significant effect on him later, when he is out of the control of the school, than the subject-matter standards the teacher maintains. These experts say that too

These experts say.

many children who work hard in class to achieve standards avoid the subject after they graduate.

Stimulus-response contiguity has sometimes been used incorrectly to justify such classroom practices as rote memorization and repetitive drill; in fact, other conditions are also necessary for learning at the human level. Furthermore, in classical-conditioning theory, the learner is regarded as essentially passive, with little control over whether certain stimuli occur in conjunction with one another. Thus, in research experiments, the experimenter decides what kind of stimulus substitution to make. Similarly, in the classroom, the teacher can decide whether to make positive or negative remarks during instruction.

In the early years of the Soviet Union, educational planners were very much impressed by Pavlov's discoveries relating to classical conditioning. Soviet leaders hoped that conditioning theory could provide a guide and a rationale for practices to improve the attitudes of Soviet children toward their new government. (Their focus was on the children because the parents were thought to require more direct methods.) Experiments such as the following were tried:

At mid-morning in a Soviet elementary school, about the time the children were ready for a milk-and-cookies break, the teacher might open the window and let in a wintry blast, turn the lights down, and call attention to the children's faint hunger pangs. Then the teacher would point to a picture of the "Little Father"—Czar Nicholas II—and state quite clearly that "this is the way Russian peasants felt when *he* was our leader." Then she would lead the children to a warm, brightly lit, cheerful room with smiling attendants who proceeded to pass out milk and cookies. While the children received these rewards, the head teacher would give them a short lecture on their new leader, Lenin, whose picture was displayed at the front of the room. "See, this is the way you will be treated under our new leader. Everybody will be well fed and happy." (So far as I know, there is no objective evidence that these rather crude attempts to implement classical conditioning in the classroom created favorable attitudes toward the Soviet regime, but it seems reasonable to suppose that they had at least some effect on the children.)

INSTRUMENTAL CONDITIONING

Learners are not always passive; often they are able to figure out what they must do in order to achieve satisfaction from their environment. Classical conditioning, as we have seen, is characterized by stimulus substitution, so that feelings of dread once aroused by punishment and disapproval from the math teacher, for example, are now aroused by the mere sight of an arithmetic book. The original stimulus has become generalized to other stimuli associated with math instruction. Instrumental conditioning, on the other hand, is characterized by response substitution: The child learns to replace an unsuccessful response with one that will result in satisfaction, or reinforcement.

It may be helpful to approach the principle of instrumental conditioning by looking first at the four fundamental components of learning: *drive, cue discrimination, response*, and *reinforcement*. These components are illustrated by the following experiment:

The subject is a girl six years old. It is known that she is hungry and wants candy. While she is out of the room, a small flat piece of her favorite candy is hidden under the bottom edge of the center book on the lower shelf of a bookcase about four feet long. The books in the center of this row are all dark in color and about the same size. The other shelves contain a radio, some magazines, and a few more books.

The little girl is brought into the room; she is told there is a candy hidden under one of the books in the bookcase and asked if she wants to try to find it. After she answers, "Yes," she is directed to put each book back after looking under it and is told that if she finds the candy, she can eat it.

Immediately after receiving these instructions, the little girl eagerly starts to work. First, she looks under the few books on the top shelf. Then she turns around. After a brief pause, she starts taking out the books on the lower shelf, one by one. When she has removed eight of these books without finding the candy, she temporarily leaves the books and starts looking under the magazines on the top shelf. Then she returns to look again on the top shelf under several of the books that she has already picked up. After this, she turns toward the experimenter and asks, "Where is the candy?" He does not answer.

After a pause, she pulls out a few more books on the bottom shelf, stops, sits down, and looks at the books for about half a minute, turns away from the bookcase, looks under a book on a nearby table, then returns and pulls out more books.

Under the thirty-seventh book which she examines, she finds the piece of candy. Uttering an exclamation of delight, she picks it up and eats it. On this trial, it has taken her 210 seconds to find the candy.

She is sent out of the room, candy is hidden under the same book, and she is called back again for another trial. This time she goes directly to the lower shelf of books, taking out each book methodically. She does not stop to sit down, turn away, or ask the experimenter questions. Under the twelfth book she finds the candy. She has finished in 86 seconds.

On the third trial, she goes almost directly to the right place, finding the candy under the second book picked up. She has taken only 11 seconds.

On the following trial, the girl does not do so well. Either the previous spectacular success has been due partly to chance, or some uncontrolled factor has intervened. This time the girl begins at the far end of the shelf and examines 15 books before finding the candy. She has required 86 seconds.

Thereafter, her scores improve progressively until, on the ninth trial, she picks up the correct book immediately and secures the candy in three seconds. On the tenth trial, she again goes directly to the correct book and gets the candy in two seconds . . . .

Her behavior has changed markedly. Instead of requiring 210 seconds and stopping, asking questions, turning away, looking under magazines, searching in other parts of the room, picking up wrong books, and making other useless responses, she now goes directly to the right book and gets the candy in two seconds. She has learned. [Dollard and Miller, 1950, p. 26.]

The dramatic manner in which this child's behavior changed is illustrated in Figure 2.1.

The first factor involved in learning is *drive*. Unless the child wants candy, the experiment will probably fail. Drive impels her to act, or respond. But, before the child began responding by removing books in search of the candy, she had to choose from a wide array of *cues*: the directions, the setting of the room, the position of the books, and so on. Possible specific cues to the response of picking up a given book are its color, size, and markings and its position in the bookcase.

Of course, the child must be capable of executing the third factor: *response*.

This brings us to the fourth factor: *reinforcement*. The child's first impulse was to look under a book on the top shelf, but this did not result in candy; she was not rewarded—that is, the response was not reinforced. Reinforcement is essential to learning, according to most behaviorist theories of learning. Because the girl received no reinforcement, the unsuccessful response was weakened and is unlikely to reappear.

She began to respond almost at random, but she had a purpose in mind. Finally, one of her responses was followed by finding and eating the candy. The response was thus reinforced. We can assume that in later trials she will be closer to choosing the right book—that is, making the right response—because of the reinforcement. In behaviorist terms, the reward has strengthened the connection between the cues and the rewarded response.

The candy must be a truly rewarding morsel for the child. Quite pos-

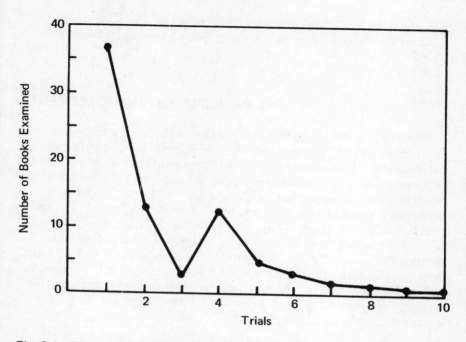

Fig. 2.1. The elimination of errors. On the first trial the child looks under thirty-six wrong books and makes other incorrect responses not indicated on the graph before finding candy under the thirty-seventh book examined. Errors are gradually eliminated until on the ninth and tenth trials the child makes only the one response of going directly to the correct book. (From John Dollard and Neal E. Miller, *Personality and Psychotherapy*, New York: McGraw-Hill, 1950, p. 28.)

sibly, after a number of successful searches for candy, she will begin to feel less interested. She may have become satiated.

The entire process can be summarized as follows:

The drive impels responses, which are usually also determined by cues from other stimuli not strong enough to act as drives but more specifically distinctive than the drive. If the first response is not rewarded by an event reducing the drive, this response tends to drop out and others to appear. The extinction of successive nonrewarded responses produces so-called random behavior. If some one response is followed by reward, the connection between the cue and this response is strengthened, so that the next time that the same drive and other cues are present, this response is most likely to occur. This strengthening of the cue-response connection is the essence of learning. [Dollard and Miller, 1950, p. 29.]

THE PRINCIPLE OF REINFORCEMENT

As we have noted, it was first believed that behavior is "stamped in" by reinforcement and "stamped out" by punishment, for this appeared to be consistent with common sense. Reinforcement theory now states that *any* event that occurs immediately after the response will function as a reinforcement—more or less. Although the reinforcing experience is generally a pleasant one, the experience may be unpleasant and still function as a reinforcement. Imagine, for example, a situation in which a child is learning to spell. Each time he spells a word correctly, he is given a small electric shock. This shock may be unpleasant to him, but, because it indicates that he has spelled a word correctly, it may increase the probability that he will give right answers in the future. In this respect, "reinforcement" is a neutral term that does not identify an experience as pleasant or unpleasant.

THE PARTIAL-REINFORCEMENT EFFECT

Most current theories of learning consider reinforcement to be essential to the process of strengthening behavior tendencies. It is generally assumed that, the greater the number of reinforced trials, the stronger will be the stimulus-response bond, until that habit has reached its maximal strength. It is further assumed that habits that are not followed by immediate reinforcement will diminish in strength. Operationally, this means that the stronger the habit, the greater the number of nonreinforced trials necessary to "extinguish" the response fully. Yet, it is well established that behavior acquired through *partial* reinforcement is more resistant to extinction than behavior acquired through 100-per-cent reinforcement schedules. Psychologists have advanced several explanations for this apparent contradiction in reinforcement theory, but these explanations tend to be rather complex and not easily subjected to experimental verification.

Although this so-called PRS (partially reinforced stimulus) phenomenon is most observable in animal behavior, there is reason to believe that it also operates to a great extent in humans. This means, in effect, that, if someone who has been performing at a certain level of motivation and receiving consistent rewards is later *not* rewarded at various times, his motivation may actually increase—at least for a while. Of course, if the frequency of reward drops to zero, motivation will also drop to zero. But, for a while, a decrease in reinforcement may raise his level of frustration and concern so that he will actually work harder at the task.

PUNISHMENT VERSUS EXTINCTION

Although instrumental conditioning is often associated with positive reinforcement, it may also involve negative reinforcement—i.e., punishment, through the administration of stimuli that the individual usually tries to avoid. Reinforcement may result from the occurrence of a positive reinforcement or from the termination of a negative reinforcement. Thus, we can increase a person's motivation to repeat a particular act by following it either with a positive reinforcement or with the removal of an obnoxious condition.

In many instances, after an undesirable act by the student, the teacher has to ask himself, "Should I follow that act with immediate punishment, or should I simply ignore (extinguish, or *non*reinforce) it?" Although the circumstances actually may decide the issue, it might be helpful for the teacher to understand what is involved psychologically. The evidence strongly suggests that punishment serves to suppress the inclination to act temporarily, whereas nonreinforcement (extinction) contributes a great deal more to the permanent elimination of the tendency to respond in that way (Estes, 1944). About all that punishment accomplishes is to postpone the occurrence of the number of non-reinforced responses that are required for permanent extinction. Of course, punishment often does work—under certain circumstances. In some cases, response tendencies can be inhibited permanently by the use of very severe, traumatic punishment. And punishment may be desirable—even necessary—when a particular act by the student, if not put to an immediate stop, would be hazardous either for him or for others around him (Rislen, 1968). Nevertheless, there is evidence that excessive punishment may fixate rather than eliminate the tendency to behave in a particular way. Punishment is most effective when it forces the student to substitute a better way of acting, for which the teacher can provide a reward and thus bring about a satisfactory outcome to the entire sequence of behavior.

BEHAVIOR MODIFICATION

Peter, a four-year-old boy with a borderline IQ (70–80), who had been diagnosed by a psychologist as having possible brain damage, exhibited extremely objectionable behavior: kicking objects or people, removing or tearing his clothes, and frequently losing his temper.

Peter's behavior eventually was changed by his mother, working with an observer trained in behavior-modification techniques. The observer would clue the mother on when to punish, ignore, or reinforce Peter's actions. Within a few days, his objectionable behavior dropped to near zero and the relationship between Peter and his mother improved. Both Peter and his mother became more sure of themselves.

An elementary-school class had difficulty settling down to work. Although the bell had rung, many children were still in the hallways or milling around the room. When they sat down to study, many of them had difficulty paying attention to their work for any significant length of time.

The behavior of the children in the elementary school was changed by rewarding students each time they exhibited desirable actions. Their reward was a brightly colored token, called a "snerkle," with which the students could rent sports equipment or art supplies and "buy" their recess. (Students who did not have enough "snerkles" had to remain in the classroom during recess.) When the students entered the classroom on time, each received a "snerkle" for being punctual. Each received another "snerkle" if he began to work immediately and more "snerkles" at approximately ten-minute intervals if his behavior—in the judgment of the teacher—had been acceptable during that period. Those who had been looking around, daydreaming, or engaging in some undesirable behavior during the ten-minute period did not receive a reward.

The behavior of both Peter and the elementary-school class was modified by a carefully administered system of rewards, or positive reinforcement. Desirable acts were immediately followed by a reward; undesirable acts were, whenever possible, not followed by rewards—that is, the behavior was ignored, or extinguished (Hawkins, Peterson, Schweid, et al., 1966).

Behavior modification is based on learning theory—specifically, the principle of reinforcement, or instrumental conditioning. This theory was not developed to provide a rationale after the fact but was used as a basis for the technique. Actually, behavior modification was not invented by psychologists; circus animal trainers have been using the technique for centuries. Recent experimental studies have dramatized its potential use for humans, on the basis of the fact that we all live in a system of reward-and-punishment contingencies. Reinforcers surround us everywhere: Whether by a smile or a slap, a new car or a traffic fine, we are all constantly being reinforced by others in our social environment. If the environment is a place of employment, these "others" are our bosses or colleagues; if the environment is a hospital, they are nurses, doctors, or other patients; if it is the family, they are our siblings, parents, or spouse; if it is a school, they are the principal, teachers, or other students. All these people are "reinforcers," for they have the power to administer rewards or withhold them. Behavior-modification strategies center upon the technique of *contingency management*, which may be defined as the rearrangement of environmental rewards and punishments that strengthen or weaken specified behavior (Skinner, 1973).

Behavior modification focuses on the symptoms or outward manifestations of behavior; it is not primarily concerned with the causes of behavior. That is to say, the rationale does not assume that the behavior is symptomatic of some more obscure force. MacMillan (1973, pp. 3–40) reports that behavior modification is being used in hospital settings with severely disturbed, retarded, and brain-damaged subjects; with juvenile delinquents in their own neighborhood environments; and with normals in a variety of fields that include nursing, clinical psychology, social work, and education.

There are basically five reinforcement manipulations that a classroom teacher can make—two positive, two negative, and one extinctive. The teacher can reinforce positively by giving a reward or removing an unpleasant situation, negatively by issuing a punishment or removing a rewarding situation, and extinctively by ignoring behavior.

From research evidence it is safe to generalize that positive reinforcement is much more effective than negative reinforcement (*Encyclopedia of Educational Research*, 1969, pp. 715–17; Altman and Linton, 1971). The teacher should use primarily the positive approaches—approval or withholding of approval—as opposed to disapproval and ignoring. This does not mean that the teacher should at all times be permissive, but he should avoid the use of punishment, which often suppresses behavior but does not remove the desire to misbehave and may result in the substitution of other unwanted responses.

An important factor in behavior modification is time. For rewards to be effective, they must occur immediately. Furthermore, it is important to correct a deviant behavior as early as possible, since any delay can cause it to become firmly established.

The teacher must maintain consistency in modifying behavior—a difficult task in a busy classroom. Once the structure is set up, with a set of rules and rewards, the teacher must follow through. If the teacher is inconsistent, the child will feel that it is acceptable for him to break the rules. In other words, the teacher's inconsistency results in partial reinforcement of a child's unacceptable behavior, which is the most difficult to extinguish.

Madsen (1973) has suggested four steps for teachers to follow in dealing with overt behaviors. It is necessary to *pinpoint* exactly what behavior is to be eliminated or established. The teacher must then arrange a hierarchy of skills and behaviors based upon specific goals. The second principle is to *record* precisely what occurs. With an accurate account, the teacher has a record of the elimination of undesired acts and can then devote time to more productive teaching. The third principle is to *"consequate,"* to set up the external environmental contingencies, such as approval and withholding of approval. The fourth principle for the teacher is to *evaluate*, having kept his techniques of behavior modification in practice long enough to determine their true effectiveness.

PROGRAMMED INSTRUCTION

The principle of reinforcement provides the psychological rationale for another development in education: programmed instruction. The learning materials used allow for constant feedback—knowledge of success—to the learner as he proceeds through the learning sequence. Programmed materials may include specially designed textbooks, audiovisual materials and equipment, and teaching machines ("hardware"). In all these forms, the material is presented as a sequence of items, or frames. Successive frames call for only small steps, or increments, in learning, so that the student will make few or no errors and will receive many reinforcements. The student must construct a response after each frame, with prompts and cues provided to ensure that he will make the correct response. This process is referred to as shaping behavior by reinforcement.

What differentiates programmed materials from conventional teaching? Two features: First, the student is required to make *observable, measurable responses;* he must be active in learning at all times. Second, he receives *immediate knowledge* of the correctness of each response. That is a very important feature because delayed reinforcement makes it difficult for the learner to know what he has done right—that is, to "fix" his behavior.

The application of the reinforcement principle to education received a very strong impetus in 1954 through an article by B. F. Skinner, "The Science of Learning and the Art of Teaching." Skinner had been active in the analysis of instrumental, or operant-conditioning, principles. He outlined the application of these principles to instruction in spelling and arithmetic in programmed sequences managed by a teaching machine.

The method may be stated as follows:

1. Clarify the final behavior desired and identify the sequence of steps essential to achieve the final objective.
2. Get the student to make the initial response through imitation, prompting, or cueing.
3. Take the student through the steps leading to the final behavior. The student must make overt responses, and the steps must be small to ensure that the correct responses are made.
4. Reinforce the responses by an appropriate schedule, so that responses are strengthened and the material is retained. For most students, knowing they have answered correctly is sufficient reward.

Programmed materials are designed so that students may work through at different rates, with the result that all may be expected to learn the material well, regardless of their cognitive abilities and other characteristics.

Skinner avoids the development of general learning theories, preferring, instead, to analyze actual behavior. The phenomena of stimuli, response, and reinforcements are identified by the roles they play. The study of learning in a particular situation identifies the events that constitute these concepts; hence, Skinner and his followers describe their work as "analysis of behavior."

According to Skinner, defining objectives in behavioral terms, designing effective classroom contingencies, and programming instructional materials may be all that is needed to solve many current problems in education (1973, p. 453). He presents a convincing argument in his extensive writings that the inefficiency of current teaching procedures is the result of poor reinforcement techniques in the classroom. For example, in 1969 he wrote:

The number of reinforcements required to build discriminative behavior in the population as a whole is far beyond the capacity of teachers. Too many teachers would be needed, and many contingencies are too subtle to be mediated by even the most skillful. *Yet relatively simple machines will suffice.* The apparatus is adapted from research on lower organisms. It teaches an organism to discriminate selected properties of stimuli while "matching to sample." Pictures or words are projected on translucent windows which respond to a touch by closing circuits. A child can be made to "look at the sample" by reinforcing him for pressing the top window. An adequate reinforcement for this response is simply the appearance of material in the lower windows, from which a choice is to be made. . . .

If devices similar to these were generally available in our nursery schools and kindergartens, our children would be far more skillful in dealing with their environments. They would be more productive in their work, more sensitive to art and music, better at sports and so on. They would lead more effective lives [p. 143].

THE IMPLICATIONS OF REINFORCEMENT

The principle of reinforcement has had a tremendous influence on psychologists engaged in the study of learning, and its impact goes far beyond the psychology laboratory. The principle has aroused widespread interest among teachers, social workers, and others in the so-called helping professions. The notion that, if an individual does something and is rewarded, the reward will cause him to repeat his behavior is, of course, a common-sense notion that has been around for a long time. Psychology has given it scientific validity and respectability (MacMillan, 1973).

Some educators, however, have been reluctant to employ tangible reinforcement with normal children in the classroom, largely because of fear that many of the children will become "hooked" on external reinforcement so that they will not perform without it (Anderson, 1967). This apprehension was not supported in a study by Rosenfeld (1972), who exposed 60 sixth-graders to both regular classroom reinforcement and extrinsic reinforcement in the form of money and feedback (knowledge of results) from a chart. The extrinsic reinforcement improved the children's math performance, yet their subsequent performance was not affected when they were given only regular classroom reinforcement. Research evidence on this question is still sparse, however, so perhaps no clear conclusion can be drawn at this time.

It is very possible that in the larger scheme of things, material types of incentives do play a more central role in the lives of the economically and culturally disadvantaged. Speculations about such matters, however, should not place excessive reliance on the experimental findings of laboratory studies. Even within the microcosm of the laboratory, their influence on behavior is too complex to be encompassed by any simple generalization, and the variables determining their effects are yet to be fully explicated. [Spence, 1971, p. 1469.]

Acceptance of the reinforcement principle in the classroom has been affected by another, much more emotion-laden factor—namely, that this principle seems to regard the child as if he were an object to be manipulated. Our religious and philosophical ideals have always held that the individual is God-given, mystical, unique. To regard him as a mere organism to be shaped and controlled by such banal means as extrinsic reinforcement collides with current child-rearing tenets and practices, as well as with our entire edifice of ideals and values about children. Giving a child a piece of candy for every vocabulary word he spells correctly strikes many people as something straight from a futuristic science-fiction plot.

We live in a time of strong feelings regarding civil and personal rights, and many people are understandably sensitive about any treatment of children that appears to be yet another instance of the creeping automation of the human personality (Thoresen, 1973). Ironically, behavioral psychology is in the business of trying to help us learn more about how to be humane and sensitive to one another. Yet, the public at large—especially rights-conscious people and political groups—is not easily convinced. Somehow, the closer psychology gets to direct application of research findings to people—especially children—the more the specter of manipulation threatens, in the opinion of many. Of course, almost all educational innovation has aroused suspicion and in some cases even malice in the public. Perhaps programmed instruction and behavior-modification techniques arouse so much controversy precisely because they are so firmly based on scientifically verifiable evidence. This makes them doubly threatening to those who are anxious about the possibility of thought control in the schools. It is evident that programmed instruction and behavior modification in the schools must gain acceptance on moral grounds—regardless of their scientific validity—before implementation can become widespread.

LEARNING AND RETENTION

Suppose that an adolescent is learning to type. If the level of difficulty of the material to be typed remains constant, his progress can be measured by the number of errors he makes per page per period. A graph showing the rate of improvement can then be plotted. The curve would represent where the student began, what he had achieved at the end of each week, and during what periods his progress was most rapid. Of course, this graph would measure only accuracy of typing. It would not indicate his proficiency relative to speed or the neatness and evenness of the typing.

Research indicates that learning curves are roughly S-shaped (Travers,

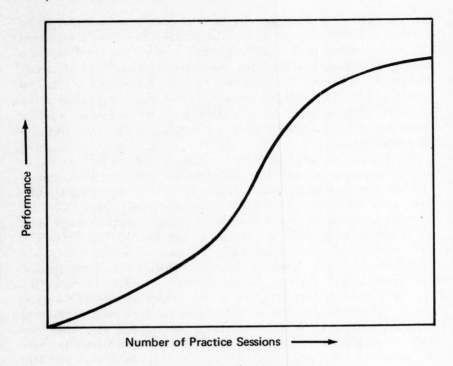

Fig. 2.2. Theoretical learning curve.

1967, chap. 10). (See Fig. 2.2.) In the learning of complex skills, progress at first is rapid, followed by an apparent tapering off—called a *plateau*—then a slight increase to what is referred to as the *physiological limit*. The decrease in progress during the second stage may be just temporary. Sometimes it means that the learner has acquired certain component skills and now must integrate these components. A beginning golfer, for example, may be able to drive the ball straight but with little power, and he may also be able to hit the ball far but with poor accuracy; now he must learn to hit the ball both straight and far. This second stage, then, generally requires a new approach to the task if the learner is to make further progress.

From a motivational standpoint the plateau is a dangerous stage, because the learner must now carefully analyze what he is doing in order to begin improving again. Mouly (1968, p. 314) offers several explanations for learning plateaus:

1. It may be necessary to reorganize previous learnings into a new pattern before further progress can evolve. In typing, for example, one has to move from typing one letter at a time to typing a word at a time and to typing a phrase at a time. Thus, a plateau may represent a period of actual progress, even though performance does not show it.

2. The learner may have to replace bad habits before he can advance to a higher level of achievement.

3. His lack of progress may be caused by decreased motivation or emotional tenseness, which prevents him from using his abilities effectively.

4. The task may not be one of uniform difficulty throughout.

5. Undue attention to one of the subaspects of the total performance may be throwing the performance out of kilter. This is particularly true when the subaspects are learned separately and have to be put together into an integrated performance.

6. Plateaus may also reflect the transition from one performance limit to another.

Even when optimal conditions have been provided and the learner is putting forth maximal effort, there will eventually be a leveling off of performance. This so-called physiological limit is not easily determined, because what may be considered the absolute peak of performance often becomes merely another landmark as new records are set. A dramatic example is the four-minute mile, once thought to be unattainable. In recent years, training techniques have improved to such an extent that it has become a fairly common event for an athlete to run a mile in four minutes—or less!

No matter how efficient the learning, however, it all would be useless effort if little were retained. Sometimes one forgets the specifics of a situation, such as a street name and house number, but retains the appearance of the particular street and house. What is learned is retained to varying degrees depending on a number of factors that operate in the learning situation.

There are several ways of determining retention. The *recall* method is familiar to every teacher. On an essay examination, the student has to reach into his storehouse of facts and concepts and reproduce the correct answer. Motor skills, too, are measured by requiring the examinee to perform certain operations from memory.

A second method, *recognition*, applies mostly to the measurement of cognitive memory. The multiple-choice item is an example of measuring retention by recognition: The student chooses the right response from four or five plausible alternatives. It is much easier to recognize the

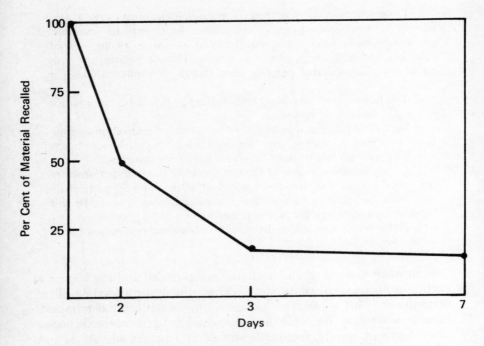

Fig. 2.3. Curve of retention for nonsense syllables. (From L. F. Cain and R. Willey, "The Effect of Spaced Learning on the Curve of Retention," *Journal of Experimental Psychology, 25* [1939] , 209-14. Copyright 1939 by the American Psychological Association. Reprinted by permission.)

right answer from among a number of cues than to recall the right answer from only a few cues, as in an essay examination. Nevertheless, recognition-type tests are capable of eliciting a wider sample of what has been learned.

The most sensitive measure of memory is the *relearning*, or *savings*, method. Suppose, for example, that an Army trainee requires twenty training sessions to learn a given level of skill in setting up and firing a mortar. After a period of time, the degree to which he remembers this skill is measured by determining how many training sessions are now required for him to reach his former level of proficiency. If it now takes the trainee only ten training sessions, or trials, to reach proficiency, the savings are 50 per cent. The soldier has remembered half of what he learned.

The amount of time it takes most people to forget what they have just learned tends to follow a distinct pattern, or curve. (A typical curve of retention is shown in Fig. 2.3.) There is a marked drop immediately after learning, followed by a tapering-off period, then a level of retention that remains fairly constant for some time.

Although there are obvious individual differences in learning ability among children, it does not necessarily follow that similar differences are present in memory—contrary to what is commonly believed. Shuell and Keppel (1971) studied the extent to which individuals differed in their ability to remember after they had been equated for degree of original learning. They found that, at least for the 99 fifth-graders in the study, differences in the rate of forgetting between fast and slow learners are very small when degree of original learning is taken into account. In other words, the slow learner can remember what he has learned just about as well as a very bright learner. In a later study, Shuell and Giglio (1973) confirmed the finding that bright children seem to have better memories mostly because they are able to learn so well and to apply what they have learned.

The fact that the slow learner has good memory potential is at least part of the reason that many curriculum experts do not advocate courses of study for slow students that are markedly different from those for the very swift. It is argued that every student can learn the basic principles of algebra, for example; it simply takes some students longer to do so, and it also takes different teaching methods.

HELPING THE LEARNER TO REMEMBER

Retention is facilitated most readily when the student understands and accepts the goal he is striving for, especially when it holds personal meaning for him. To use a term that we return to later (Chapter 5), it means bringing the activity into the child's "perceptual field." This is most easily done with school subjects and skills that the child perceives as directly useful to him. A sixth-grade boy will retain the technique of pitching a curve ball learned in a physical-education class if he feels that it gives him a good chance for a key position on a Little League team. Learning the fundamentals of set theory in modern math has less urgency for him, and he is likely to forget the specifics rather quickly unless he has been provided with some opportunities to use them.

Practice sessions that are distributed, or spaced, over a period of time are usually better for retention than massed practice. Probably the reason is that spaced learning promotes a deeper grasp of the content. Also, short sessions have advantage in that longer practice periods may cause fatigue and tension and thus may reduce the learner's concentration and resourcefulness in achieving a good performance. Duncan

(1951) found that, when students were given rest periods equivalent to two thirds of the total practice time, there were no detrimental effects on final performance even though the rested group had only one third as much actual practice as the control group.

Furthermore, distributed practice tends to be a more efficient method of learning when there is a great deal of material and much of it is not particularly meaningful, when the probability of erroneous responses in the early stages is high, or when motivation is likely to be low.

On the other hand, changing from one activity to another is time-consuming, especially when it requires getting out a lot of equipment, "suiting up," or a warm-up period. These disadvantages have to be weighed against the disadvantages of lengthening the learning sessions. The time between sessions should be neither so long that excessive forgetting takes place between sessions nor so brief that wrong responses do not have sufficient time to drop out, as, for example, in the learning of vocabulary and grammar in a foreign language.

Although research has generally favored short, spaced learning sessions over massed practice as the best aid to retention, this is by no means an unassailable principle. Many schools have found that in some circumstances "total immersion" in an activity can occasionally be highly beneficial. For this reason, many schools have adopted flexible time patterns to allow some extended class periods during each week. In physical-education classes, for example, teachers have found that the traditional fifty-minute period often allows insufficient time for meaningful activity. In fact, since so much of physical education involves changing and showering, a large part of physical-education instruction seems to be devoted to locker-room skills! A once- or twice-a-week double or triple session allows the class to carry through an entire sequence of activities: getting equipment and donning proper attire, warming up, intensive play, and a critique of the game.

Another problem of interest to teachers is whether more is learned— and retained—by reading and rereading material than by devoting some of that time and effort to recitation. Experimental research rather conclusively indicates that, because of the immediate feedback and the overt rather than the passive nature of the learning, recitation activities are more beneficial than rereading, particularly from the standpoint of delayed recall. Forlano (1936) found that one can profitably spend up to 80 per cent of the total learning time in recitation.

OVERLEARNING

If learning is defined as the ability to perform an act, recite a page of verse once from memory, or repeat a list of words, then any amount of practice beyond the required level is called *overlearning*. If a child learns multiplication tables in twenty repetitions, thirty repetitions make it more likely that he will be able to recall and repeat the tables after a period of time has elapsed. Experimental results show that over-learning results in more accurate retention over a longer period of time than practice which ceases at the point of initial learning (Holland and Porter, 1960).

The gain from overlearning tends to decrease as additional practice continues, although in some cases overlearning may cause the individual literally to be unable ever to forget what was learned. For example, many veterans can recall almost instantly the serial number assigned to them when they were in military service, although they never had any need for it in civilian life.

In the primary grades, where specific skills, such as reading and arithmetic, are emphasized, overlearning is employed through drill, repetition, and review. At the secondary level, however, there seems to be too little overlearning, probably because teachers are not so inclined to concentrate in one area of learning, preferring, instead, to direct students toward the acquisition of many broad concepts and problems.

I once had a vivid experience with overlearning while teaching En-glish grammar to high-school sophomores. One day, after casually re-marking on the traditional taboo against ending a sentence with a preposition, I inadvertently committed the offense myself. A clever student named Barbara quickly pointed out the error—much to my embarrassment! Red-faced, I tried to make a joke of it and found an opportunity, later, to catch her in the same offense. During the next few years, in the many conversations I had with her, the incident developed into a game of friendly retaliation. Each of us would listen to the other for a sentence ending in a preposition to impale him, or her, *with*. Years later, Barbara said that, as a result, she had never forgotten that point of grammar in either speaking or writing; it was indelibly inscribed in her memory.

TRANSFER OF TRAINING

"He doesn't practice what he preaches" is a common expression. True, much of what people are "taught" is really not "learned" in the sense that it is ever used in the situations for which it was intended. As Socrates astutely remarked, for someone to know virtue does not guarantee that he will practice it. Every English teacher has ruefully noted that students frequently spell words correctly in a spelling test and then misspell them in a theme assignment. The entire educational process is based on the assumption that there will be a transfer of training from what is learned in formal education to situations outside the classroom. In this sense, unfortunately, much education is quite inefficient.

According to McGeogh and Irion (1950), "Transfer of training occurs whenever the existence of a previously established habit has an influence upon the acquisition, performance, or relearning of a second habit." For example, transfer is presumed to occur when skill in tennis helps one to learn badminton, or when newly acquired typing skill seems to have an effect on piano keyboard technique.

The notion of transfer is not new in educational practice; its historical predecessor is the doctrine of *mental discipline*, which stressed the necessity for developing the "sinews of the mind." According to this nineteenth-century theory, the "faculties" of the mind can be trained in much the same fashion as the muscles of the body are strengthened through exercise. It was believed, for example, that there is a faculty for memory, a faculty for reasoning, a faculty for artistic expression, and a faculty for judgment. (Contemporary research indicates that this element of the earlier theory was not entirely erroneous; certain generalized areas of the brain do function primarily in certain mental activities.) Just as one's biceps can be strengthened by lifting barbells, the mind, it was believed, can be strengthened by taking on "heavy" academic subjects. The harder the mental exercise, the more disciplining effect it would have on the faculties. The subjects thought to be best for training the mind were Latin, Greek, mathematics, and science.

Psychologists early in the twentieth century put the mental-discipline theory through extensive experimental tests. One of the areas investigated was the claim that Latin is especially good for developing the mind. If so, then students who take courses in Latin should become better problem solvers and abstract reasoners than those who do not. Actually, students who take Latin *are* better problem solvers—but not as a result of studying Latin. Most of them tend to be better students to begin with. When compared to students of like ability and motivation who have not been exposed to Latin, they reveal few differences in subsequent problem solving and abstract reasoning.

Studies have even raised questions about the supposed effect of learning Latin on English vocabulary. Douglass and Kittelson (1935) found no significant differences in students' knowledge of English grammar, spelling, and vocabulary between those who had studied Latin and those who had not. A similar study conducted by Pond (1938) also found no relationship between the learning of Latin and improvement in English vocabulary.

It is important to add that, although the proponents of mental discipline have abandoned the claim that certain academic subjects "train" the mind, they continue to believe strongly that a positive attitude toward academic subjects and learning in general is transferred, that the mastery of difficult subjects contributes to a stronger self-concept and a willingness to think reflectively (Bagley, 1922). This claim appears to have considerable merit, although it has not been amenable to experimental testing.

As the doctrine of mental discipline lost credibility, early behaviorists began to formulate a systematic theory of transfer. Thorndike was one of these. As mentioned earlier, Thorndike believed that learning is the formation of a bond or connection in the nervous system between an input on the stimulus end and an output on the response end. According to this theory, transfer of training takes place when one stimulus-response connection transfers to another one much like it. The effectiveness of the transfer is related to the extent to which tasks resemble one another. For example, skill in playing the piano may transfer to typing. In other words, transfer occurs to the extent that the learner can carry certain aspects of his previous learnings to a new situation, which is then only partially novel. Sometimes this involves learning a principle in one context and then seeing how it can be applied in another.

An early demonstration of the principle of transfer of training was a famous study by C. H. Judd (1936). Two groups of boys were asked to throw darts at targets under water. One group was given an explanation of the principle of refraction but the other was not. After they had mastered the task of hitting the target under 12 inches of water the boys were asked to throw darts at another target lying under 4 inches of water. Since the boys were standing at an angle to the target, the change in the level of water also changed the amount of refraction. This changed the apparent position of the target. The group that had been told the principle of refraction adapted more rapidly to the second task than did the other group. They had *transferred* the use of the principle from one task to another. Taking a known principle and extending it to cover new situations, Judd emphasized, was the essence of transfer. In Judd's view, transfer was most likely to occur when a generalizable principle was involved. He nevertheless emphasized the importance of specific, concrete experiences. Actual experience in shooting at one water level was necessary before the experimental group could do better than the group that lacked knowledge of the principle.

This ability to transfer a principle from one situation to another is very important in learning. Also of great importance in transfer is a positive attitude on the part of the student, a conviction that his previous skills and knowledge are useful for solving future problems.

The learner must be taught to be transfer-conscious by being provided with numerous opportunities to try out what he knows.

Early experiments on transfer, such as those carried out by Thorndike, suggest that there is no way of ensuring that transfer of training will occur. From the vast amount of research on the subject, the following points have implications for the classroom:

1. Students should master subjects as thoroughly as possible if there is to be carryover from the classroom to other situations. This means that teaching a subject in depth probably is more beneficial than attempting to cover a wide area of subject matter. However, the disadvantage of this method is that there will be significant gaps in the student's knowledge. With the current knowledge explosion, the pressure to "cover the ground" may be too great for the teacher to resist.

2. To facilitate transfer, the student should be exposed to a wide range of problems that differ somewhat from one another. This will encourage flexibility in thinking, since the student develops an expectation that each problem will have to be solved in a way that is somewhat different from the solution of previous problems.

3. The teacher should put heavy emphasis on principles and their application. Principles are likely to be retained and used when students are given opportunities to try them out in a variety of problem situations.

4. Finally, as we have pointed out, much of the transfer that educators and parents expect as a result of education does not appear to take place. A significant factor is motivation—the *need* to transfer, or use, what is learned. (As we will see in Chapter 5, perceptual theory offers explanations and some possible solutions to the problem of getting the learner to transfer what he has learned.)

COMPLEX BEHAVIOR: SKILLS AND PROBLEM SOLVING

Problem solving, reasoning, and *thinking* are terms used more or less synonymously to refer to a broad variety of mental skills, including inductive and deductive processes, the synthesis of isolated experiences, the ferreting out of relationships, the reorganization of cognitive structure, and the like. Previously, we have been discussing learning in the sense of acquiring knowledge and skills—such as spelling words or learning to type. These involve learning to make correct responses in the presence of certain stimuli, such as a test question. Problem solving refers to learning of essentially the same kind but different in degree and emphasis. As formulated by John Dewey in 1933, problem solving comprises the following steps of critical thinking:

Awareness of the Problem. Problem solving is initiated not by the emergence of a problem in an objective sense but, rather, by what Dewey called a "felt need," the perception of a problem as related to one's needs and purposes. Such a problem is more than an idea to be manipulated; it is a challenge to the student's self-concept. If he is sufficiently ego-involved to feel discomfort because the problem is not solved, he will apply all his effort and judgment toward seeking the solution. If he is not thus involved, the problem is really not his but is merely labeled by the teacher as "problem."

Development of the Hypothesis. Having become aware of a problem, the learner must be able to state precisely what its components are and what steps must be followed to solve it. The hypothesis may come as a sudden insight, or it may be developed step by step.

Testing of the Hypothesis. Does the hypothesis work? Does it fit all the facts? Is it consistent with this principle, with this finding? The factors that make for effective hypothesis testing include intellectual and experiential background, flexibility, originality, and—not least—a critical judgment that prevents the individual from jumping to wrong conclusions.

Generalization. Problem solving is not complete until the individual has identified the areas and conditions in which his solution holds and the areas and conditions in which it does not. In other words, can these findings be generalized beyond this situation? If so, it can provide a basis for both understanding and scientific progress.

MEDIATIONAL RESPONSES

When the individual has mastered these steps, what has he learned, in a psychological sense? Psychologist Harry Harlow says that what has developed is a *learning set*. The learner, in effect, has figured out what to look for, what to expect, and this will help him when the next problem appears.

The phenomenon of learning set has been demonstrated by Harlow in numerous experiments involving both monkeys and human subjects. In the typical Harlow experiment (1949), a monkey is trained to discriminate between two objects: a cube and a solid triangle. Under one of them is a raisin—his reinforcement. The monkey soon learns that, in every trial, the raisin is under the cube and not under the triangle. Having mastered the problem, he is then confronted with another one. This time both objects are cubes, but one is black and one is white. He must now learn a new discrimination, which he does, followed by another problem, and so forth. After a long series of such problems, the monkey reaches the stage where he makes the discrimination with great speed and requires very few trials compared with the first problem. He has learned that the raisin is always under the same one of the two objects in every problem. According to Harlow, he has acquired a "learning set" for solving problems of this kind.

Research along similar lines suggests that children, too, reach a stage in their development where they are able to abstract the essential principle, or rule, involved in a problem and use it to solve other problems of a similar nature. Some behavioral psychologists claim that this involves *mediational responses,* which in children correspond to that stage in language and conceptual development when they begin to use words as a means of understanding and communicating events and ideas rather than merely as a way to transmit and receive sensory information.

Even if the child understands the concept of *animal* as applying to most of the four-footed creatures he has had contact with, he may not be ready to understand that "animal" is a *class* of creatures having certain characteristics in common. As he gains more experience, however, he realizes that animals are part of an entire group of living creatures, including man, who inhabit various places on the earth.

Experimentation with chickens, pigeons, rats, and other infrahuman organisms has demonstrated that at least some creatures learn to respond consistently to such geometric forms as triangles, squares, or circles, even when the shape or color of the form is changed from time to time. This suggests that these animals can grasp the abstract concepts of squareness, triangularity, or circularity. In perceptual terminology, they have achieved an insight into the principle that governs these shapes. This principle helps the learner to grasp the common element in squares, triangles, or circles of various sizes and colors. Osgood (1963) has argued that a rat's ability to distinguish triangles of various sizes and colors from squares or circles constitutes a common "mediating response" that the learner makes to all sets of stimuli belonging to a particular conceptual category. It is a concept of squareness that the animal responds to; it has learned to recognize square shapes, even though they are altered in size or color. In fact, when the square is altered and begins to approach unrecognizability as a square, the animal exhibits difficulty deciding whether to continue responding to it as if it were a true square.

Further support for Osgood's contention that concept formation is

FIRST DISCRIMINATION   SECOND DISCRIMINATION

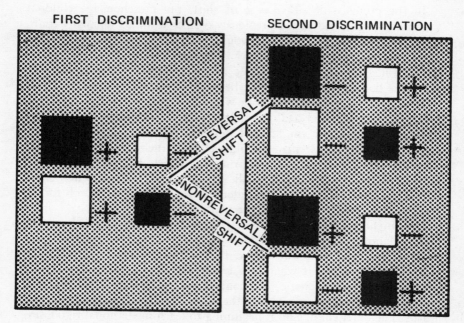

Fig. 2.4. Examples of reversal and nonreversal shifts in discrimination learning. In a reversal shift, after learning to select the large stimuli in the first discrimination, the subject is reinforced for selecting the small stimuli in the second discrimination. In a nonreversal shift, he is required to respond to another dimension (brightness) in the second discrimination. (From H. H. Kendler, *Basic Psychology*, 2 d ed., New York: Appleton-Century-Crofts, 1968, p. 376.)

dependent upon the learning of a common mediating response is provided by studies of children's behavior conducted by Howard and Tracy Kendler (1959, 1962, 1964). Children in two age groups were involved in an experiment based on *reversal* and *nonreversal shifts*. (See Fig. 2.4.) The stimuli were squares of different sizes and colors. Their responses to the "correct" stimulus—for example, the larger square—were reinforced by the awarding of a colored marble. After they were accustomed to responding in this way, two types of shift were made. With the reversal shift, if they had been selecting the *larger* square, the rules of the game were changed. They now had to respond to the smaller square in order to get the reward. Thus, size was the relevant characteristic, regardless of color. In the *nonreversal* shift, color, not size, was the relevant characteristic.

In the presence of either type of shift, the preschool-age children continued to respond to the previously correct stimulus for many trials. Like the lower animals, these young children made simple, direct responses, and this pattern of behavior, once established, had to be extinguished before a new response could be made. However, the preschoolers had less difficulty with the nonreversal shifts than the older children did. Presumably, black or white had been right *half* the time, so that the young child had only half a "habit" to extinguish. With the older child, for whom the reversal shift was easy, the nonreversal shift caused difficulty. Apparently, the older child learned more than a simple response; he learned a rule, or principle, which helped him on the reversal shift: "large but not small." This helped him to switch sizes. With the nonreversal shift, the older child was forced to search for an entirely new rule: "black but not white."

We might say that the elementary school is the level at which, for want of another term, children learn to think. They no longer respond to stimuli in a simple, direct way; they are beginning to gain insight into the significance of what they learn. They are becoming aware of an important characteristic of a concept: its *generalizability*. Whereas the very young child may learn that $2 + 2 = 4$, this is about all he learns. The older child, who is beginning to learn mediational responses, is likely to understand that "2-ness" plus "2-ness" equals "4-ness." This concept will help him to use numbers as a tool for wider applicability, such as $20 + 20 = 40$, $200 + 200 = 400$, and so on.

According to the Kendlers (1964), the relative speed with which both rats and children execute reversal and nonreversal shifts is evidence of mediational behavior in forming concepts. Appropriate mediating responses facilitate the transfer of conceptual understanding from one situation to another. And as children grow older, from about three to ten years of age, their ability to execute reversal shifts increases.

REFERENCES

ALTMAN, K. I., and T. E. LINTON. 1971. Operant conditioning in the classroom setting: A review of the research. *Journal of Educational Research*, 6, 277–85.

ANDERSON, R. C. 1967. Educational psychology. In P. H. Mussen and M. R. Rosenzweig (eds.), *Annual review of psychology*. Palo Alto, Calif.: Annual Reviews.

BAGLEY, W. C. 1922. *The educative process*. New York: Crowell-Collier & Macmillan.

CRONBACH, L. J. 1963. *Educational psychology*. New York: Harcourt, Brace & World.

DAY, L. M., and M. BENTLEY. 1911. A note on learning in paramecium. *Journal of Animal Behavior, 1*, 167.

DEWEY, JOHN. 1933. *How we think*. Boston: D. C. Heath.

DOLLARD, J., and N. E. MILLER. 1950. *Personality and psychotherapy*. New York: McGraw-Hill.

DOUGLASS, H. R., and C. KITTELSON. 1935. The transfer of training in high school Latin to English grammar, spelling, and vocabulary. *Journal of Experimental Education, 4*, 26–33.

DUNCAN, C. P. 1951. The effect of unequal amounts of practice on motor learning before and after rest. *Journal of Experimental Psychology, 42*, 257–64.

Encyclopedia of Educational Research. 1969. New York: Macmillan.

ESTES, W. K. 1944. An experimental study of punishment. *Psychological Monographs, 57*, 263.

EYSENCK, H. J., and R. JURGENS. 1959. Learning theory and behavior therapy. *Journal of Mental Science, 105*, 61–75.

FORLANO, G. 1936. School learning with various methods of practice and rewards. *Teacher College Contributions to Education*. New York: Teachers College, Columbia University.

HARLOW, H. F. 1949. The formation of learning sets. *Psychological Review, 13*, 673–85.

HAWKINS, P., et al. 1966. Behavior therapy in the home. *Journal of Experimental Child Psychology, 4*, 99–107.

HOLLAND, J. G., and D. PORTER. 1960. *The influence of repetition of incorrectly answered items in a teaching-machine program*. Paper presented to the American Psychological Association, Harvard University, Cambridge, Mass.

JUDD, C. H. 1936. *Education as cultivation of the higher mental processes*. New York: Macmillan.

KENDLER, H. H., and T. S. KENDLER. 1962. Vertical and horizontal processes in problem-solving. *Psychological Review, 69*, 1–16.

KENDLER, T. S. 1964. Verbalization and optional reversal shifts among kindergarten children. *Journal of Verbal Learning and Verbal Behavior, 3*, 428–36.

KENDLER, T. S., and H. H. KENDLER. 1959. Reversal and non-reversal shifts in kindergarten children. *Journal of Experimental Psychology, 58*, 56–60.

MCGEOCH, J. A., and A. L. IRION. 1950. *The psychology of human learning*. New York: Longmans, Green.

MACMILLAN, D. L. 1973. *Behavior modification in education*. New York: Macmillan.

MADSEN, C. K. 1973. Values versus techniques: An analysis of behavior modification. *Phi Delta Kappan, 54*(9), 598–601.

MOULY, G. J. 1968. *Psychology for effective teaching*, 2nd ed. Atlanta: Holt, Rinehart & Winston.

OSGOOD, C. E. 1963. Psycholinguistics. In S. Koch (ed.), *Psychology: A study of science*. New York: McGraw-Hill.

POND, F. L. 1938. Influence of the study of Latin on word knowledge. *School Review, 46,* 611–18.

RISLEN, T. R. 1968. The effects and side effects of punishing the autistic behaviors of a deviant child. *Journal of Applied Behavior Analysis, 1,* 21–34.

ROSENFELD, G. W. 1972. Some effects of reinforcement on achievement and behavior in a regular classroom. *Journal of Educational Psychology, 63,* 189–93.

SHUELL, T. J., and J. GIGLIO. 1973. Learning ability and short-term memory. *Journal of Educational Psychology, 64*(3), 261–66.

SHUELL, T. J., and G. KEPPEL. 1971. Learning ability and retention. *Journal of Educational Psychology, 61,* 59–65.

SKINNER, B. F. 1954. The science of learning and the art of teaching. *Harvard Educational Review,* Spring, *24,* 86–97.

———. 1969. Why we need teaching machines. In R. C. Sprinthal and N. A. Sprinthal (eds.), *Educational psychology: Selected readings*. New York: Van Nostrand-Reinhold.

———. 1973. The free and happy student. *Phi Delta Kappan, 55*(1), 13–16.

SPENCE, J. T. 1971. Do material rewards enhance the performance of lower-class children? *Child Development, 42,* 1461–70.

STAATS, C. K., and A. W. STAATS. 1957. Meaning established by classical conditioning. *Journal of Experimental Psychology, 45,* 74–80.

THOMPSON, R., and J. V. McCONNELL. 1955. Classical conditioning in the planarium, dugesia dorotcephala. *Journal of Comparative and Physiological Psychology, 48,* 65–68.

THORESEN, C. E. 1973. Behavioral humanism. *Behavior modification in education, 72nd Yearbook of the National Society for the Study of Education,* Part I. Chicago: University of Chicago Press.

THORNDIKE, E. L. 1911. *Animal Intelligence*. New York: Macmillan.

TRAVERS, R. M. W. 1967. *Essentials of learning*. New York: Macmillan.

CHAPTER THREE

Cognitive Development

AS WE HAVE SEEN, the early years of psychology were marked by the development of associationist theories of behavior, best exemplified by Thorndike's formulation of a body of laws regarding learning and instruction. But by the 1920's there was growing debate over a number of issues in learning. Thorndike's conception of learning as chiefly trial-and-error came under attack from several sources, most notably in Wolfgang Kohler's *Mentality of Apes* (1925). Kohler had conducted a series of interesting studies during the years 1913–17. While visiting the island of Tenerife, off the coast of Africa, during World War I, he was interned by the British. He was allowed to carry on research, and during his enforced stay he began experimenting with some of the other inhabitants of the island—chimpanzees.

Kohler's research had an important effect upon American learning theory because it emphasized the importance of insight—*Gestalt*—as an alternative to trial-and-error. The German word *Gestalt* translates into English somewhat clumsily as "configuration," meaning an awareness of a problem or a situation in terms of its entirety, or "wholeness."

Gestalt theory implies that a learner acts as intelligently as he can under the circumstances that confront him, so that insightful solution of problems is the typical solution if the problem is not too difficult and all the essential factors are open to inspection. Fumbling and trial-and-error are resorted to only when the problem is too difficult for the learner to perceive the answer spontaneously. This reversed the early associationist position that trial-and-error is the typical method of attack, and reasoning is essentially "mental" trial-and-error. Most of

Thorndike's experimentation was with cats in a problem box, where the animal was confronted with a situation that required a solution for which he was rewarded. The problem tended to be a random operation, so that, if the cat fumbled around long enough, he eventually achieved the solution. When this achievement was immediately reinforced by a satisfying consequence, Thorndike was able to demonstrate that the next time the animal was confronted with the same problem, the number of trials needed for him to achieve the solution tended to be reduced. The reward raised motivation, and the animal profited from the experience. A question remained about what this process consisted of, however, for there was no way of knowing to what extent past experience was involved in the initial solution.

Kohler concentrated on two kinds of problem for his chimpanzees to solve. In the box problem, bananas were hung from the ceiling of the cage, out of the ape's reach. The animal was provided with two boxes, neither of which by itself was high enough for the ape to stand on and reach the fruit. After a period of maneuvering and otherwise "fruit-less" activity, the ape appeared to sit back on his haunches and stare intently at the situation. Then, with apparent purpose, it placed one box on top of the other, climbed on top of the construction, and snared the bananas.

The stick problem was similar. The bananas were placed outside the cage, beyond the reach of the ape. The animal was given two sticks, each one too short by itself to reach the fruit. When the two sticks were put together, however, they made an implement long enough to rake in the bananas. The ape went through essentially the same process as with the boxes, trying various means of reaching the bananas and not succeeding. Then, after a period of apparent bafflement, during which the ape just sat and contemplated the situation, it got up, inserted one stick into the other, and snared the food.

These famous experiments opened up entirely new areas for research on learning. Psychologists regarded the findings as strong evidence that much learning—perhaps *all* of it—consisted of the learner's perceiving the problem in its entirety, recognizing the relationship of all the separate parts to the whole. Unlike the associationists' view that learning consists of the orderly building up of individual bits, one upon another, Gestaltists demonstrated that learning is, rather, a process of stepping back to size up the entire situation, or "field," in order to determine how all the elements fit together to achieve a solution. The whole is greater than the sum of its parts.

With regard to classroom practice, this conception of learning constituted a significant change. Associationists had given respectability to the practice of learning in a step-by-step fashion, with emphasis on drill and other repetitive activities. The Gestalt approach, in effect, reversed this; the process starts from the top, or total situation, and proceeds backward to individual elements.

Because associationism had so little to say about insightful learning in humans, Gestalt psychology came as a welcome development. Perhaps it is hard to understand now why such a common-sense notion as insight should have evoked so strong a reaction. Associationism had gained enthusiastic supporters because of what appeared to be a rigorously scientific approach to the study of human behavior. Unfortunately, as we have noted, this body of theory, if interpreted narrowly, suggests that the individual is a passive organism pushed and pulled by his environment, to which he reacts in generally mindless and mechanical ways. The return to a more balanced, humane view of learning that resulted from research on insight and creativity gave fresh hope and inspiration to many psychologists and teachers. Thinking and understanding were now assigned an important place in theories of behavior.

THE ROLE OF EXPERIENCE IN LEARNING

A basic tenet of associationism was that past experiences have a great deal to do with present learning behavior. Although learning was originally described as trial-and-error, it was easily demonstrated that the first attempts the learner made at solving a problem were most likely to be based on his past experiences. The learner utilized first what had succeeded in the past. When this failed, he cast about for other possible ways of solving the problem, and these, too, tended to have something in common with past learning. Only when everything from the past had been tried and the learner realized that he was confronting an entirely novel situation did he think about a fresh approach. Thus, according to the associationists, experience plays a significant role in learning.

The Gestaltists, however, were not convinced that learning was inextricably bound up with the past. The factor of experience, they claimed, did not adequately explain the phenomenon of originality. It was inconceivable that Kohler's apes, for example, had experienced situations in the past that were even remotely similar to the box or stick problem. In any case, sooner or later every learner will be confronted by a situation that has no precedent in his experience. If he wants the reward badly enough, he will be forced to seek a totally new solution. Gestaltists said that this is really what complex learning is all about. The learner sizes up the situation, and he may even mentally or actively try several solutions based on past experiences. When these fail, he is forced to take a hard look at the entire situation. He perceives what all the elements are and puts them together in a Gestalt, or configuration, that reveals the significant organization upon which the solution is based.

According to the Gestaltists, this does not mean that experience is *never* a part of solving problems. In fact, experience plays a great part in most thinking behavior, but it may or may not be an essential ingredient for thinking. The individual will quite naturally act on what has worked in the past; but, when the past is no help, he is forced to seek an original solution.

The *need* to seek a solution, however, *is* a necessary ingredient. The learner must feel some discomfort or disequilibrium, which energizes him and helps him to focus on the problem.

The role of experience in learning is critical, for it affects important aspects of school curriculum planning. But, if learning strategies are based on a Gestalt approach, then the background of the student is only an aid to learning. The teacher can regard every student as a brand-new learner. This would mean less emphasis on review activities; the teacher could design classroom objectives without necessarily taking into account the objectives of the previous grade levels. Whereas the elementary- and secondary-school curriculum must contain at least a minimum sequence of learning objectives through the grade levels, there is a middle ground of choice for the teacher, who may or may not wish to construct classroom objectives specifically articulated to the school curriculum.

DEVELOPMENTAL PSYCHOLOGY: THE HIGHER MENTAL PROCESSES

As we have seen, Gestalt psychology began the shift toward internal factors in the process of learning, suggesting that human learning takes two general forms: associative and insightful learning. Both forms of learning are considered to apply at any stage in the life of the human. In other words, adults and children learn in the same way.

A long time ago, Jean-Jacques Rousseau proposed what was in his time a novel idea: that the child is not simply a truncated adult, and that the child's mind is not some kind of mini-copy of the adult mind. Although it might seem unnecessary at this period in the history of psychology, a reminder might be useful. Many educational authorities are advancing the idea that adult mental processes—in logic, for instance—can be taught earlier and earlier in the child's development, to the point, presumably, that children in first grade can learn set theory. The assumption is that the only difference between the child and the adult is in their experiences, and one only has to teach the subject logically for the child to reach adult status.

This argument is rejected by developmental psychologists on the ground that the child is essentially different from the adult in a variety of ways, among which are neurological differences between early life and adult maturity, and differences in ways of perceiving the world and in ways of processing the information received about it. Developmental psychology describes the characteristic behaviors found at various ages or stages of development and the general principles of growth over a period of time, including the interaction of various psychological, physiological, and environmental factors. The focus is on the *cognitive* behavior of the individual, on the assumption that behavioral acts result from the manner in which the organism interprets the environment (Kendler, 1971).

Developmental psychology is concerned with human behavior from before birth (prenatal) until death and includes the psychologies of infancy, childhood, adolescence, maturity, and old age (gerontology). These require a decided shift toward maturational factors, which has enormous implications for the design of school programs for young children. If maturational growth factors are the dominant influence on the child's learning, then educational events should be designed to coordinate with the child's readiness to learn. If environmental forces, by contrast, are the dominant emphasis, the school years should be filled with systematically planned events of learning, and few allowances need be made for the particular stage the child is in.

JEAN PIAGET

All teachers have at least a rudimentary knowledge of how children learn. Some of this is common sense, some relates to bits and pieces of learning theory, but probably most of their knowledge is derived from student teaching and reminiscences of early experiences in school. Consequently, most of what teachers know relates to learning as an adult might interpret it, not to the act of learning from a child's frame of reference.

Jean Piaget, a Swiss psychologist, has devoted most of his life to the study of individual children and how they go about solving problems and incorporating knowledge about the world in which they live. Piaget is a biologist by training. His initial interest in the ways in which marine life adapts to its environment led to his current work with children. Piaget believes that mental development is a process of adaptation to the environment—that this is the essential, biologically motivated element in the process of mental growth. This implies that the organism has an innate drive toward understanding and interpreting the world in which it lives.

STAGES OF DEVELOPMENT

The keystone of Piaget's theory is his concept of stages of development, which he has formulated as follows:

Stage I: Sensorimotor development—from birth to about two years

Stage II: Preoperational stage—from two years to about seven years

Stage III: Concrete operations—from six or seven years to about eleven years

Stage IV: Formal operations—from about eleven years of age throughout the rest of life

Stage I: The Sensorimotor Stage (Birth to Two Years). During the first two years of life, the child learns to coordinate perceptual input with motor responses in such a manner as to be able to control his limited world of self and immediate environment. Piaget has identified six substages that the infant goes through in this process of establishing his relationship to the environment. Incoming visual, motor, auditory, and other sense perceptions are organized into mental schemata that permit the child to understand himself in relation to his world. These schemata are limited by the child's mental capacity, his developmental stage, and the set of experiences he has had with the world.

In forming his conception of the world, the child does more than reflect what is apparent to his senses. His view of reality is, in fact, an interpretive reconstruction of the world, not simply a copy of it. By reasoning about the information he receives, the child is able to organize his sensory experience and begin to develop that awareness of the permanent, integrating characteristics within apparent change that is the essence of adult thought.

These mental schemata are organized for different purposes, depending upon the child's stage of development. At first, the child develops a mental picture to understand his functional relation to the world.

Later, he organizes mental pictures to act upon the environment. It is during this stage of development that the child first understands that objects have some degree of permanence independent of himself. With this mental set he is able to act with intent and foresight and thus contemplate future action.

Stage II: Preoperational Stage (Two to Seven Years). The preoperational stage is especially significant to teachers.' It is during this stage that the child acquires language. Language permits him to deal symbolically with the world rather than having to act out through motor activity. The language he attaches to events is of particular importance, for the child's mental schema of a language concept may not be consistent with the interpretation the teacher gives to this same word. Forced or premature language instruction with an inadequate mental association often hinders the child's later development of the ability to interpret and deal with the world abstractly. Teachers tend to assume that, if a child uses a word, he has an adequate mental representation of that word. This can be a significant instructional problem to the child and the teacher.

It is during this preoperational stage of development that the child begins to acquire schemata of time, space, and distance. He gradually learns a set of operations dealing with these concepts. The schemata he attaches to time, space, and distance are dependent upon his environment, his experiences with these variables, and the developmental growth that permits him to isolate himself and his actions from the environment. During this stage of development, the child appears to be limited to mental manipulation of a single variable at a time. The water-in-a-glass experiment is a classic example from Piaget of the child's inability to hold one concept constant while manipulating another variable. When the child is asked to comment on water poured from a glass of one shape into a container of another shape (for example, a flat pan), he says that there is more or less water in the pan, depending on whether he compares the height of the water in the glass with the height of water in the pan or with the width dimension of the pan. This inability to deal with the conservation property is a limitation every teacher should be aware of when teaching children of this age.

Stage III: Concrete Operations (Seven to Eleven Years). During this stage of development the child begins to establish a logical set of mental operations; that is, he learns to handle one variable or concept at a time and to interpret relationships. For example, a child can reason about the effects of elevation on rainfall but may be unable to account for wind direction, relative humidity, and temperature at the same time. The child at this developmental level interprets the environment and forms mental schemata primarily on the basis of the world of reality. This tendency to deal with the world in concrete rather than abstract terms is significant for the teaching process. It implies that, for adequate mental development at this age, abstract and logical reasoning should not be stressed. The child's schemata (concepts), symbols, and interpretations are mostly literal representations of his experiences with the world. For this reason the teacher should provide educational experiences that are relevant to the child's life, time, and space experience, not abstract or rote. According to Piaget, the child is unable at this stage of development to deal with logic (except intuitively) and to utilize abstractions or other nonexperienced relationships; this limits the appropriate sets of teaching to the child's world. Piaget's work suggests that inner-city, suburban, and rural children during this stage of development should have different educational experiences, reflecting their different environmental circumstances.

Stage IV: Formal Operations (About Eleven Years). At this stage, the child begins the process of learning to reason as an adult. The child's previous experiences can now be brought into the teaching process. He is now able to handle several variables while manipulating another variable to determine its effects on a basic principle or set of operations. For example, during this period of time a child can accurately reason about the effects of elevation upon rainfall while controlling or holding constant such factors as wind direction, temperature, and relative humidity. He can then select another variable in this set of operations while holding elevation constant and thus, by logical reasoning, deduce the effects of a number of factors on rainfall. What is significant to us here is that the teacher can teach logical reasoning at this stage—but not before, according to Piaget. As Piaget states, the child cannot be taught successfully that which he is developmentally not ready to receive. Assuredly, the child can be taught, but it is detrimental or inappropriate psychologically to force learning upon him until he is capable of grasping the significance of what he is learning. Furthermore, learning that is forced upon the child prior to readiness may seriously interfere with appropriate learning later, when he is developmentally ready.

An understanding of these stages of development is essential to an understanding of the basic concepts of intelligence and intellectual development. Piaget believes that, as development proceeds, intelligence operates at each level with different purposes. Intelligence, as seen by

Piaget, is a set of specific instances of adaptive behavior, of coping with the environment, or organizing and reorganizing thought and action. Intelligence is largely a process that entails continuous modification both of the organism (the child) and of the perceived environment with which he interacts. Every act of intelligence presumes some kind of structure that the child has attached to his world.

The child's ability to change schemata whenever necessary to fit his orderly growth and development is called *adaptation*. Adaptation as conceived by Piaget is made up of two interrelated components—*assimilation* and *accommodation*. Assimilation is the process by which the child can expand his understanding of the world within the framework of his existing imagery of that world. An example of assimilation would be the addition of new elements to a class of objects; the schema of "lakes" would not be changed by adding the knowledge of new lakes foreign to the previous understanding of the child.

The other component of adaptation, accommodation, involves changing the present schemata to incorporate learnings, understandings, or interpretations not previously available to the child. To accommodate requires the child psychologically to restructure, reorder, or change a schema to include new knowledge that does not fit the previous mental set. This process is vividly illustrated when a child begins to understand that pouring a quantity of water from one vessel into another does not change the quantity of water. This insight will cause the child to restructure all schemata he had previously held that did not account for this preservation of quantity.

The concepts of assimilation and accommodation as two forms of adaptive intelligence can be stated as follows:

Adaptive Intelligence

Schema A + new knowledge that does not affect the understanding of that schema $\Big\}$ = assimilation = Schema A_1

Schema A + new knowledge that changes the mental imagery of the schema $\Big\}$ = accommodation = Schema A_2 or new Schema B

In the first example, the child is able to incorporate new knowledge into the old schema. He thus preserves his mental imagery but can extend it to include new knowledge.

In the second example, the child is unable to incorporate the new knowledge into the schema. He is forced to make an accommodation in order to adapt intelligently to his environment. He therefore either alters his schema to include a new schema, A_2, or incorporates his original schema into his new mental imagery, thus changing it to an entirely new schema (Schema B), which was not previously available to him.

Obviously, accommodation is a much more complex process than assimilation. Furthermore, the younger the child, the more often he must make accommodations rather than assimilations as a basis for adaptation. This explains the necessity of using direct experiences with the environment as a basis for teaching children. The demands upon the child to add new learnings that do not fit his present schema are not easily met through abstract experiences. The child needs relevant and direct experience with his environment in order to develop appropriate mental imagery for his dealings with the world around him. Any attempt to induce learning through abstractions, telling, or other teaching techniques that do not involve the child with concrete realities in the first years of his life will lead to inappropriate, inaccurate, or inadequate mental imagery. This concept is perhaps the greatest contribution Piaget's works have made to classroom-teaching practices.

Any experience to which the child is unable or not ready to adapt is useless in terms of his cognitive development. However, every mental encounter with an environmental object involves some kind of cognitive structuring or restructuring of that object in accordance with presently available schemata. This principle is the answer to the "readiness" problem so often of major concern to teachers. Behaviorist "readiness" theories or propositions suggest that the teacher should break down the environmental object into its component parts and teach from parts to wholes. Piaget argues that this is not appropriate if the initial teaching purpose is to develop a concept of the environmental object in its totality. An example of this is the teaching of numbers. If the teacher is explaining the concept of "four," the learning experiences should consist of many object groups that constitute "four." Any attempt to break down four into its components (for example, $2 + 2$) interferes with the development of a schema for four. Piaget believes that the learner should not be coerced in this learning. The teacher should not bring about a rote learning situation if the child does not have a basic understanding of "four." If the teacher resorts to a rote teaching method, he may be interfering with the child's later normal development of the ability to deal with the mental schema of "four." Perhaps this may account for the inability of many children to understand mathematics. They can perform the operations in rote fashion, but they do not grasp the principles involved.

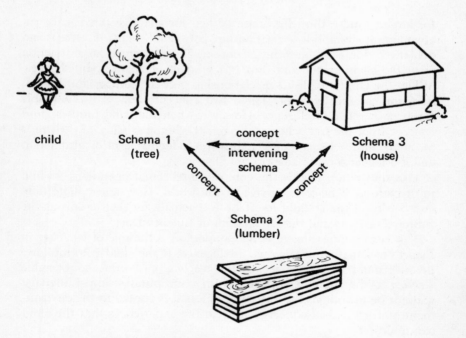

Fig. 3.1. Piaget: The formation of a concept.

THE DEVELOPMENT OF CONCEPTS

Piaget emphasizes that experience plays a vital role in the evolution of intelligence. As the child develops, he becomes capable of taking more environmental objects into account and using more complex techniques to solve problems. He becomes progressively more adaptive. The acquisition of language is an important part of this process, because language permits the child to deal with new concepts.

Concepts, in turn, are the adaptive mechanism through which the growing child copes with reality. They are the crucial tools that allow him to relate to his environment and the bases on which he perceives (identifies) objects in his environment. Concepts are the means by which the child organizes the environment; they help him to attack or cope with the problems of living.

A concept is a particular kind of mental structure. It is a relationship between objects, events, principles, or a combination of these factors. For example, in Figure 3.1, the child has one schema for tree, another for lumber, and a third for house. When his adaptive intelligence enables him to establish a relationship between Schema 1 (tree) and Schema 2 (lumber), he forms a concept. The concept is an abstraction from the environment and thus is a product of adaptive intelligence. When the child establishes a relationship between lumber and houses, he forms another concept. These two concepts are relatively simple forms of adaptive intelligence. However, when the child forms a third concept from the tree schema (1) and the house schema (3), there is an intervening schema (2) that involves a higher level of abstraction and is a higher form of adaptive intelligence.

This illustration reveals the complex intellectual operations a child must perform if he is to survive in the world. How much more difficult it is for a young child to establish schemata for such events as the Boston Tea Party and the Declaration of Independence!

This last example illustrates how important is the role of language in Piaget's explanation of adaptive intelligence. If the child is to interpret or understand abstract concepts, the teacher must bring considerable *Realien* to the child's environment for conceptualization. Language will not be meaningful to the child unless it is rooted in the environment and learned in concert with real-life experiences that the child can interpret.

In any transaction with the environment, the child inevitably brings to bear certain pre-existing schemata in order to make the experience intelligible. This presents certain difficulties to the child. His intelligent adaptation to a new experience is limited by (1) the previous schemata available to interpret the new experience and (2) the quality of the new experience. When previous schemata are rich enough to interpret the new experience, the child can assimilate it. The other form of adaptive intelligence—accommodation—occurs when the existing schemata are inadequate to interpret the new experience. The quality of experience that the child has is as vital to the process of restructuring schemata as is the quantity of schemata available to him.

In summary, concept formation consists of the following factors:

1. Acquiring appropriate schemata for the forming of concepts—for example, the relationship of lumber and trees.
2. Acquiring appropriate behaviors to accompany each concept—for example, knowing what to do if one wanted to obtain lumber from a tree.
3. Learning whether existing concepts are adequate for intelligent behavior—for example, if one wishes to build a house, should he start by planting a tree?
4. Unlearning inappropriate or inadequate concepts—for example, the

decision to buy lumber before the act of planting a tree in order to build a house.

5. Acquiring new concepts—for example, lumber can be obtained from sources other than planting a tree, namely, lumber yards and other building supply sources.

It is evident that the building of appropriate schemata to perform appropriate behavior is very complex. Much of this is taken for granted in the teaching-learning process. A teacher should understand the child's stage of development if appropriate teaching acts are to occur. In addition, experiences should be provided that reveal the sets of schemata available to the child which bear upon the problem and provide opportunities for the child to apply his adaptive intelligence. It is only through such applications that the child understands whether he can assimilate the experience into his present schemata or must restructure those schemata in order to function intelligently. The child can assimilate only what past experience has prepared him for. Changes in his assimilatory structures direct new accommodations, which, in turn, stimulate further structural reorganization.

MENTAL DEVELOPMENT IN THE CHILD

Functional intelligence is an adaptational and organizational process. The process of adaptive intelligence accomplished through the complementary processes of assimilation and accommodation is the crucial ingredient in Piaget's explanation of the mental development of the child. Piaget sees adaptation as the result of a quest for equilibrium in the organism's interaction with its environment.

Assimilation to available schemata is possible only in a state of equilibrium. When available schemata are insufficient for intelligent adaptation to the environment, disequilibration occurs, which causes the individual to decenter from his available schemata so as to solve the problem presented in the environment. This decentering is the crucial factor in accommodation. (The meaning of decentering is similar to that of problem solving.) Unable to assimilate a new experience, the organism must then decenter in order to adapt to the environmental condition. This produces a problem-solving set that calls for new schemata from the state of disequilibration to a state of equilibration. This transformation of objects of perceptions to acts of intelligence can be phrased as follows: Assimilation and accommodation proceed from a state of chaotic undifferentiation to a state of differentiation. The ability to coordinate differentiated schemata is the underlying process of intelligence, according to Piaget.

Piaget has shown that the thinking of children progresses in stages from motoric intelligence in the sensorimotor stage to deductions and the use of logic in the formal-operations stage. It is during the concrete-operations stage (seven to eleven years of age) that the child begins to reflect, reason, and understand logical relationships. Prior to this stage, much of the child's thinking is self-centered and vague about relative judgments and cause and effect.

All intelligence is a form of adaptation to the organism's environment. The child adapts to the world by changing it and being changed by it. He assimilates the world to his available schemata and accommodates himself to the world through the creation of other schemata. Learning results from the psychological interaction of the organism with the real objects in the environment. Human thought is more than a copy of external reality; it transforms and transcends that reality by mental operations upon the world.

If learning is the functioning of an organism interacting with its environment, it is limited by the developmental level of the organism, its past experiences available in the form of schemata, and the present conditions of the environment. Learning is represented by the presentation of new schemata or additions to old schemata that permit the individual to move from a state of disequilibration to one of equilibration with the environment.

An important assumption of Piaget's theory is that children are innately curious about their environment; they naturally seek knowledge and understanding about the world in which they exist. This assumption has great significance for the teacher and is the basis for the following guidelines for teaching:

1. The teacher must first provide an educational environment that allows the child to satisfy his curiosity.
2. The teacher must provide an educational setting that utilizes the physical, social, political, and economic world of the child as the basis for subject matter.
3. The teacher must teach from an awareness of each child's developmental level rather than rigidly following society's demands.
4. The teacher must assume that this is an orderly process of mental growth that cannot be accelerated beyond the child's ability to adapt.

The contributions that Piaget has made to teaching are considerable. He has given us a means by which we can interpret how the child's mind develops. If his theories have validity, then certainly the classroom setting should be one that utilizes discovery and experimentation, deals with the *now* world of the child, and generally provides real-life experiences.

LEARNING THEORY: QUO VADIS?

By this time, it would be surprising indeed if the reader were not considerably confused about theories of learning and development. Is learning dependent on external or internal factors? Is learning largely the accumulation, through conditioning and reinforcement, of increasingly complex response patterns; or does the human being evolve through a maturational sequence of learning styles, each representing a distinct stage of development? Does the environment entirely "shape" the child's mental behavior; or does he already have, at birth, a mental blueprint for thinking and perception that needs only to be filled in with symbolic language and appropriate experience in order for it to become a fully functioning cognition system?

Psychological theories—whether behaviorist or developmental, external or internal in emphasis—can be regarded as systems of verbal constructs that are believed to describe the learning process. Unlike the physical sciences, in which most phenomena are studied directly, almost all the relevant phenomena in psychology must be inferred logically from overt behavior. It amounts to knowledgeable speculation on internal processes, based on clues suggested by outward behavior. Let us assume, for example, that we are confronted with a ten-year-old child who is working diligently at an arithmetic problem. What is going on inside the mind of this youngster? If we could unscrew the top of his head and peer in, what would we see? Obviously, the first thing we would see is a brain mass that is alive and functioning. One way to measure any mental activity would be to make an electroencephalograph, to observe the nervous pattern of lines recorded on a flowing graph sheet. The pattern might change as the boy decides to read, write a theme, or talk with a friend, but would it tell us whether he is solving problems by drawing on past experience or by discovering solutions that are entirely new and unique to him? Is he learning by building up ideas and concepts step by step through a process of connecting the old to the new, or is he using powers of insight, or structuring, to rearrange the jigsaw pieces of learning into new and significant wholes?

Much current research on human thinking processes is directed toward seeking the answers to these questions. As a consequence, investigators are shifting increasingly from an associationist, or S-R, view of learning to an information-processing conception; from the older position that learning is a matter of establishing connections between stimuli and responses to the view that stimuli can be processed in many different ways by the human central nervous system, and that understanding the nature of learning is a matter of figuring out how these processes operate. Exclusive preoccupation with conditioning theories of behavior is giving way to increased interest in the study of higher mental processes (Bruner, 1959, 1961; Segal and Lachman, 1972). The theories of Piaget, of course, are prime examples of this shift in emphasis.

Almost all psychologists agree on certain basic, observable facts of learning—for example, the effects that immediate reinforcement has upon motivation, the shape of learning curves. But vigorous disagreement arises when attempts are made to fit a given learning process into a tightly knit theory that can account for all the variables and provide the basis for research designs. In the setting of the classroom, the importance of learning by conditioning, insight, creativity, and understanding are universally agreed upon. But the major question still remains: How are these things achieved psychologically? Like the phenomenon of electricity, learning behavior is a great deal easier to measure than to define. We know what learning is by its effects; its true nature remains a mystery.

REFERENCES

BRUNER, J. S. 1959. Learning and thinking. *Harvard Educational Review,* 29, 184–92.

———. 1961. The act of discovery. *Harvard Educational Review, 31,* 21–32.

KENDLER, H. 1971. Environmental and cognitive control of behavior. *American Psychologist, 26,* 962–73.

KOHLER, W. 1925. *Mentality of Apes.* New York: Harcourt, Brace & World.

PIAGET, J. 1954. *The construction of reality in the child.* Translated by Margaret Cook. New York: Basic Books.

SEGAL, E. M., and R. LACHMAN. 1972. Complex behavior or higher mental processes: Is there a paradigm? *American Psychologist, 27,* 46–56.

CHAPTER FOUR

Language Development and Reading

READING is one of the few academic skills in which society demands that all students be successful. Unfortunately, however, many children do not become good readers. The evidence is clear: The schools are not producing as many good readers as the society would like. Every survey completed at any grade level beyond the first grade reveals large numbers of retarded readers (one year behind in the lower grades and two years or more at the higher grade levels). The percentages of retarded readers range from 10 to 25 (Bond and Tinker, 1973). Although reading difficulties are to be expected among slow learners, there are many instances of poor reading among average and intelligent students as well.

As the child advances through school, his need for competence in reading increases. In fact, we can almost predict his over-all academic success according to his reading ability (Bond and Tinker, 1973). Because a basic education is now essential for most occupations, reading is rapidly becoming the most vocational subject in the curriculum.

In spite of volumes of research on the subject, there is no commonly accepted explanation of the reading process. Authorities agree on many of the particulars, but a comprehensive theory that accounts for all, or even most, aspects of reading has not been forthcoming. Teaching practices have been based more or less on what appears to work best in actual classroom situations. Scientific investigation of the structure of language and the behavioral, perceptual, and cognitive processes involved in language development has not made a major impact on instructional practices in reading (*Encyclopedia of Educational Research*, 1969, p. 1075).

Current authorities refer to reading as the process of "decoding" the printed page—that is, recognizing the oral equivalent of the written symbol. The principle on which the decoding concept rests is that language is basically spoken communication, and writing or print is merely a graphic representation of speech. But this is by no means the total explanation. Reading involves the communication of meaning by the use of symbolic language, which is highly abstract. Since the sounds and appearances of words themselves are suggestive of meaning, the process of reading, therefore, involves a hierarchy of skills ranging from auditory and visual discrimination to such higher-order mental activities as organizing ideas, making generalizations, drawing inferences, and so on (DeBoer & Dallmann, 1970, p. 13).

By the time they first enter school, most children have learned to use the symbols of spoken language to the extent of their needs and their level of development. In a sense, their repertoire of spoken language is a first step toward learning to read. Some children, in fact, have made a beginning in the substitution of visual for auditory symbols. The apparent ease with which almost all children learn oral language seems hard to reconcile with the fact that learning to read is so difficult for so many children, even by the age of six or seven. Loban (1963) states that, by school age, most children's speech is already a close approximation of the adult speech in their communities. Studies of the vocabulary of school beginners indicate that the average child knows at least 8,000 words, and that some know more than 20,000. Yet, after a year or more of intensive study, many of these same children can recognize only the simplest words and grammar patterns on a printed page. Obviously, the transition from speaking a language to reading it poses instructional problems of considerable complexity.

The teacher continues to be the most significant influence on the child's reading progress (Robinson, 1968). Major comparative studies have found marked differences in the effectiveness of various methods and materials, with the teacher being the significant factor. It is implicit in this book that every teacher—regardless of his subject-matter field—should be aware of at least the fundamentals of the psychology of language and thought in relationship to the process of reading and the instructional strategies currently in use. The purpose of this chapter, therefore, is threefold: (1) to identify the nature of language and thought in the reading process; (2) to present important factors that influence reading achievement; and (3) to discuss concept formation and its relationship to reading.

LANGUAGE AS BEHAVIOR

An early behaviorist, J. B. Watson (1920), defined thought as "sub-vocal speech." According to this, when we think "if," for example, we must be "using" the word, because there is no "if" but the word. Therefore, mental events—thinking—are a form of behavior, or responses to stimuli. The behaviorist regards language and thought as a learned repertoire of sensory images and symbolic language. We respond with ideas and mental images because we have learned to do so, and this process can be explained by behaviorist learning theory.

As we saw in Chapter 2, behavior theory states that four conditions are necessary for learning to take place: drive, cue discrimination, response, and reinforcement. If language is learned, then the process must include each of these requirements.

DRIVE

Why do children learn to talk? Are they destined to learn a language? The answer is yes, if we consider *any* form of communication—writing, speech, or gestures—as "language." The normal child is born with the capacity to make sounds—about six or seven distinct sounds at infancy. From these, he learns the other sounds required for speech—called *phonemes*.

Before he learns to talk intelligibly, the child naturally engages in a great deal of vocal play. He hears his own sounds and begins to recognize the sounds of others. Hearing oneself and others is very important in language development; the totally deaf child never exceeds by very much the infantile sounds that can be made soon after birth (Stroud, 1956). In addition to these basic sounds, the child begins to "point" to objects and people by the use of his vocal cords. Approval and recognition from his parents help him to make these naming responses. Very soon, he learns to make demanding responses as well, which are usually followed by something he wants—food or water, for example. His basic survival requirements impel him to do whatever is necessary to get what he wants—usually by means of speech and gesture. According to the behaviorist, when a response to a stimulus is repeatedly reinforced, the response tends to acquire drive value. What began as a primary drive for sustenance gradually becomes a secondary drive for recognition, acceptance, love, stimulation, and so on.

CUE DISCRIMINATION

A drive impels a person to respond. Cues determine when and where he will respond and which response he will make (Dollard and Miller, 1950, p. 32). Most young children quickly learn how to control their responses so as to elicit pleasant consequences. In fact, this ability to know when to act is necessary if the child is to cope with the increasingly complex world about him. In order to achieve this, the child requires good sensory equipment.

RESPONSE

By about the thirtieth month of life, the average child has mastered about twenty-seven distinct phonemes (Stroud, 1956). After this, he does not learn many more separate sounds, but his sound production and the complexity of his speech patterns increase. He learns to select from a wide array of speech sounds, and their correct use is rewarded by ever increasing control over the environment.

REINFORCEMENT

The child learns the language he hears. Language behavior, such as calling objects by their correct names, tends to be reinforced by generalized responses from the listeners, who show in both direct and indirect ways that they understand and approve. In this way, according to the behaviorist, verbal behavior is "shaped" by the reinforcement contingencies of the verbal environment in which we live.

The acquisition of language can also be described by the principle of classical conditioning. As we have seen, this principle states that a stimulus not only acquires the power to elicit a response but, once having done so, can then pass the response on to a new stimulus. Thus, when a child encounters a word that is paired with an aspect of the environment, the word takes on meaning. For example:

Let us say that a child has through first-order conditioning already acquired a meaning for the word BAD. That is, the child has received aversive stimulation in contiguity with the presentation of the word stimulus. Let us also say that the child later on reads a new word, EVIL—a word that he has never seen before; thus, to him a nonsense syllable. He is then told by a parent or teacher that EVIL means BAD, and he repeats this to himself several times.

These experiences would constitute conditioning trials in which the word BAD would serve as the unconditioned stimulus and the word EVIL as the conditioned stimulus. Through this conditioning the new word, EVIL, would come to elicit the same meaning response as the word BAD. [Staats, 1968, p. 24.]

The principle of reinforcement is not so heavily stressed in describing language acquisition by means of classical conditioning. The emphasis is on contiguity, or pairing of stimuli. But whether or not reinforcement is considered essential, all behaviorist theories of language focus on overt behavior, with considerably less concern for the nature of the language itself. And whether he explains it by the reinforcement principle or by a process of conditioning, the behaviorist contends that language and thought are largely learned. At the common-sense level, behavior theory provides a fairly convincing explanation of how children acquire a vocabulary and learn basic sentence patterns. For example, children who were deprived of contact with other humans from birth on invariably have very limited speech facility, and limited mental development as well.

But language is infinitely variable. There is virtually no limit to the possible length and variety of sentences in English. Also, the information load of language appears to have infinite potential for complexity. Behaviorist psychology's attempts to describe the process of language acquisition have received strong buffeting from another group of people interested in language and thought—the psycholinguists.

PSYCHOLINGUISTICS

As we have seen, the typical behaviorist analysis states that the child receives reinforcement upon hearing himself make sounds similar to the ones that the rewarding parent makes. This is supposed to account for the child's progress from babbling to adult forms of communication. Nevertheless, the study of the structure of language, as well as of its use by children, has convinced some investigators that a *natural* propensity for language patterns is activated in the child as he listens to the speech of adults (Chomsky, 1965).

According to the psycholinguistic position, the human brain comes already supplied with a kind of universal grammar, just as the procedure for pecking is preprogrammed in the brain of a newborn chick. Language is therefore largely an innate human attribute, only partly a learned one. The child constructs sentences because he already has the rules of grammar (Chomsky, 1964). Learning to talk is much like learning to walk; both are inevitable, given the characteristics of the human organism, unless there is physical or mental impairment.

> We know very little about the actual processes by which children learn language, but there has been an increasing awareness over the past few years of just how much the child brings to the task by way of his own internal organization and innate human characteristics. He certainly is not "taught" language in any formal sense, but acquires it naturally, so to speak, in the course of maturing and developing in an environment where he is adequately exposed to it. Interestingly enough, we now see that this natural process of acquisition continues actively into the early school years, and perhaps beyond. [Chomsky, 1972, p. 32.]

The child may have no explicit awareness of the rules, but he can intuitively distinguish between strings of words that are sentences and those that are not. He recognizes *"The large boy runs slowly"* as a sentence but not *"boy slowly large runs The,"* because the former group of words follows the familiar adjective-noun-verb-adverb sequence of English sentences.

This theory of language acquisition, sometimes referred to as the *linguistic-relativity hypothesis,* is based on the assumption that thought has a relation to the language patterns that convey it (Carroll, 1964). According to this theory, the thinking processes expressed in language may vary from culture to culture depending on the characteristics of the language. One language contains concepts that others do not and thus produces a different perception or "view" of the world. For example, an Eskimo can make more than eleven kinds of verbal response with respect to snow, whereas a Brazilian has only a few general terms for snow. As a consequence, an Eskimo is likely to "think" differently about snow than a Brazilian would. Some anthropologists and psychologists have therefore argued that the nature of a language affects thought processes. If a child cannot say *not,* it is argued, then he will lack the concept of a negative.

Lenneberg (1966) has detailed the reasons for regarding language as innately determined behavior:

1. Linguistic universals such as phonetic systems and syntax are common to all languages.

2. Historical investigations of languages reveal that, although spoken languages change, at no time does one find evidence of human speech that can be described as unphonetic or agrammatical.

3. Specific language disability—characterized by delayed speech onset, poor articulation, and marked reading and second-language learning disability—in which general intelligence remains unaffected appears to be inherited.

4. The developmental schedule of language acquisition follows a fixed sequence, so that, even if the entire schedule is retarded, the order of attainment of linguistic skills remains fixed.

5. Finally, comparisons of children learning non-Indo-European languages with children learning English indicate a high degree of concordance between milestones of speech and motor development.

The trend of research in psycholinguistics is to regard the grammar of a language, not as a set of formal prescriptions for determining whether a sentence is correctly constructed, but as logic, a set of rules by which the child derives meaning from language. The grammar serves as a link between the surface structure of a message and the deeper structure, which contains the meaning. The surface level refers to the physical manifestation of language as it strikes the eye or the ear; the deeper level refers to meaning or semantic interpretation. Learning the former does not automatically bring understanding of the latter. To put this in another way, the meaning of a sentence is not the sum total of the meanings of the individual words of the sentence. Because there is no simple relationship between the surface structure of words and their total contextual meaning, it has thus far proved impossible to design a computer program that can read and respond to human language in any interesting way. This also explains why human communication is so different from any other known animal-communication system.

LANGUAGE DEVELOPMENT: PIAGET

The view that the child has a developing sense of language structure has been given support by Piaget (1963), who approaches language and thinking largely from the standpoint of the child's cognitive capacity. According to Piaget, the child's use of speech and language, and subsequently the process of deriving meaning from printed words, does not substantially affect the development of his personal symbolic structures (the means by which the child, in interacting with the environment, processes external reality into an object of knowledge). They are independently made. The behaviorist position, by contrast, holds that language and thought are learned from the adult environment. As the child comes to understand language, says Piaget, he has to assimilate and then accommodate the lingual signs to his symbolic structure; but, if he has to find his own meaning, the symbolic structuring must come first and not be confused by adult language patterns. The child follows his own symbolizing, then translates his thoughts into language and comes to terms with adult signs. For example, children who lack language mechanics may sometimes express ideas by the way in which they manipulate objects in play and in solving problems. According to Piaget, unless the teacher starts with the child's spontaneous structures, adult language may confuse the child's thinking or cause him to learn verbal statements without knowing what they mean.

The major problem with linguistic theories of language is that they fail to explain how these grammatical rules, or symbolic structures, are acquired. Perhaps they are acquired very early in life in somewhat the same way that some lower animals learn by an imprinting process. As stated above, children reared in isolation do not develop any intuitive grasp of grammar. Perhaps in the early months or years of a child's life, language structure becomes a part of his cognitive equipment as an aspect of his over-all maturational development, and this helps him to grasp the meaning of language as he grows older.

BEHAVIORISM VS. PSYCHOLINGUISTICS
IN BEGINNING READING

What are the implications of these theories of language acquisition for the teaching of reading? Are instructional procedures based on the assumption that language and thought are learned behavior different from procedures that reflect a belief in the child's innate capacity for mastering language? The answer is yes as regards strategy of reading instruction. But with respect to tactics—the day-to-day instructional procedures—the answer is probably no, because reading teachers tend to use techniques from any theoretical source as long as they work.

It can certainly be asserted that what the child ultimately learns in reading are *words*. As he advances in reading, he learns word groups and arrangements and begins to associate them with meaning. In a sense, the child acquires palpable *things*; his rate of achievement can therefore be determined by counting what he has acquired. Fundamentally, the behaviorist is interested in how many verbal units the child has acquired and how quickly he can retrieve them (Seymour, 1969). Thus, if language is in fact overt behavior that the child learns in the same way any other behavior is learned or skill mastered, then to bring about growth in language skills the focus must be upon the teacher as a trainer early in the child's life. Whether he realizes it or not, the teacher manipulates many conditions of learning that help to determine the behaviors the child acquires.

> . . . the teacher could be an active participant in arranging circumstances to most efficaciously produce an abundant, rich, adjustive behavioral repertoire using a minimum of aversive stimulation and a maximum of positive reinforcement. Good working behaviors, good studying behaviors, the ability to work without immediate reinforcement; reasonable, cooperative, a not overselfish behavior; a good language system about the world, his own behavior, and that of others; a good system of reinforcers, including words of positive and negative reinforcement value; social stimuli that appropriately control striving and nonstriving behavior; social behaviors that reinforce other people as well as oneself; these seem to be some of the behaviors that teachers help determine by the conditions they present to the child. [Staats, 1968, p. 467.]

Nevertheless, considerable *covert* mental activity must occur as the child processes the words he acquires. In the beginning stages of learning to read, the child must necessarily depend on his knowledge of sound-letter relationships. But in order to advance he must rely less on "decoding" procedures and more on the underlying linguistic structure of what he reads. In a comparative study of good and poor readers in the fourth grade, Weinstein and Rabinovitch (1971) found that one difference between the two groups was in their ability to make use of the information inherent in the grammatical structure of a sentence. This is the ability even beginning readers have to avoid misreading in such a manner as to break the phonological and grammatical rules of their native language. The child does not read *two* as *wto* (an impossible phonological arrangement in English), although he might quite possibly perceive it as *to, too, tow,* or *toe.* In addition, he relies heavily on his knowledge of the grammar of his spoken language to anticipate the message on the written page.

According to psycholinguistic principles, it is suggested that the young child read materials whose sentence structure is as much like his own spoken language as possible. For example, in oral language children rarely begin a sentence with a preposition; therefore, this sentence construction should be delayed in reading. Also to be avoided in beginning reading materials are complex sentences, the passive voice, and heavy use of nominal constructions. Nor is it necessary for the child to learn the alphabet before learning words or comprehension. Learning to read will be easier if the child learns some words first by rote (as most children do).

In summary, psycholinguistics, in teaching reading, focuses on where the child is in his language development and then structures the learning steps from the child's own point of view (Seymour, 1969; Goodman, 1972; Hall, 1972).

THE "CLOZE" PROCEDURE

A technique called the "cloze" procedure has been used by some reading authorities to identify the psycholinguistic processes underlying the reading act (Weaver, 1965; Bormuth, 1968). The cloze procedure is based on the principle of *closure*, from Gestalt psychology: the tendency of the individual to complete a structure by supplying a missing element. The principle is applied to the reading process as follows:

Every "nth" word in a printed passage is omitted and the reader is asked to complete the passage by supplying the missing words. Words can be omitted on a random basis or in a systematic pattern. Both lexical words and structural words can be omitted. (In linguistic terms, lexical words carry primary meaning and are roughly similar to verbs, nouns, adjectives, and adverbs. Structural words indicate relationships, as articles, prepositions, conjunctions, and auxiliary verbs.) Thus, the reader's closure must fill in the gaps in both language and thought; what he supplies gives some clues to the nature of his psycholinguistic processes (see Fig. 4.1).

Although this technique thus far has had only limited use by reading specialists, it has strong possibilities for research in language, diagnosis of reading difficulties, and instruction (Spache, 1968). The procedure has been used successfully as a test of reading comprehension, as a measure of the readability or difficulty level of a reading selection, and as a method of improving reading (Geyer and Carey, 1972). Bormuth (1968, p. 429) identifies the steps for the use of the cloze procedure in measuring the readability of a reading selection:

1. Passages are selected from the material that is being evaluated.
2. Every fifth word in the passage is deleted and replaced by an underlined blank of a standard length.
3. The tests are duplicated and given, without time limits, to students who have *not* read the passages from which the tests were made.
4. The students are instructed to write in each blank the word they think was deleted.
5. Responses are scored correct when they match exactly the words deleted (minor misspellings are disregarded).

The cloze procedure appears to have potential for the analysis of other

A Trip

It was Saturday morning. Bill and Dan

_____ going camping. It was eleven _____

to the camp grounds so _____ decided to ride

their bicycles. _____ tied their sleeping

bags, their _____, and their pots and pans

_____ their bicycles. They had sandwiches

_____ lunch, steak for supper, and _____

and eggs for breakfast.

They _____ not sure of the way, _____

there were signs along the _____ so they weren't

worried.

They _____ for about an hour when _____

suddenly hit a bump on _____ side of the road. He

_____ to the ground. Bill was _____ but

not seriously. They discovered _____ Bill's front

tire had a _____. Bill and Dan thought about

_____ home, but they decided to _____ the

tire. They pushed Bill's _____ to a gas station

and _____ it.

Fig. 4.1 An example of a CLOZE reading exercise.

psycholinguistic abilities (Hafner, 1965) as well as reading comprehension. For example, a reader's failure to supply the correct missing words may be used to measure his listening ability, to analyze the part that reasoning plays in reading, to diagnose his ability to handle both lexical and structural linguistic components, to learn more about cognitive styles, and to find out more about how the human brain functions as an information storage and retrieval system.

GETTING READY TO READ

Havighurst advanced the idea that there are certain tasks that every child needs to accomplish. He called these "developmental tasks."

> A developmental task is a task which arises at or about a certain period in the life of the individual, successful achievement of which leads to his happiness and to success with later tasks, while failure leads to unhappiness in the individual, disapproval by the society, and difficulty with later tasks [1972, p. 2].

Certainly, reading qualifies as a crucial developmental task, one that children must accomplish to satisfy their own needs and the demands of society.

When is a child "ready" for this task? Should he begin formal study whenever we choose to teach him? Is he "ripe" for reading when he expresses strong curiosity about the little marks on the pages of books? Does the child develop a "hunger" for reading at a particular stage in his development? Is it wise to withhold reading opportunities from the child until he is at least in first grade, or is it a case of "the sooner the better," since it takes about four years of reading practice for the average child to reach the level of functional literacy and about ten years to attain minimal reading proficiency?

These are only a few of the questions that are asked about introducing children to the act of reading. Although the concept of reading readiness is nearly thirty years old, its nature and purpose are not universally clear to teachers and parents.

According to Spache and Spache,

> . . . there is more to readiness than the vague term "maturity" or prereading training. Readiness also includes the planned experiences intended to prepare the child for various reading tasks as well as to help him to continue to grow to meet new demands. . . . Therefore, readiness, in the largest sense, is a continuous process during the

entire reading program, although it receives its greatest emphasis during the beginning school years [1969, p. 44].

Durkin (1968, pp. 53–54) claims that the issue is not so much a matter of when but of how to begin reading. The answer concerning when to begin will be affected not only by the kinds of reading instruction provided for the children but also by where the children are; most kindergarten and first-grade children are neither totally unready nor totally ready to begin to read.

Sutton (1964) reported the findings of an extensive study of readiness for reading at the kindergarten level. She selected 134 kindergarten children in Muncie, Indiana, for an investigation of the visual and auditory perceptual abilities considered to be prerequisites for reading. All children who expressed an interest in beginning reading received instruction. Those who showed no interest in reading could choose activities such as drawing, painting, looking at picture books, or playing with puzzles. Within four weeks, 41 children had completed one or more prerequisites. By the end of the school year, several had completed their fourth book, a first-grade primer containing 160 pages and a vocabulary of 158 words. Most of the other children were beginning to express interest in beginning reading.

According to the findings of Sutton's study, the child who learns to read at an early age is more likely to be a girl, with some or most of the following characteristics:

1. It is likely that she has one or more older brothers who read to her occasionally.
2. She comes from a relatively high socio-economic level. This, in turn, may affect the quantity and quality of her learning experiences.
3. Her father probably earns a living through largely mental endeavor rather than manual labor.
4. Her parents are interested in school affairs and in the educational progress of their children.
5. Her parents have read to her since she was one and a half years old or younger.
6. She is interested in words and asks questions about them.
7. She is conscientious, self-reliant, and able to concentrate.
8. She has a good memory.
9. She is probably not "happy-go-lucky" in temperament.
10. It is likely that she can recognize most of the letters of the alphabet.

In a follow-up study done several years later, Sutton (1969) found that those children in the Muncie investigation who had achieved a measure of reading skill in kindergarten had a continuing and increasing reading advantage over their classmates throughout the primary grades.

Durkin (1968) suggests that the kindergarten year can be used to assess the child's readiness for reading, but that in some cases the assessment procedures could function as a beginning step to reading itself. For example, without diminishing their value as forms of free expression, finished products in art provide a good opportunity to teach kindergarten children to sign their names, to write captions, and to read the words written by others. At the same time, this situation may give the teacher an opportunity to identify those children for whom writing and spelling might provide the easiest route to reading, those who can remember whole words after little exposure, and those who have difficulty performing the motor skill of writing. Still another opportunity for both instruction and assessment is provided when the teacher reads to the children. In discussing some of the words and their characteristics, the teacher can present letters and sounds while identifying children who seem to know the alphabet as well as those who have skill in making visual and auditory discriminations.

This suggests that the question of when to begin reading is related to the varying capacities and interests of young children interacting with the types of learning opportunities that are provided.

EARLY READING

Occasional magazine articles and a book by Doman, *How to Teach Your Baby to Read* (1964), have created considerable excitement among parents and consternation among educators. Doman presents a case for teaching two-year-olds how to read. The method consists of using cards with colored letters, a vocabulary for familiar objects, and, finally, instruction on the alphabet. According to advertisements for the materials, if the steps are followed properly, mother and child will reach the "joyousness" promised in the last chapter of Doman's book.

Most experts in the reading field, however, do not take very seriously attempts to teach reading directly to preschoolers. Their emphasis is, rather, on reading-readiness activities—getting children interested in reading and prepared to read—especially in the kindergarten (Stanchfield, 1971; LaConte, 1969). For example, Operation Head Start did not attempt to teach preschool children to read; it concentrated on socializing activities. Likewise, "Sesame Street" provides some instruction in the alphabet, but its main thrust continues to be toward exercising the perceptual and discriminative skills of children and the development of positive interpersonal attitudes and relationships.

Although there is pressure to push the teaching of reading downward into the kindergarten and preschool years, research has pointed to the dangers of too-early academic routines on children. Studies show, for example, that imposing routine stimulates aggression among small children, that the training is not retained or transferred outside the classroom, and that much of the social learning is incidental to class instruction. Furthermore, studies note the variations in individual attention span, the need for physical activity, and the inability of small children to share an adult's time and attention with others. At least partly as a result of these findings, early childhood education emphasizes, instead, the social and emotional development of the individual child (Spache, 1968).

INDIVIDUAL DIFFERENCES

Individual differences in learning and achievement are dramatically apparent in first grade. Although the children are generally within 11 months of one another in chronological age, their mental ages may range from 60 to 150 (that is, from about 3 years to 7 years, 6 months). The children may vary on other characteristics as well—verbal fluency, physical vitality, attentiveness, and emotionality—but the differences in capacity to learn pose the most immediate problem to the teacher.

Figure 4.2 presents the range of reading ability found in typical classrooms at grade levels two through six at the beginning of the school year (Bond and Tinker, 1973). The combined scores of children from several classrooms are used at each grade level. The graph shows the median scores made by the best readers of all the classes at a given grade level, the median score of the poorest readers, and the median score for the grade that is the same as the grade level. It also shows the best and poorest scores, in grade level, of the middle third of the children starting that grade. For example, in the several classes starting the second grade, 3.8 is the best reading-grade ability, 2.0 the middle score, and 1.3 the lowest—a spread of 2.5 grade levels. For the middle third of second grade, reading ranges from 1.8 to 2.2, a four-month spread between the poorest and the best reader.

From the third grade on, differences in reading ability between low, middle, and higher groups are proportionately about the same for each successive year; but, when measured by grade levels, the spread is markedly wider. For example, at the sixth grade there is a 2.8 grade-level spread in the high group alone. In other words, the older the children, the wider become the differences in reading ability and therefore

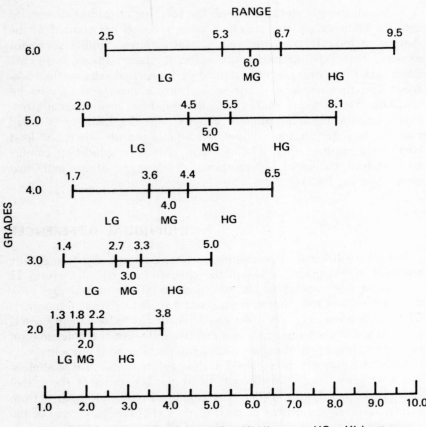

Fig. 4.2. Achieved reading level found in typical classrooms of grades two through six at the beginning of the school year. (Reproduced with permission of the publisher from Guy L. Bond and Miles A. Tinker, *Reading Difficulties,* 3d ed. [New York: Appleton-Century-Crofts, 1973], p. 51.)

achievement. If we add to this the motivational factor arising out of differences in personality adjustment and social-class characteristics, we can expect that the children will spread out even more widely each year. By the time children reach the upper elementary or junior-high-school level, even if every child is reading *according to his ability,* approximately one-fifth of the children will be "retarded" readers in the sense that they read at a level two or more grades below their chronological age.

In spite of the obvious differences in ability to read, most teachers still expect all the children in their classes to read from the same page of the same book. *The Harvard Report on Reading in Elementary Schools* (Austin and Morrison, 1967) provides evidence that group instruction by reading ability, with some provision for individual instruction, is still the dominant practice. Completely individualized instruction, with no provision for group instruction, is apparently never used, and only a handful of schools use this method even to a moderate degree.

WORD ANALYSIS

Current debate in reading instruction centers on the question of how word analysis should be taught in beginning reading—whether by helping children to learn the sounds represented by the written letters or by emphasizing the meaning of the written message. The terms usually applied to the two approaches to teaching reading are "code emphasis" and "meaning emphasis."

Code Emphasis. This approach, sometimes referred to as the "phonics" method, focuses on the learning of sounds represented by each letter or combination of letters. It is based on the belief that beginning reading is essentially a process of discrimination. The child is required to make the necessary sight-sound discriminations, a skill that helps him to unlock the sounds of words and, if they are familiar, to determine their meaning. The assumption is that direct associations are established between the sight of the written word and its meaning (Witty, 1961). The written word serves as a sign for an idea with which the child is familiar and which is a part of his oral language experience. The associations that occur between the sight, sound, and experience relevant to the word result in the establishment of meaning and visual familiarity. This is fundamentally a behaviorist explanation for the learning process.

Repetition is important in this process in order for the child to learn symbol-sound patterns well enough to transfer at least some of these discrimination skills to the task of learning new words. Readiness is created as the child develops familiarity with certain symbols and sounds. Motivational satisfaction is considered to result from the feeling of adequacy and independence that the child acquires as he learns to make discriminations among words rather than from the satisfaction of immediately reading a story.

The weakness of code emphasis is that a child may develop such a strong learning set toward regarding symbol-sounds as ends in themselves that he fails to modify this set sufficiently to permit the attention to word wholes and other larger units of meaning that is necessary for fluent reading.

Meaning Emphasis. Often referred to as "sight-word" or "look-say" method, this is the approach whereby the pupil does not focus entirely on the letters of the alphabet and their sounds but centers on the whole word. This is based on the belief that reading is essentially a cognitive process that requires the reader to come to grips immediately and directly with the thought units in our language—the word, the phrase, the sentence, and other more complex patterns of thought. In a sense, the reader is directed toward meaning first, with sound-symbol discrimination incidental to making meaning. In its concern for the cognitive or meaning aspects of learning and for word wholes and word patterns as the vehicles for meaning, this approach reflects Gestalt theories of learning and has strong support from psycholinguistics.

With meaning emphasis, the principle of readiness requires that the child bring the appropriate language and experience background to the task of attaching meaning to words. Word recognition is encouraged by controlling word frequency, while overlearning and therefore retention are promoted by the high degree of controlled encounters with words and by extensive reinforcement of the meaning of these words in a variety of contexts to strengthen the association of sight-sound meaning. Presumably, transfer of learning begins to occur as the child develops a generalized attitude toward the importance of meaning in reading. A key feature in meaning emphasis is the immediate motivation satisfaction that is assumed to occur as the child realizes that he is actually "reading a story." To succeed in the act of reading is assumed to be satisfying, and deriving meaning from the story is considered to be intrinsically rewarding.

Research evidence is not clear as to whether code emphasis or meaning emphasis is better for beginning reading. However, according to several studies (Austin and Morrison, 1967; Bond and Dykstra, 1967; Chall, 1967; Hunt, 1969), with very few exceptions, schools use a beginning reading method that utilizes both code and meaning emphasis in combination. Further, evidence supports the contention that, given sufficient time, 85–90 per cent of the children in the primary grades progress satisfactorily regardless of method.

From an extensive survey of research on reading, Della-Piana and Endo (1973) conclude that it may be unlikely that schools will find one best method of reading instruction, but it is not unlikely that the best methods will be developed for specific outcomes, population, personnel, and time-cost factors. Della-Piana and Endo urge that teachers try to develop the expertise to find the best method for each child under existing conditions.

FACTORS INFLUENCING SUCCESS

As the child begins the process of learning to read, a number of physical, social, emotional, and intellectual factors come into play that affect his performance. The intellectual factor is pre-eminent, but it is by no means the only important factor. To a large extent, it makes sense to say that reading is a function of total development. Although reading achievement correlates most highly with mental development, any other factor, or combination of factors, may have a significant influence on the child's progress in reading.

CHRONOLOGICAL AGE

Chronological age has traditionally been the chief criterion for admission to school and the start of instruction in reading. Yet, the bulk of research refutes the value of having all children begin reading at about the same age. Most studies indicate that the age of beginning reading instruction is much less important for early or later reading success than are intellectual, personality, and social factors (Spache, 1963; Hirst, 1970). Nevertheless, most school systems find it administratively expedient to consider children "ready" to read when they enroll in first grade and not before.

MENTAL AGE

Very early studies promoted the belief that a mental age of six and a half years was desirable for beginning reading instruction. Later, however, Gates (1937) demonstrated that this mental age was essential to reading success only under certain classroom conditions and with certain instructional procedures. Most authorities now agree that mental age is an important factor in overcrowded, understaffed schools, but that in better schools it is less important than the cultural background and social maturity of the child. Given appropriate stimulation and opportunity, many children can learn to read before having reached the mental age of six and a half (Spache, 1963).

SEX

Numerous studies have found sex differences, usually favoring girls, in reading achievement, especially during the early years of reading instruction. In a study of nearly 15,000 children, Prescott (1955) reported somewhat superior performance by first-grade girls on the *Metropolitan Readiness Test* as compared to first-grade boys. However, this and other studies suggest that the commonly reported early sex differences favoring girls in reading may be due largely to environmental and instructional influences and are not inherent.

INTELLECTUAL CAPACITY

Reading achievement tends to be related to intelligence at all levels in the elementary school. Strang (1943) found correlations of .80 and .84 between language scores on the *California Tests of Mental Maturity*, a group intelligence test, and scores on the *Gates Basic Reading Tests*. Bond and Tinker (1973) cite numerous other studies that indicate relationships between intelligence (measured as mental age) and achievement in reading. Nevertheless, the fact that the child has high intellectual capacity does not guarantee that he will be successful in reading, especially at first.

The early stages of reading development require the exercise of mechanical skills such as visual and auditory discrimination. But, as children get into the upper grades, reading requires finer discriminations, logical reasoning abstract analysis, inference, and other comprehension skills that involve a high level of intellective ability. Thus, mental age and reading achievement become more closely related as the reader advances to more mature materials and as he reads for more mature purposes.

To a certain degree, below-average intelligence places a limit on reading achievement. There appear to be relatively few cases of "overachievers" in reading—that is, children who read at grade levels considerably higher than their mental age. However, when instruction and materials are appropriate for their needs and capabilities, children can be taught to read somewhat above the level of their mental capacity.

PHYSICAL FACTORS

Any impairment in vision—skills, discrimination, or perception—can seriously affect reading. Hinds (1959) states that the visual skills essential for reading are (1) near-point binocular vision: clearness of vision at a distance; (2) binocular coordination: accurate parallel action of the eyes; and (3) accommodation and convergence: adjustments of the eye by changes in the shape of the lens and posturing of the eyes.

Visual discrimination is an area of strong interest to reading experts.

This refers to the skill required to distinguish wordlike shapes. There have been attempts to link discrimination difficulties to laterality, or handedness, to cerebral dominance, and to reading in reverse, but there appears to be little relationship. Visual-discrimination difficulties can result in reading failures, such as inability to recognize significant details in words and thus to remember their shapes, seeing only jumbles of details, seeing separate letters as wholes but being unable to distinguish one letter from another, and attaching no significance to the orientation of the shape and therefore being liable to confusions in direction, reversals, and the like.

In their world of sight, children show a tendency to see a great deal but to observe very little. It is obvious that children cannot react to all or even a great proportion of the stimuli within their sight. Even adults are notoriously unreliable in reporting details of something they have seen. Reading involves not simply receiving light rays on the retinas of the eyes but sorting and organizing the information conveyed by the words. It is a joint physical-intellectual process. Ocular defect may be a handicap in discrimination, but some children read well despite such defect. And it is also true that some children have considerable difficulty in visual discrimination and yet have no apparent ocular deficiencies.

A venerable piece of equipment for sharpening visual skills is the tachistoscope, a device that can present information to the eyes for very brief periods of time. In its simplest form, the tachistoscope is a slide projector that throws a picture upon a screen for a controlled amount of time, usually only a fraction of a second. When the device was first used, in the 1890's, it was discovered that the eye could perceive visual stimuli after being exposed for very much less time than was generally thought necessary for perception. What could be perceived in a single brief presentation depended on what was presented and on the viewer's prior knowledge. If nonsense syllables were presented, only four or five letters would be reported. But, if familiar words were presented, especially in sentences, then four or five words—a total of perhaps twenty letters—might be perceived in one exposure.

The process of reading begins as the child learns to distinguish the shapes and details of letters and words—to discriminate significant elements. Use of the tachistoscope and other pacing devices helps the reader to begin focusing on "chunks" of words, which are "seen" by the mind in telegraphic form. Soon he develops increasing skill in seeing words and word groups as "wholes."

Another factor in reading readiness and achievement is *hearing*—especially during early reading. This involves acuity (the ability to hear sounds of varying pitch and loudness) and discrimination (the ability to distinguish similarities and differences in phonemes). Some authorities consider failure in this skill to be a primary cause of reading disability, especially when instruction in phonics is emphasized (Smith and Carrigan, 1959). However, auditory discrimination appears to be particularly difficult for the young child, since the skill normally is not fully developed before age eight.

A place to start in auditory-discrimination activities is to expose children to likenesses and differences in sounds and to help them perceive the sound of recurring rhyming words. The ability to discern differences as well as likenesses is essential to auditory discrimination. Games involving alliteration will help children to become alert to words that begin with the same consonant sound.

EMOTIONAL AND SOCIAL MATURITY

Children starting first grade bring different emotional and social characteristics to reading. Some children will be confident, poised, and eager to begin reading. Some will be shy, even fearful, and will be hesitant in getting started. Some will be "self-starters," while others need gentle but constant encouragement and guidance. Still others will show marked feelings of insecurity or social inadequacy, as well as other emotional difficulties. The causes of emotional instability can often be traced to turmoil and frustrations in the home or neighborhood. Increasingly, teachers are recognizing the importance of personal and social factors in beginning reading achievement. An important objective of the kindergarten is to accustom the child to the give-and-take of a social group of his peers, since reading is taught primarily in group situations.

Emotional and social immaturity can be a cause of poor reading, but this cause-and-effect situation is often reversed in first grade. Frequently, inability to succeed in reading is a cause of personality problems. Aggression, withdrawal, irritability, negativism, and other forms of unsocial or antisocial behavior are common symptoms of children frustrated because they cannot succeed at activities so rewarding to others in the classroom.

Although the teacher must consider the possibility that emotional factors are preventing the child from learning to read, he must bear in mind that reading difficulties are not necessarily rooted in emotional problems. Summarizing the evidence on the relationship between emotional problems and reading disability, Bond and Tinker (1973, p. 143) conclude:

1. In a relatively small proportion of the cases, children are emotionally upset and maladjusted when they arrive at school. The origin of their personality difficulties may be something constitutional or may come from unfortunate environmental conditions. Many of these children will encounter difficulties in their attempts to learn to read.
2. In a relatively large proportion of reading cases, the children will have formed well-adjusted personalities before they arrive at school. The frustration from failure to learn to read results in some degree of personality maladjustment. In these cases, reading disability causes the emotional difficulty.
3. Emotional maladjustment may be both an effect and a cause of reading disability in many cases. The emotional disturbance produced by failure to learn to read may then become a handicap to further learning. A vicious circle is formed, i.e., there is a reciprocal relationship between the emotional conditioning and the reading disability.
4. If the personal and social maladjustment is due to reading disability, it tends to disappear in most cases when the child becomes a successful reader.
5. A few children need to be referred to a psychiatric social worker, a clinical psychologist, or a psychiatrist for psychotherapy. These include two types of reading disability cases. First, there are the children who are so emotionally upset that they do not respond to the best efforts of the remedial teacher. They must achieve better adjustment through specialized aid before they are ready to learn effectively. Second, with a few children, the emotional maladjustment associated with reading is so ingrained in their responses that it remains after they learn to read well. They continue to feel nervous and insecure about their reading ability. Special therapy is needed to help them achieve more satisfactory emotional adjustment.
6. Adverse attitudes toward reading, the teacher, and school activities are due frequently to failure in reading. These undesirable attitudes are symptoms of personal and social maladjustment.

CULTURAL EFFECTS

There is widespread concern about the educational handicaps of children with cultural and socio-economic deprivations. This is not a new problem; sociologists have long noted the relationships between academic success and such factors as parental attitudes, income, and occupational level; deviant cultural or language patterns; and racial, ethnic, and social-class group patterns of behavior and thought that conflict with the dominant middle-class-oriented educational goals (Ennis, 1964; Ziller, 1964). The restricted environment of lower-social-class children frequently results in poor visual-discrimination skills (Aliotti, 1970);

inability to use adults as sources of information, correction, and reality testing and as instruments for satisfying curiosity; an impoverished language-symbolic system; and a paucity of information concepts and relational propositions (Deutsch, 1963).

Research clearly substantiates the fact that children of lower-social-class background enter first grade already behind their middle-class counterparts in a number of skills highly related to scholastic achievement. They are simply less prepared to meet the demands of the school and the classroom situation (Deutsch, 1965). The achievement differences between lower-class and middle-class children are smallest at the first-grade level and tend to increase through the elementary-school years. While the school does not contribute to the initial problem (except through its effects on the next generation), neither does it appear to do a great deal to overcome this initial handicap. For this reason, increasing interest has been shown in preparing the child to meet the school's demands before he enters the first grade, before failure and frustration result in maladjustive behavior.

Of course, many parents in the lower socio-economic classes aspire to upward mobility and have positive and constructive attitudes and behavior that they pass on to their children. And, although cultural deprivation is more readily found among lower socio-economic groups, the middle class has a goodly share of it as well (Kuschman, 1966).

It must be emphasized that to be "culturally deprived" does not mean that a particular child lacks a culture. It means, in this case, that the culture in which he is growing up has language patterns that largely restrict his communication and his mobility to a given social class. The active verbal engagement of the social groups around him is the reinforcing influence in the child's language development. Language utterances are one of the manifestations of an individual's life-style. Unfortunately, the life-style of large segments of lower-social-class families contributes to a restricted language pattern. If a child asks for something, he frequently gets a simple "yes," "no," "later," "uh-huh," or just a nod. A paucity of activities that stimulate conversation is a characteristic of homes that are culturally deprived so far as getting the child "ready" for formal reading instruction is concerned. According to Deutsch:

> The negative properties associated with lower-class and minority-group status tend to become reinforced, and for these children, language becomes an effective tool only when it has adequate feedback properties in communicating with peers and others who share the particular subculture. In other words, it becomes intra-class contained. The breakdown in communication here is probably a major operative vari-

able which leads for example to the high dropout rate: the student is no longer in communication with anything that is meaningful to him in the school. When teachers report they are frustrated with the learning attitudes and potentials of many of the disadvantaged children, they are responding objectively to a reality condition that, through their expectations, they have helped to produce [1964].

Uhl and Nurss (1970) studied the styles of solving reading-related tasks of 211 second-grade boys and girls, approximately one-third black and two-thirds white, from each of two socio-economic levels. They found that low-SEL groups were not as effective as high-SEL groups in using language to mediate, or solve, cognitive and nonverbal tasks. The dialect speech patterns of low-SEL children were related to poorer performance on tests of vocabulary, memory span, and academic achievement. The greatest similarities between the two groups appeared to be on the visual-discrimination tasks—that is, those tests least affected by language skills. Uhl and Nurss recommend that when low-SEL children are introduced to reading, maximal attention should be given to their oral listening comprehension, oral sentence completion, and rhyming.

Scott (1968, 1970), however, in a study of culturally deprived kindergarten and second-grade pupils, concluded that compensatory programs emphasizing oral-language activities may not provide the necessary experiential foundation for later reading success, unless there is also considerable visual-perception training.

It is widely believed that language retardation in the culturally deprived child can be counteracted through an enriched program of preschool education that emphasizes practice in visual and auditory discrimination and the acquisition of a vocabulary of basic concepts. Most authorities advocate that much time should be spent in reading and talking to children, in furnishing an acceptable model of speech, and in developing listening, memory, and attention skills. This view is disputed somewhat by linguists who are concerned more with meaning and fluency than with form, and also by some sociologists who feel that too much emphasis on correct speech can widen the communication gap between teacher and pupils. The need for an early introduction to language skills as a prerequisite for learning to read becomes more urgent in view of what many experts believe to be the eventual irreversibility of learning deficiencies that result from prolonged cultural deprivation.

As Ausubel states,

The child who has an existing deficit in growth incurred from past deprivation is less able to profit developmentally from new and more advanced levels of environmental stimulation. Thus, irrespective of the adequacy of all other factors—both internal and external—his deficit tends to increase cumulatively and to lead to permanent retardation [1969, p. 281].

THE DEVELOPMENT OF CONCEPTS

We acquire knowledge and experience in two ways: through our senses, by direct experience; and indirectly, through ideas conveyed by symbolic language. Both ways are useful. Words alone cannot portray the richness of a sunset over water, a Beethoven string quartet, or an exhilarating moonlight swim. These are sense-laden experiences, and words are largely unnecessary. But the world of direct experience is necessarily quite limited. The complexities of modern living require us to deal with what is not immediately present to our senses. As Walter Lippmann (1949) wrote: "The real environment is altogether too big, too complex, and too fleeting for direct acquaintance. . . . We have to reconstruct it on a simpler model before we can manage with it. Men must have maps of the world."

But one must know how to interpret a map. Language helps the child to form ideas about experiences and objects both concrete and abstract, but direct and indirect experiences and activities are necessary for the child to understand the meaning of words. Language is a tool with which to grasp ideas, but the child must have a storehouse of perceptual experiences in order to understand the meaning of the tool.

Although earlier psychologists used somewhat different terminology from what is found in more recent writings by psychologists, both saw similar characteristics of perception. Lange wrote: "The mind apprehends outer impressions in accordance with its wealth of knowledge gained through former activity. . . . We see and hear not only with the eye and ear, but quite as much with the help of our present knowledge, with the apperceiving content of the mind" (1902, pp. 5, 21). William James noted that "whilst part of what we perceive comes through our senses from the object before us, another part (and it may be the greater part) always comes . . . out of our head" (1890, p. 103). Stroud put it this way:

The brave who reads the moss on the trees, hoofprints of horses, bent twigs, twisted grass, smoke signals, pictographs inscribed on the face of a rock, is in each case making a similar psychological reaction. He is going beyond the sense data actually given. He is reacting upon the basis of the signal properties of the stimuli. His reactions are dependent upon his optical mechanism, but not determined by it, as are brightness and color; he is "seeing" with his existing store of knowledge [1956, p. 51].

Concepts are the unifying and integrative force that, through the cognitive processes, provides the intellectual wherewithal for dealing with a wide variety of experiences. As learning progresses, the child should rapidly shift from recognition of printed words to concept development, which, according to Stauffer, "merits a first-order rating in the teaching of reading as a thinking process" (1965, p. 101).

THE NATURE OF CONCEPTS

As the child progresses beyond the "naming" stage, we need to distinguish between his use of words in a denotative sense and in a connotative way. Explicit dictionary definitions of nouns—especially specific objects—are examples of denotative meanings. To learn the denotative meaning of "dog," the child must know which patterns of properties are important in determining whether or not an animal is a dog. But, in addition to its denotative meaning, "dog" has a connotative meaning: "dogness," which is a more abstract and complex version of the child's knowledge of a dog. Such qualities as "friendly," "faithful," "vicious," "man's best friend," and "floppy" are connotations that a child might have about dogs that depend on the personal experiences he has had with dogs. Although these terms are associated with "dog," they are noncritical attributes and are mostly irrelevant as far as denotation is concerned. Children acquire these connotative meanings through association, the process referred to in Chapter 2 as classical conditioning.

There are, to cite another example, many teachers with whom a given child comes in contact, differing from one another in appearance, personality, intelligence, attitudes, and many other ways. Yet, they have certain characteristics in common by which the child can identify them all as teachers and thus understand how to make appropriate responses to them. The verbal concept, or construct, of "teacher" serves as a cue for the child to behave in ways that benefit him while in the presence of a teacher. Of course, this requires a reasonably accurate and realistic concept of teachers. The child who conceives of all teachers as ogres is likely to make many serious errors in his relationships with teachers. A major determinant in developing concepts that are accurate and rich in both denotative and connotative attributes is the quantity of information and experience the child accumulates.

The important concepts a child must learn are usually quite complex.

It has been suggested that concepts can be classified as conjunctive, disjunctive, or relational.

A *conjunctive concept* must include all the relevant characteristics or attributes. The child learning the concept "elephant" finds that an elephant can be recognized by its distinctive trunk, floppy ears, and immense size. A creature that is like this in all respects but has no trunk is not an elephant.

With a conjunctive concept the learning task is not especially difficult. For example, if the child does not understand what a coconut is, the easiest thing to do is show him one, cut it open, and let him take a sip of the juice inside or a bite of the meat. If the specific item is not available, or if it is not practical to bring it into the classroom, a photograph of the item is the next best thing.

A *disjunctive concept* has one of several alternative characteristics. A foul in basketball represents a member of this concept class. A foul may be called for charging, shouting at the referee, or disrupting the game. Multiplicity of meaning makes disjunctive concepts difficult to learn.

Relational concepts involve relationships or contrasts between elements. "Larger than" and "similar to" are examples of relational concepts. Pigeons, rats, and monkeys are capable of solving relational problems, but not so rapidly as humans. Concepts involving relationships are common in everyday life, but young children often experience considerable difficulty in understanding, for example, that the same town is west of one city and south of another.

In addition, as Horn (1937) pointed out, children often do not give reasonable interpretations of certain quantitative concepts, such as "many," "few," and "average." Apparently, children find it difficult to think in relative terms and would prefer to be able to assign definite ranges of numbers to such words.

In teaching a child these relational concepts, the main problem is to provide numerous examples so that the child can contrast them with what he already knows. Thus, an "average" number of children in class could be contrasted to the total number of children in class. It should be pointed out that 100 items might be "many" in some situations and "few" in other contexts. It may help to use an unusual context in order to illustrate concepts of large and small in sharp relief. Imagine an astronaut meeting manlike creatures on the moon whose average height is 6 inches!

Concepts that are both disjunctive and relational pose a more serious problem for the teacher. Words such as "love," "hate," "teamwork," and "democracy" must be taught by successive approximations.

Each time the child is told that activities in gym class are examples of teamwork, he gets closer to a concept of teamwork. The more abstract the concept, the more examples and experiences are required for a clear understanding. It is very much like adjusting the focus on a camera. Each experience or bit of information relating to a concept functions as a partial approximation. When enough of these bits and pieces are brought together, they can form a concept that accounts for most, if not all, of the possible attributes involved in that term. The objective is to get the child closer and closer to the real thing.

E. L. Thorndike once said that normal children need at least thirty exposures to a word before they know it "cold." With words that are highly abstract—such as "democracy"—thirty exposures is the minimal requirement for learning, providing only the sensory recognition of the appearance and sound of the word. Understanding its *meaning* is quite another matter, considering that highly educated, verbally sophisticated adults can hardly come to agreement on what the term "democracy" means.

Generally speaking, concept attainment becomes more difficult as the number of relevant attributes increases, as the number of values of these attributes increases, as the information load that must be handled by the subject in order to solve the concept increases, and as the information is increasingly carried by negative rather than positive instances (Carroll, 1964).

A rich background of concepts both simple and complex is necessary for progress in reading. For this reason, the development of concepts must begin early in the reading program. The teacher's major task is to help children learn correct concepts by selecting from a wide array of instructional methods. The more ways in which a child can experience a concept, the more that concept becomes an established part of his repertoire of concepts, and the more useful it becomes as background for growth in reading comprehension. Teachers at the secondary-school level especially tend to load too many complex concepts on students rather than concentrate on teaching fewer concepts in depth.

McCullough (1959) has described four general conditions favorable to reading comprehension and concept formation:

1. *Removing impediments.* The first problem of the teacher is to discover and eliminate the deficiencies that make it impossible for the child to profit by his attempts to read. His guidance will be directed toward developing the confidence a child needs if he is to profit by his reading; developing the new word meanings without which progress is blocked; training to help the child grasp how sentences, para-

graphs, and stories are organized; and aiding his interpretation and critical evaluation.

2. *Content.* Another condition involves the content of the reading, the sorts of ideas dealt with. Content ranges from easy to difficult for a particular child. The teacher must know what the topics are and how difficult they will be to understand. Only then can he assign to his pupils what is appropriate to their present level of proficiency.

3. *Preparation.* A third condition is to prepare the pupils for what is to be read. Involved are: the pronunciation and meanings of difficult new words; preliminary reading and discussion; audio and visual materials; a problem-solving approach; introducing supplementary materials from the library that can be read; and, of course, explaining the purpose of the reading and arousing interest in it.

4. *Motivation.* Motivation is highly important. This may come partly from the desire to do well, related past experiences, previous acquaintance with a topic, curiosity about the answer to a question, a longing for approval, current interest in a subject, and the enthusiasm of the teacher and the other pupils.

WORDS AS MEDIATORS AND CONTROLLERS

The child's ability to solve problems is related to the use he makes of language in verbal mediation. Jensen (1963) defines verbal mediation as "verbal behavior which facilitates further learning, which controls behavior and which permits the development of conceptual thinking."

In the child of one and a half to two years—about as young as a child can be to respond to language at all—language has little effect other than to arouse orienting responses. If an adult says something to the child, the child may stop whatever he is doing and look at the speaker or at the object named by the adult, or he may look for the object named by the adult even if it is not immediately present; but he will not do what the adult tells him to do. If the adult says "Give me the ball," the child will just look at the ball.

As the child develops, language begins to activate an information-processing mechanism. The effect of verbal instruction then seems to be to make the child do whatever he is ready to do. In other words, if the child is ready to give the ball to the adult and the adult says "Give me that doll," the child will give the ball to the adult. This is what he was ready to do, and the language merely triggers the response.

When a child acquires a word which isolates a particular thing and serves as a signal for a particular action, the child, as he carries out an adult's verbal instruction, is subordinated to this word. The adult's word, associated with love and authority, is incorporated into the child's mental processes and becomes a regulator of his behavior. [Evcloff, 1971.]

Finally, the most advanced and interesting function language has is that of preselection, or self-instruction, which means that the child, by means of the language stimulus, is now able to understand in *advance* what he is expected to do. By about five and a half or six years, the child can withhold or inhibit a response that is inappropriate in accordance with a set of mental controls produced by previous instruction. In Piaget's (1963) words, operations of thought are "internalized" actions. He points out that the most important mediating responses (language) are implicit executive responses—responses that act to modify the environment. In other words, language helps the child "learn how to learn" and thus to cope more adequately with his environment.

This is a deficiency especially critical in many ghetto and rural-slum children. To be sure, their language has a structure, coherence, and clear meaning to those who use it. But it is a functional language. It is well suited to adaptation and survival in a poverty culture, but it does not provide a means of grasping the significance of concepts and functions that deal with ideas and events not immediately available to the senses. Skill with words and the comprehension of ideas and concepts that sprout from the thoughts behind the words are probably the most essential prerequisites for formal learning. Yet, these are exactly the skills most lacking in the culturally deprived slum child.

THE STATUS OF READING

In recent years, the ultimate objectives of reading instruction have moved far beyond purely utilitarian concerns to an emphasis on reading as a continuing source of personal value and social understanding. A child may value reading because it helps him to find answers to study questions provided by the teacher. Or he may value reading for its power to carry him to new realms of personal experience beyond the classroom. There are examples too numerous to relate of individuals whose entire lives were changed through reading. (Ralph Ellison, the black writer, once told an audience at a writers' conference that, as a boy, he was what is now termed "culturally deprived" until his mother, a cleaning woman, brought home a copy of Thackeray's *Vanity Fair*.

Ellison devoured that book, and his entire life began to change from that time.)

It is far easier, of course, to motivate most students to read when the purposes are directly utilitarian than it is to promote the "mind-stretching" values of reading. Teaching the mechanics of reading requires largely a systematic reinforcement strategy, but to bring about such important outcomes as "personal value" and "social understanding" requires the teacher to view reading instruction as the stimulation of creative thought processes.

Certainly we do not know as much about the basic nature of reading as we should like. Smith (1969) has pointed out that words are more than mere tools for signaling; they are the basic materials with which we think. If reading were an entirely physiological process, the limits of every child's reading ability could be measured and set. But reading is largely a cognitive process, and we have no reliable measure of its limits for any particular child. This being so, it is highly likely that the ability to read well can be developed in every normal child.

REFERENCES

ALIOTTI, N. C. 1970. Ability to read a picture in disadvantaged first grade children. *Reading Teacher, 24,* 3–6.

AUSTIN, M., and C. MORRISON. 1967. *The first r: The Harvard report on reading in elementary schools.* New York: Macmillan.

AUSUBEL, D. P. 1969. The influences of experience on the development of intelligence. In J. M. Seidman (ed.), *The child: A book of readings.* New York: Holt, Rinehart & Winston.

BOND, G. L., and R. DYKSTRA. 1967. *Final report, project x 001.* Washington, D.C.: Bureau of Research, U.S. Office of Education, U.S. Department of Health, Education, and Welfare.

BOND, G. L., and M. A. TINKER. 1973. *Reading difficulties: Their diagnosis and correction.* New York: Appleton-Century-Crofts.

BORMUTH, J. R. 1968. The cloze readability procedure. *Elementary English, 45,* 429–36.

CARROLL, J. B. 1964. Words, meanings and concepts. *Harvard Educational Review, 34,* 178–202.

CHALL, J. 1967. *Learning to read: The great debate.* New York: McGraw-Hill.

CHOMSKY, C. 1972. Stages in language development and reading exposure. *Harvard Educational Review, 42,* 1–33.

CHOMSKY, N. 1964. Current issues in linguistic theory. In J. A. Fodor and J. J. Latz (eds.), *The structure of language: Readings in the philosophy of language.* Englewood Cliffs, N.J.: Prentice-Hall, 50–118.

91 / *Language Development and Reading*

————. 1965. *Aspects of the theory of syntax*. Cambridge, Mass.: MIT Press.

DeBoer, J. J., and M. Dallmann. 1970. *The teaching of reading*. New York: Holt, Rinehart & Winston.

Della-Piana, G. M., and G. T. Endo. 1973. Reading research. In R. M. W. Travers (ed.), *Second handbook of research on teaching*. Chicago: Rand McNally.

Deutsch, M. 1963. The disadvantaged child and the learning process. In A. H. Passow (ed.), *Education in depressed areas*. New York: Teachers College, Columbia University.

————. 1964. *The role of social class in language development and cognition*. Speech presented at the 1964 Annual Meeting of the American Orthopsychiatric Association, Chicago, Illinois.

————. 1965. Facilitating development in the pre-school child: Social and psychological perspectives. *Merrill-Palmer Quarterly*, 249–63.

Dollard, J., and N. E. Miller. 1950. *Personality and psychotherapy*. New York: McGraw-Hill.

Doman, G. 1964. *How to teach your baby to read*. New York: Random House.

Durkin, D. 1968. When should children begin to read? In H. M. Robinson (ed.), *Innovation and change in reading instruction*. Chicago: University of Chicago Press.

Encyclopedia of Educational Research. 1969. New York: Macmillan.

Ennis, P. H. 1964. Recent sociological contributions to reading research. *Reading Teacher, 17*, 577.

Eveloff, H. H. 1971. Some cognitive and affective aspects of early language development. *Child Development, 42*, 1895–1906.

Gates, A. I. 1937. The necessary mental age for beginning reading. *Elementary School Journal, 37*, 397–408.

Geyer, J. R., and A. R. Carey. 1972. Predicting and improving comprehensibility of social studies materials: The roles of cloze procedure and readability adjustment. *Reading World, 12*(2), 85–93.

Goodman, K. S. 1972. Reading: The key is in the children's language. *Reading Teacher, 25*, 505–9.

Hafner, L. E. 1965. Implications of cloze. In E. Thurston and L. Hafner (eds.), *The Philosophical and sociological bases of reading. Fourteenth Yearbook of the National Reading Conference*. Milwaukee: National Reading Conference.

Hall, M. 1972. Linguistically speaking, why language experience? *Reading Teacher, 25*, 328–31.

Havighurst, R. J. 1972. *Developmental tasks and education*. New York: David McKay.

Hinds, L. R. 1959. Longitudinal studies of certain visual characteristics, readiness, and success in reading. *Reading in a Changing Society, 4*, 84–86.

Hirst, W. E. 1970. Entrance age—a predictor variable for academic success? *Reading Teacher, 23*, 547–56.

HORN, E. 1937. *Methods of instruction in social studies.* New York: Scribners.

HUNT, L. C., JR. 1969. Decoding or meaning? It's more than a matter of method. *Today's Education,* 58(4), 21–22, 62.

JAMES, W. 1890. *The principles of psychology,* II. New York: Holt.

JENSEN, A. R. 1963. Learning in the pre-school years. *Journal of Nursery Education,* 18, 133–39.

KUSCHMAN, W. E. 1966. Education and society in disadvantaged suburbia. *School and Society,* 94, 386–87.

LaCONTE, C. 1969. Reading in kindergarten. *Reading Teacher,* 23, 116–26.

LANGE, K. 1902. *Apperception: A monograph on psychology and perception,* ed. Charles DeGarmo. Boston: D. C. Heath.

LENNEBERG, E. H. 1966. The natural history of language. In F. Smith and G. A. Miller (eds.), *The genesis of language: A psycholinguistic approach.* Cambridge, Mass.: MIT Press.

———. 1970. On explaining language. In H. E. Fitzgerald and J. P. McKinney (eds.), *Developmental psychology.* Chicago: Dorsey Press.

LIPPMANN, W. 1949. *Public opinion.* New York: Macmillan.

LOBAN, W. 1963. *The language of elementary school children.* Champaign, Ill.: National Council of Teachers of English.

McCULLOUGH, C. M. 1959. Conditions favorable to comprehension. *Education,* 79, 533–36.

PIAGET, J. 1963. *The language and thought of the child.* Cleveland: World Publishing.

PRESCOTT, G. A. 1955. Sex differences in metropolitan readiness test results. *Journal of Educational Research,* 48, 605–10.

ROBINSON, H. M. 1968. The next decade. In *Innovation and change in reading instruction. The Sixty-seventh yearbook, National Society for the Study of Education,* Part II. Chicago: University of Chicago Press.

SCOTT, R. 1968. Perceptual readiness as a predictor of success in reading. *Reading Teacher,* 22, 36–39.

———. 1970. Perceptual skills, general intellectual ability, race, and later reading achievement. *Reading Teacher,* 23, 660–70.

SEYMOUR, D. Z. 1969. The difference between linguistics and phonics. *Reading Teacher,* 23, 99–102.

SMITH, D. E., and P. M. CARRIGAN. 1959. *The nature of reading disability.* New York: Harcourt, Brace.

SMITH, N. B. 1969. The many faces of reading comprehension. *Reading Teacher,* 23, 249–59.

SPACHE, G. D. 1963. *Toward better reading.* Champaign, Ill.: Garrard.

———. 1968. Contributions of allied fields to the teaching of reading. In H. M. Robinson (ed.), *Innovation and change in reading instruction.* Chicago: University of Chicago Press.

SPACHE, G. D., and E. B. SPACHE. 1969. *Reading in the elementary school.* Boston: Allyn & Bacon.

STAATS, A. W. 1968. *Learning, language, and cognition*. New York: Holt, Rinehart & Winston.

STANCHFIELD, J. M. 1971. Development of pre-reading skills in an experimental kindergarten program. *Reading Teacher, 24,* 699–708.

STAUFFER, R. G. 1965. Concept development and reading. *Reading Teacher, 19,* 101.

STRANG, R. 1943. Relationships between certain aspects of intelligence and certain aspects of reading. *Educational and Psychological Measurements, 3,* 355–59.

STROUD, J. B. 1956. *Psychology in education*. New York: Longmans, Green.

SUTTON, H. 1964. Readiness for reading at the kindergarten level. *Reading Teacher, 17,* 234–39.

―――. 1969. Children who learned to read in kindergarten: A longitudinal study. *Reading Teacher, 22,* 595–602.

UHL, N. P., and J. R. NURSS. 1970. Socio-economic level styles in solving reading-related tasks. *Reading Research Quarterly, 5,* 452–85.

WATSON, J. B. 1920. Is thinking merely the action of language mechanism? *British Journal of Psychology, 11,* 87–104.

WEAVER, W. W. 1965. Theoretical aspects of the cloze procedure. In E. Thurston and L. Hafner (eds.), *The philosophical and sociological bases of reading. Fourteenth Yearbook of the National Reading Conference.* Milwaukee: National Reading Conference.

WEINSTEIN, R., and N. S. RABINOVITCH. 1971. Sentence structure and retention in good and poor readers. *Journal of Educational Psychology, 62,* 25–30.

WITTY, P. 1961. A forward look in reading. *Elementary English, 38,* 151–64.

ZILLER, R. C. 1964. The social psychology of reading. *Reading Teacher, 17,* 583–88.

PART 2

Psychology and the Child

CHAPTER FIVE

The Perceptual World
of the Child

THE PSYCHOLOGY of perception emphasizes internal, psychological forces —needs, wants, anxieties, values, attitudes, interests, and so on. Perceptual psychology is concerned not with their direct effects on behavior but with the ways the individual interprets or perceives what these forces mean to him. Teachers have traditionally held that teaching is a matter of standing authoritatively before a class, aiming a learning gun at the students, and zapping them with knowledge. Students may "learn" something this way, but they will internalize very little unless the teacher pulls them into it in a personal way. Somewhere in the learning process the student has to feel that it all has some significance to him personally. This occurs when something in the child's own experience connects with what he is confronted with in the classroom. Thus, the classroom must become a place where the exciting experience of exploring and discovering personal meaning is the central activity. Without it, the result is likely to be the all-too-frequent instance of the teacher who lectures, discusses, and reviews abstract ideas and concepts period after period, feels assured that the students really know it, and yet, when he tests them a week or two later, finds that most of the learning either was forgotten or was never acquired in the first place.

FROM S-R TO S-O-R

Behaviorism provides a comprehensive explanation of many forms of learning: trial-and-error and discrimination learning, maze learning, rote memorization, the acquisition of skills, and so on. It provides a way of describing environmental influences upon the organism (the input) and the organism's responses (the output) by focusing on the stimulus-response (S-R) factors, with relatively little concern for the intermediary processes.

An associationist system can account for the learning behavior of simple stimulus-bound creatures, such as rats and pigeons, or it can explain the learning of simple movements, such as turning right or left toward a specific stimulus. The child's acquisition of basic skills generally follows this process. Learned behavior such as this does not seem to depend on earlier experience to any great extent.

Much of the learning behavior of young humans—babies—is similar to that of lower animals—simple and direct. As children, humans are as much sensory creatures as the lower animals are throughout their lives. Only gradually does the human child expand its sense-bound behavior patterns and begin to respond more selectively to changes in his environment. Whereas a bird, dog, rat, or baby reacts to every noise or shadow, the older child ignores most of the noises and shadows that surround him except those to which he attaches some importance. The outstanding characteristic of human learning is the relative rapidity with which the maturing child begins to make sense of the tremendously complex world about him. How is it that an older child or adult can recall a set of directions that is stated only once, whereas a small child may need to hear a number of repetitions? The reason is that the very young child is still at the stage of learning basic elements of language and concepts, whereas the older child or adult already has learned most of the essential components of the task and needs only to learn the sequence. Because adults are familiar with virtually all the elements they are called upon to use in acquiring new knowledge, they need only attend to the novel features.

As children get older, background factors become more prominent. Some things will be easier for the child to learn because he has already acquired S-R associations. Other things may be difficult, however, because he still has inadequate or even wrong associations that are aroused by the stimuli the teacher is manipulating. The effects of background and experience become extremely important as teachers deal with the maturing child. Generally speaking, the older the child gets, the more difficult it becomes to affect his behavior by controlling the environment in which he is operating. We can "control" him, but we cannot be certain what stimuli he will choose to respond to. In fact, at any given time, most people are responding to many stimuli. For example, when an adolescent receives a sharp, specific stimulus in the form of a school bell reminding him to go to gym class, he may really be reacting to an entire array of stimuli—thoughts of boredom, the sudden desire to talk to a classmate in gym class, the chance to try out his new gym shoes, the hope for improvement in dribbling a basketball, as well as the conditioned habit of going somewhere else when a school bell rings!

Since most human learning situations are complex, they bring into play a multiplicity of motives and experiential factors, all reinforcing and interfering with each other in various ways. When an S-R event is a reflex action—such as the blinking of the eye following a puff of air—it is assumed that little occurs between the stimulus and the response. But in higher forms of thinking, such as a presented problem in math (the stimulus) and its solution (the response), what occurs between these events involves cognition and insight, which are unique to each individual. Perceptual psychology is based on the premise that what takes place between a stimulus and its elicited response is not just another component of the learning process but the nucleus of learning itself.

REALITY AND PERCEPTION

A basic premise of perceptual psychology is that behavior is the result, not of the situation as it actually exists, but of the individual's perception of the situation at any given moment. What one perceives is more than what is seen in a physical sense. Two persons witnessing the same event may "see" very different things. Yet, what each "sees" is reality to him, the only reality by which he can guide his behavior.

To understand perceptual psychology, it will be helpful to assume that there are two ways to describe reality. When we ask the fundamental question of what life is all about—what is real and what is imagined, what truly exists and what can be considered to be the stuff of the spirit or mind—the answer may be formulated according to two general philosophical schools: realism and idealism.

REALISM

The realist believes that all matter constitutes true reality—from the observable bodies of the universe to the physical world about us, including our own physical beings. Aristotle was among the first to develop the idea that reality is, in fact, the material elements of our existence. This is the fundamental premise of the physical sciences.

According to this conception, all matter exists in measurable amounts and can be neither added to nor subtracted from; it remains essentially the same and changes in form only.

An important characteristic of the philosophy of realism and the methodology of science is that both call for definitions that can be understood by everyone. A scientific definition of a piece of blackboard chalk would consist of a description of the atomic structure of that chalk plus a series of mathematical statements and chemical terms that identify its size, weight, shape, function, and so forth. The important point is that this definition must result in agreement among all concerned regarding its basic nature and ingredients. It should be so clear to the scientist (or to anyone else interested in a scientific description) as to cause little or no ambiguity. A very clear, objective description of that particular piece of chalk would be almost, but not quite, identical to anyone else's definition of that piece of chalk. This is sometimes referred to in research as an *operational definition*. Like the recipe for a cake, a good operational definition helps one to understand exactly what directions have to be followed, and what ingredients assembled, in order to arrive at an almost identical understanding of a particular object, or concept (Bridgman, 1969).

In effect, the realist says that our piece of chalk has potentially one, and only one, true "reality." This method of defining objects in the world around us is very important in science and has been instrumental in providing the basis for the so-called scientific method of inquiry. As we will see in Chapter 6, operational definitions play an important role in the development and construction of various instruments used in the identification and measurement of human learning and ability.

IDEALISM

The Greek philosopher Plato, an idealist, approached reality from quite another direction. The idealist says that the material things around us are not "real" in themselves but are merely copies of reality. The chair we sit on is but a pale reflection of the spirit, or essence, of an ideal "chair" which exists in a perfect state somewhere in the realms of the mind or spirit. In other words, true reality, according to Plato, involves something more than the scientific description of the material world around us.

Let's return to our example of the chalk. Picture a teacher holding that piece of chalk in front of his students. Everyone "sees" the same object; that is, identical light rays are bouncing off the retina of their eyes. After all, if you've seen one piece of chalk, you've seen them all! Now, as the teacher displays the chalk prominently before the class, he says, "In the next few minutes, with this piece of chalk I intend to write a very difficult examination on the blackboard." To each pair of eyes focused on that chalk, what now is the "reality" of this object? As the students begin to contemplate what is in store for them, this apparently innocent object takes on a rather menacing image, a reality that is unique and significant for each person viewing it! Its objective characteristics are not important now. What is important is what that piece of chalk has in store for each student. In most of his contacts with the environment, the significant factor that affects the individual is not the outward, material appearance or nature of objects and ideas; rather, it is the personal meaning that he attaches to them. In fact, the meaning he attaches may have almost no relation to objective reality. A thirsty man in the desert will run as eagerly to a pool of water that is only a mirage as he will to a real pool.

REALITY: A DYNAMIC CONCEPT

By this idealist concept, reality is not static but dynamic. Our insignificant piece of chalk now has a special meaning. The perceiver becomes aware of qualities in the chalk which, in turn, affect his thoughts and feelings, and these remind him of other aspects of chalk, and so on. It is a back-and-forth, interactive process. Perhaps the most famous expression of this concept in artistic form is the line by writer Gertrude Stein: " Rose is a rose is a rose . . ." When one looks at a rose, it causes him to react, and as he does he gets interested and involved in the rose, while the rose, in turn, expands and evolves aesthetically before his gaze—like a multifaceted jewel. Perception is an interactive relationship characterized by change; it is a reality based on the dynamic nature of personal experience. In a sense, this process is like repeatedly putting one's foot in a river; each time it is a *different* river. All the phenomena of our existence are in a never-ending state of interaction and change.

But, you may say, our intellectual training and our habit of accepting what our senses tell us cause us to think in terms of only one reality for any given object before us. It is "good common sense" to regard this pencil in my hand as having one and only one reality. The notion that it is a different object to each person who is perceiving or using it is not "scientific." After all, is it common sense to say that one object can be many objects at the same time?

From the logic of science, man has developed the habit of assuming that similar things are truly alike. This is a result of our efforts to classify things. If we can say that all the objects in a certain group are the same, we do not have to deal with so many different objects. For example, if each child in kindergarten brings one oak leaf to school, we can put all the leaves in one category or class. It is possible to show that different children carry different notions of the size and other characteristics of an oak leaf, that there is no such thing as a "standard" oak leaf. But abstractions that are kept reasonably close to the concrete objects upon which they are based can be useful tools. When we consider them as reality in themselves, we confuse the tool with what we make with the tool. An abstraction is a sort of statistical average of all our clues with regard to an object in our surroundings. Like any statistical average, it can be precisely right only once in an infinite number of cases. In most cases, it is somewhat less than accurate. The teacher must realize that each child has a perceptual awareness of an abstraction that may differ considerably from the one the teacher intends.

PERCEPTION AND THE INDIVIDUAL

The basis of perceptual psychology is a focus on the individual's inner core of feelings and beliefs and how these inner forces influence his view of the world about him and his relationship to that world. A person's behavior is the direct result of his total perceptual field at the moment he thinks and acts. More specifically, at every moment his behavior can be described as the result of how he sees himself, how he views the world about him, and the interrelationship of these two (Combs, 1967). It is evident that the conditions under which children grow and develop are not so important in understanding their behavior as is the way in which they react to, or "see" (perceive), these conditions. And of all the perceptions that exist for an individual, none is so important as those he has about *himself*. The individual's self is the center of his entire thinking-feeling world, and all his actions spring from his perceptions of self and the world.

The perceptual field is the universe of naive experience in which each individual lives, the everyday situation of the self and its surroundings that each person takes to be reality. To each of us, the perceptual field of another person contains much error and illusion— it seems an interpretation of reality rather than reality itself. But to the individual, his perceptual field *is* reality—it is the only reality he knows (Combs, 1967).

Perception, then, is the process by which we obtain first-hand information about the world. As a concept, it overlaps with cognition; but perception involves more—the distinctive effects of experience.

Perception also has a responsive aspect; it entails discriminative, selective responses to the stimuli in the immediate environment. A rather gross selectivity at birth becomes progressively refined with development and experience. Gibson (1969) defines perceptual learning as an increase in the ability to extract information from the environment as a result of experiences with stimulation from the environment.

As Combs (1967) states the position, all behavior, without exception, is completely determined by, and pertinent to, the perceptual field of the behaving organism. This concept is fundamental in understanding the child in the classroom.

FACTORS AFFECTING PERCEPTION

We make contact with external reality through the vehicle of perceptual processes. It is a personalized world that we see "through a glass darkly," in the words of Saint Paul. A number of variables intervene between individual perception and objective reality—among them, physiological factors, time and experience, values and goals, the existence of threat, and what we shall call "need prisms."

PHYSIOLOGICAL FACTORS

Among the more obvious factors affecting perception are physiological and biological disorders, such as mongolism and microcephalia, as well as mechanical or disease damage to the central nervous system. Malnutrition, visual disabilities, and chronic fatigue may also affect perceptual processes. It must be stated, however, that individuals who suffer impairment of various sense modalities may have as rich and varied a perceptual field within their own limitations as we have within ours. These people may have different, but not necessarily fewer or poorer, perceptions than "normals." Their perceptions develop from the sense modalities they do have.

It should be understood that perceptions are *psychological* (a broader term than *visual, auditory, tactile,* and *olfactory*). Perceptions are the way in which we interpret external events and forces, mediated through our inner forces. A totally blind person has a "perception" of any familiar stimulus, although it is not a visual image. The stimulus is associated in his mind with something, but what that something is cannot be understood adequately by those with normal sight. In other words, "perception" is the total battery of responses, of which the formation of visual images is only one.

TIME AND EXPERIENCE

Generally speaking, what an individual is able to perceive in any situation depends to a considerable extent on how long he has been exposed to the event. In most situations, the more time the individual has to observe, the more he is able to perceive. The more often one hears a piece of music or inspects a painting, the more details, themes, relationships, special effects, and meanings he will perceive. This process of discerning increasing detail out of the total field of awareness is called *differentiation*.

The time required to perceive an event or an idea may vary from a split second to generations. Studies have shown, for example, that it is possible for a person to differentiate single words exposed in tachistoscopes at speeds of as little as one hundredth of a second. Even at these speeds, viewers report seeing "something there." On the other hand, it has taken centuries for man to perceive the relationship of the earth to the solar system. Human beings lived with gravity for thousands of years before it was perceived and stated as a principle of physics.

Most perceptions the individual makes reflect his previous experiences. Prior learning provides the basis for discrimination. The more background and experience one has with football, the more he will perceive in a Saturday afternoon game.

Values and Goals. Some values and goals are differentiated as positive and satisfying and therefore will be highly sought. Values that are negative, demeaning, or threatening will be avoided. When a person's values and goals are known, it often becomes possible to predict with great accuracy how he will behave in given situations.

The kinds of interests people hold are a function of the values and goals that are important to them. We are interested in whatever serves to satisfy our needs. A boy will try out for Little League competition because he likes baseball and because he hopes to get personal recognition by performing before others. He may find that the pressure to excel is more than he expected. But the reaction of his team members and the encouragement of the coach will help to sustain him. When he develops some skill and begins to regard himself as an important member of the team, his motivation will become self-sustaining.

THREAT

Any perceived threat to our physical or psychological well-being will directly affect our perceptions. The individual may react to threat in a number of ways. He may prevent it from coming into focus by pretending it isn't there. He may fall back on rationalizations or other ways of distorting the situation in order to make it less threatening or ego deflating.

When threat becomes severe, it can lead to narrowing of the perceptual field, so that the anxious individual is unable to focus on the broader circumstances of the problem. He becomes fixated on his own fears. This situation, called "tunnel vision," results in stereotyped, rigid, sometimes bizarre behavior. In some cases, it can force a temporary change of personality. During the sinking of the ocean liner *Titanic*, for example, some passengers reportedly reverted to an almost primitive state, forgetting their own families in their eagerness to get into a lifeboat, donning women's clothing in order to qualify for a seat, and otherwise perceiving only their drives for self-preservation. In athletic competition, one of the standard tactics of play is to undermine the confidence of the opposition so as to reduce its resourcefulness and cause it to make mistakes—to "psyche" one's opponent, as tennis star Bobby Riggs does so well. Coaches overcome this by rigorous training. The athlete anticipates threatening situations by developing almost instinctual response habits. This gives him the confidence to try out innovative alternatives whenever necessary.

NEED PRISMS

As the foregoing section suggests, we do not notice everything about us. From the thousands of features in our environment at any given moment, we choose to notice those that the self feeds upon. The direction of the growth of the self depends upon these choices.

Why does a child select what he does out of his surroundings, and why does he classify, or ascribe meaning, in his own way? No two persons do this in precisely the same fashion, since individuals differ in past experience and in what they want to achieve or become. To a large degree, one will pay attention to those elements in his environment that hold the most promise of advancing his purposes or to those that are most threatening, which he senses may frustrate his purposes.

In the words of Combs and Snygg (1959, p. 46), man's basic need is that "great driving, striving force in each of us by which we are continually seeking to make ourselves ever more adequate to cope with life." Everyone is perpetually concerned with· the search for a more competent self. Whether he is successful in this search will be determined largely by the perceptions he is able to make in the course of his life. His perceptions help him to behave in ways that are likely to lead to the satisfaction of his fundamental need for adequacy. The basic need for adequacy is composed of many lesser needs, all of which contribute to the total personality growth of the individual.

As an illustration, consider the self-concept to be surrounded by something we might call *need prisms*. These need prisms function as the means by which information is relayed from within the person to the external world and from the external world to the person's inner self (Fig. 5.1). Each prism corresponds to a need that tends to bend, or distort, information being sent or received by the senses. For example, if I were to overhear a student comment on my "very readable and scholarly textbook on educational psychology," I would probably "hear" the comment quite clearly. I might even mentally note the "high caliber" of students at my university. On the other hand, if another student mutters in my presence, "What a dull, uninspired book this is!" it is quite likely that I may not even "hear" what he said. If, like almost everyone else, I have a strong need for approval from others, my need prisms will generally function to screen out comments that are personally upsetting.

Of course, it would be beneficial for any author to evaluate all views of his book objectively, but it is always difficult to accept with enthusiasm what is threatening or inconsistent with what we believe or hope about ourselves and our efforts. Our need prisms are always functioning to shape incoming information in order to make it a little more palatable. They might even grossly distort some input so that perceptions are much closer to what we would like them to be. In many cases, this is the mechanism by which individuals cope with forces that might otherwise be overwhelming. Information and perceptions that are consistent with what we believe will be processed and retained; information and perceptions that are *not* consistent with our beliefs and desires will be either rejected or changed into a more acceptable shape. Fundamentally, we tend to act in ways that protect our self-esteem.

The need prisms of our personalities are in a state of continual change—daily, even hourly. If a person gets hungry, a restaurant sign, a chance word, a look at his watch—almost anything will painfully remind him of food. If inadequate diet is chronic, he may spend a great deal of time thinking about food. Psychologists have long been fascinated with the question of how needs affect perceptions. Studies have found that college students asked to estimate their academic aptitude tend to answer in ways that protect their feelings of adequacy.

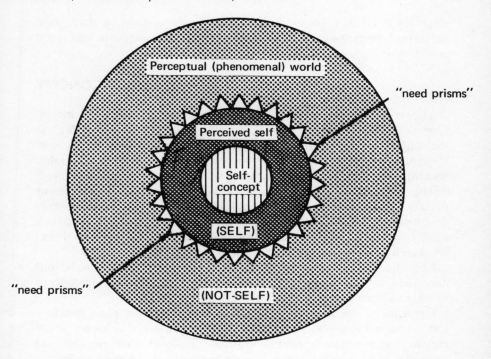

Fig. 5.1. The relationship of needs to the self-concept.

It has been noted that children from poor homes estimate coins as being larger than the estimates of the same coins made by children from wealthy homes. The poor child's perceptual distortion of the size of coins can often reveal quite clearly what is on his mind.

Each child brings with him to class his own pattern of need prisms, a kind of personal agenda. As the teacher makes assignments and discusses learning activities, each child processes a perception of the information. To begin with, the teacher himself evokes a particular image in each child. To some he is strong and loving, to others he is menacing and punitive, to still others he is simply an enigma. What the teacher communicates will be reacted to in even more variable ways. The child who has a strong need for a good grade will eagerly grasp everything the teacher says and bend it in the direction of his hope that this will be his lucky day. His need for grades makes him avidly receptive to any opportunity for an A. On the other hand, the low-achieving child may not even "hear" the assignment, or he may make an instant perception of it as impending disappointment and even punishment.

THE SELF-CONCEPT

The core of the individual's perceptual field is his self-concept. Originally proposed by Lecky (1945) and adopted by Rogers (1961) as the central idea of nondirective counseling and psychotherapy, the self-concept is of major importance to the classroom teacher in understanding the child's behavior relating to motivation and adjustment.

The self-concept is a system of attitudes, feelings, and perceptions that the individual has about himself. All attitudes are important determinants of behavior, but attitudes concerning the self are much more basic than those in which the individual is less ego-involved and are therefore more potent in determining behavior.

Can the individual's self-concept be measured? Not precisely, but one could conceivably gain an approximation of his own self-concept by the following procedure:

Get a reasonably accurate photograph of yourself and place it before you on the table. Now, look at that picture and ask, "*Who are you?*" If you can honestly express what you think of that person, and especially how you feel about him or her, you would have at least a partial estimate of your self-concept. Of course, it is not likely that anyone could describe himself really accurately—even if he wanted to do so very much. Few people know themselves that well; in fact, most people learn something new about themselves at frequent times throughout their lives—even in their advanced years.

In addition to the basic feelings the individual has about himself, which are largely the legacy of his childhood, he eventually supplies a great many objective facts about himself, which add realism to his feelings and understanding of himself. The feedback he receives in competition with others contributes to the development of the self-concept. Without some basis for comparison, the individual has no way of knowing what he can do or cannot do.

The core of the self-concept, however, is always the feelings we have about ourselves, and this self-evaluation greatly influences our behavior in almost everything we do. This is an important principle for the teacher, for the way the child feels about himself will have much to do with the kind of learning he can achieve.

The child's self-concept colors his interpretation of his environment and may interfere with or facilitate his perception of certain events.

Thus, we can expect that children from different backgrounds wit. different sets of values will differ in the interpretation they give to pieces of literature and perhaps even historical materials. Further, as we will see, the child's self-concept and his resultant perceptions of external reality have a direct relationship to his motivational level. In many cases, as the teacher or counselor gains an understanding of the nature of a child's self-concept, he can predict that child's future motivation and degree of personal success in the classroom.

DETERMINANTS OF THE SELF-CONCEPT

How does the self-concept begin? Is the self-concept a little man in a bowler hat inside each of us telling us what we are and how we should behave—like a conscience? Is the self-concept influenced by heredity and fixed for all time; or is it learned? Actually, it is acquired in both ways, but the part of it that is learned is what concerns us most. There are three major determinants of the self-concept: genetic inheritance, family, and the external environment.

Although one's genetic inheritance is largely fixed, its effects can be altered to some extent in specific cases. For example, nutritional factors can sometimes significantly alter the growth patterns of individuals, medical or therapeutic treatment can sometimes offset the effects of certain kinds of physical handicaps, and the self-concept can be seriously eroded by a temporary crisis involving physical development. A common example is the effect of late (or early) maturation of adolescents of both sexes (Jones and Mussen, 1958).

The child's closest family members—his primary group—are the first and usually the greatest influence on his self-concept. The ways in which parents and others in the immediate family who are very close to him regard the child will be a very significant influence on his attitudes toward himself. In fact, the help that parents can give, or the burdens they impose, can set irrevocable and irreversible patterns of personality development (Ausubel, 1969). The ideal situation is to have parents who have a zest for life, who are confident of its rewards, who feel that they are worthy persons, who know they are useful in their work and community, and who regard each other as autonomous. admirable individuals. Such parents can ignore the primacy of their own needs and accept their child for what he is and what he is becoming.

As the child grows and interacts in the environment outside his home, significant others in the broader world about him such as teachers, friends, and neighbors become contributors to the development of his self-concept. Later, in his adolescence, the child will come into contact with individuals and social groups even further removed from his immediate personal circle, and these influences will also contribute to his personality development through the setting of competitive standards and especially the inculcation of social values and attitudes.

DEVELOPMENT OF THE SELF-CONCEPT

Early Infancy. Every infant is born without knowledge of himself or the world about him. At first, his world is totally undifferentiated. As he experiences hunger, dampness, pain, and as he gains control over physiological equipment and functions, he gradually begins to differentiate between "me" and "not me." As the infant becomes more a person and less a mere organism, the process of living itself becomes as important to him as the actual satisfaction of his needs. This is the beginning of psychological development, and the treatment he receives as a consequence is an important determinant of personality characteristics. Erikson (1963) has postulated that, if an infant's needs are met fully and dependably, he becomes aware of the world as a good, stable, and encouraging place to be—a place to be trusted. But, when his needs are not met, the world becomes for him a frustrating, threatening place where no trust is possible. Thus, the infant's basic attitudes of trust or distrust are developing, and these attitudes will determine how he will approach and regard others and the events of his life.

Late Infancy and Preschool. By the end of the second year, the child's self-concept becomes much more precise as he learns to speak and to understand the meaning of "mine." In fact, at this age almost everything he comes in contact with he sees as "mine." This stage merges into the period where he is able to replace his name with "I." Then, as he grows increasingly aware of his powers and self-worth, he enters the stage where resistance to parental guidance becomes the familiar "no" of the two-and-a-half- to three-year-old. Now his parents have to tread the fine line between teaching him self-control and providing opportunities in which he can practice using his own initiative.

For the three-year-old, increased awareness of himself is developing into an integrated self-concept. This is a very important stage, because he is now capable of a wide variety of behavior, including some that must be corrected by his parents. He must gain a clear idea that, although what he *does* may often be a "no-no," he *himself* is loved and accepted no matter what his actions are. Separating his perceptions of himself from his actions is extremely important in the growth of a positive self-concept. There is a big difference between telling a child that he is acting in annoying, even obnoxious, ways and telling him that *he* is an annoying, obnoxious person. Of course, every parent occasionally gets angry at his child and calls him a pest or whatever, but a steady stream of labeling over a period of time will inevitably leave a mark on his self-concept.

Nursery-School Years. The nursery or kindergarten classroom provides one of the first opportunities for the positive development of self-concept in the young child. It is essential that each child in the classroom be recognized as an individual, and that he or she be called by name as soon as and whenever possible. This can pay off when a child remarks, "I like my teacher; she already knows my *name.*" Adults are pleased and feel a sense of acceptance when they are courteously introduced. This is also true of the young child as he ventures forth into the larger social world from the secure familiarity of his home. It is also helpful if the teacher learns something about each child's family and his home life.

As important as recognizing the child's name, and hence his presence in the group, is the repetition of his name in writing. At first, his name can be placed on objects that belong to him, such as his painting smock, his "cubby," or the book or toy he brings from home. A printed name card pinned to his shirt gives the child tangible evidence that this is *his* classroom, a place where he is important and belongs.

Teachers should encourage the children to put their names on their products as well. When the child signs his work, he displays his name for all to see: "This is a part of me; I created this and am proud of it." Writing his name can also help the child to progress to writing captions under pictures, with the teacher's guidance, and can enable the teacher to assess the child's readiness for language development.

Ample space should be provided for displaying children's work. The kindergarten or nursery-school classroom's walls, windows, and light fixtures should be resplendent with the self-expression of its young occupants. Teachers should view the labeling of children's belongings and their products, not as a convenience, but as a way to foster the child's sense of belonging and to build his ego. Children are most affected by things or events when they feel part of them and involved in them. Lists of names of those responsible for passing out supplies, cleaning up, and evaluating activities are also appropriate for the young child's classroom.

Childhood. Much of the child's early sense of identity develops from identification with his parents during the preschool years. When he enters school, he encounters additional reinforcement from his teachers, but an even more powerful influence is the peer group. He is now faced with a larger reference group, more objective evaluation, and less personal attention. He has to accept the give-and-take of the classroom—the rights, privileges, and possessions of others. The typical ten-year-old does not have absolute measuring rods to help him decide how bright, handsome, or likable he is. He naturally and spontaneously uses his immediate peer group as the reference for these evaluations. The larger the peer group, the less likely it is that a child will conclude that he is high in rank order, and therefore the less likely that he will feel that he is unusually smart, handsome, or capable of leadership. For example, consider two boys, each with an IQ of 130 and similar intellectual interests. One lives in a small town, the other in a large city. It is likely that the former child will be the most competent in his peer group, while the latter is likely to be fifth or sixth best. Thus, differences in perceived rank order in many objective qualities are often relative to the circumstances of the individual's immediate environment.

Adolescence. The "middle years" in the process of growing up are the period that most adults appear to understand least. One reason is that frequently the adolescent turns his back on adults and actively shuts them out from his world. Even if the child wishes to communicate his feelings and perceptions, he often does not have enough command of the language to do so. He is more likely to "act out" his emotions in ways that are often hard for adults to understand and accept fully. Of course, many adolescents can express themselves quite well and have close relationships with their parents, but many others do not. In fact, some may never have the verbal-conceptual skills to communicate to parents and others their innermost feelings and attitudes.

Yet, the need for self-expression is characteristic of almost every growing child. Parents and teachers who work with young people of this age should not let their concern with doing things to them—educating them, civilizing them, and so forth—divert them from attempting to understand the inner state of those young people.

The physiological changes experienced by the adolescent stimulate self-doubts about his appearance, behavior, morality, and relationship with others.

The central theme of adolescence is the finding of one's self. The adolescent must learn to know a whole new body and its potential for feeling and behavior, and fit it into his picture of himself. He must come to terms with the new constellation of meanings presented by the environment. He must define the place he will occupy in adult society. This means an intensified self-awareness—largely manifested as *self-consciousness*—and a new push for independence.

In early adolescence, the individual continues to seek independence —although with new vigor and in new areas—almost in the way he did in the middle years: he wants more privileges, more freedom from adult supervision and restraint so that he can follow the dictates of the gang. . . . For the young adolescent is still primarily concerned about his status with his immediate peers; he strives to be as much like the others as possible, largely as a result of feeling out of step with them. Individual differences are now more clear-cut than at earlier ages, but a uniqueness which is still only half-understood is not completely welcome.

The older adolescent shares the younger one's concerns but is, in addition, confronted by the problem of where he stands with respect to the entire adult world of independence, marriage, jobs, politics—in short, he must now find an identity as himself rather than as a member of either his family or his gang. We can say that the young adolescent is concerned with who and what he is, and the older adolescent with what to do about it. [Stone and Church, 1968, p. 270.]

Adolescence is the stage at which the effects of a positive or negative self-concept can become starkly noticeable. How the adolescent views himself influences his behavior in quite obvious ways. It is now that the self-concept functions as a "self-fulfilling prophecy." For example, the child who enters middle school with high expectations of happiness and success is most likely to apply himself energetically to school challenges and responsibilities; his energy and motivation will therefore raise the probability of his success. His expectations, which are so much related to his positive feelings about himself, will help him over the rough moments in class.

Having a positive view of self is much like having money in the bank. It provides a kind of security that permits the owner a freedom he could not have otherwise. With a positive view of self one can risk taking chances; one does not have to be afraid of what is new and different. A sturdy ship can venture farther from port. Just so, an adequate person can launch himself without fear into the new, the untried, and the unknown. This permits him to be creative, original, and spontaneous. What is more, he can afford to be generous, to give of himself freely or to become personally involved in events. Feeling he is much more, he has so much more to give. [Combs, 1962, p. 53.]

Conversely, the child with a negative self-concept half-expects to do poorly and therefore may work at his responsibilities with little enthusiasm. This, in turn, may lead to failure, news of which is received as more or less expected—thus fulfilling the psychological "prophecy" with which he began.

The cumulative effects of the self-concept are most poignantly apparent with respect to one's feelings toward others. How the child views others reflects what he feels about himself. If he has a strong, positive feeling about himself, he will tend to regard others in an equally positive way. Since he is positive in his behavior toward others, he is likely to be treated better by others as a consequence, which, in turn, reinforces his attitudes toward himself. Conversely, if the child has qualities in himself that he rejects, he is also likely to reject these qualities in others. This can lead to conflict and dislike by others.

In summary, the individual develops feelings that he is likable, desirable, acceptable, and able from having been liked, wanted, accepted and successful. And, more important, from the experience of being so regarded by others. As Eliza Doolittle, the flower girl in Shaw's *Pygmalion*, says, one becomes a "lady" not necessarily by acting like a lady but by being *treated* like one.

SELF-CONCEPT AND READING

Lecky's theory of self-consistency uses the principle of homeostasis to explain the tendency for people to defend their self-concepts against change. In effect, the individual tends to behave in ways that maintain his perceptions of himself. Often our level of performance or attainment may have more to do with what we *believe* we are capable of doing than with our actual mental or physical capabilities. For example, Lecky (1945) worked with children who were poor spellers, but who were otherwise normal. He noted that the children apparently made the same number of spelling errors per day regardless of the difficulty of the material. When the spelling tests were reduced in length, the children made about the same number of mistakes on each page, again regardless of the difficulty of the material. Lecky observed, furthermore, that these children did not make such mistakes in spelling when they were dealing with a foreign language. He concluded that the children must be spelling in terms of their self-concepts regarding their ability to spell.

Similarly, it now seems clear that many children are poor readers largely because they *believe* they cannot read. Beretta (1970) found that good readers among children tend to be high on measures of acceptance, personal and social adequacy, security, and consistency of self. She concluded that self-concept is as much a factor in reading success as intelligence or mastery of basic skills.

A child who believes he cannot read tends to avoid attempting to read. Escape from reading becomes rewarding. Thus, he gets little reading practice, and so is unlikely to improve. Then, when he performs poorly, the teacher remarks how much he needs to improve, which confirms what he has believed all along—that he is a poor reader!

High-school grade-point average (or class rank at graduation) is still a valuable predictor of success in post-high-school education—but not necessarily because it indicates the student's intelligence or fund of knowledge. The predictive value of the grade-point average is based on the transfer of a positive academic self-concept. The successful high-school student has the habit of success—and this is what he takes with him into his post-high-school education. He has acquired good study skills, he tends to have clear goals, and he knows how to cope with his instructors and the educational system. Study skills are indispensable in any form of academic competition.

SELF-CONCEPT AND VOCATIONAL CHOICE

Another manifestation of self-concept is vocational choice. A prominent career-development theorist, Donald Super, has advanced the proposition that preparing for and choosing an occupation essentially involves a process of developing and implementing a self-concept. Super and his associates believe that the "self-concept seems to lend itself admirably to the formulation of broad principles explanatory of occupational choice and vocational adjustment" (Super *et al.*, 1957).

This process involves considerable role playing—"trying out" various occupational roles related to the kind of self-perception the individual has. The process begins during the middle-school years, when adolescents imagine what it would be like to be a nurse, pilot, auto racer, astronaut, scientist, and so on. They begin to think of educational choices in relationship to tentative career interests, but in broad fields only. Although many youths at this stage continue to perceive occupational roles in terms of stereotypes, they are also exploring the kinds of entry occupations that lead to their preferred occupational goal. Thus, the boy who visualizes himself as a professional auto racer may decide to take an auto-mechanics course. The girl who has a career goal in the field of business may choose typing and shorthand courses as the first step.

Since self-concept relates to social-class level, occupational choice also reflects social-class values. Thus, a lower-middle-class youth is likely to consider the occupation of teacher, businessman, draftsman, or accountant rather than a status-oriented occupation such as literary critic or art historian.

The function of the school counselor is to help the individual decide what courses of study to take and what vocations to find out about consistent with what the student believes he can do.

> The process of vocational development is essentially that of developing and implementing a self-concept; it is a compromise process in which the self-concept is a product of the interaction of inherited aptitudes, neural and endocrine make-up, opportunity to play various roles, and evaluations of the extent to which the results of role playing meet with the approval of superiors and fellows. [Super *et al.*, 1957.]

SELF-CONCEPT AND SEX-ROLE IDENTIFICATION

There is a growing interest in the issue of sex-role stereotyping, especially in its effects on academic achievement and vocational choice. Research evidence has generally indicated that the male sex role is more highly valued than the female sex role, by both males and females. Connell and Johnson (1970) found that males who perceive themselves in strong sex-role terms have greater feelings of self-esteem than do males with a weaker sex-role identification. However, they also found that the degree of sex-role identification perceived by females has little correlation with their feelings of adequacy. Males with weak sex-role identification had significantly lower feelings of self-esteem than females, regardless of the sex-role identification of the female.

The problem faced by women in our society is that they receive positive social reinforcement either by adopting "male" characteristics, such as competence and independence, or by fully embracing the stereotyped role that society has historically structured for women. For the male, only the conventional male role provides consistent positive reinforcement.

With respect to academic achievement and motivation, being a girl does not appear to have adverse effects—on the average. The problem arises during the process of choosing a career and future life-style (Baumrind, 1972). The two life patterns that confront the woman— the feminine nurturant career and the aggressive and competitive masculine career—create conflict during the critical adolescent years of self-concept development. This conflict promises to become even more serious as women achieve full legal and professional parity with men and less guilt is associated with dividing a woman's role between career and family. The school has a vital role to play in this process by eliminating excessive sex-role stereotyping in school subjects. Unfortunately, only in recent years has research effort been devoted to the issue of sex-role identification, achievement, and vocational choice.

SELF-CONCEPT AND THE SCHOOL

Popular versions of psychoanalytic theories of growth and development have fostered the idea that the self-concept is largely a result of dramatic events of acceptance or rejection that occur in a child's life as he grows up. This is consistent with common sense, since the really important events from childhood are the easiest to recall and become symbolically associated with particular feelings. An event is significant because powerful and pervasive feelings can cluster around one or several starkly recalled aspects. But this is probably an oversimplification. More likely, self-concept is shaped by the gradual effects of many experiences over long periods of time. A child learns that he is acceptable or unacceptable from the cumulative effects of the minor instances of acceptance or rejection that he experiences every day. Every child is rejected at one time or another by parents or peers; sometimes, rejection may even serve a useful purpose. Depending on the emotional strength of the child at any stage in his development, the beginning of a series of deprecating feedback could make serious inroads in his self-concept. Delinquent adolescents invariably have a history of failures and setbacks of various kinds, with some dramatic, precipitating events that bring them to the attention of juvenile authorities.

A common characteristic of many children, especially adolescents, is that they have a self-concept that is not very positive; in some instances, the denial of self is rather conscious. A high-school girl whose self-concept was quite negative reported in a counseling session: "They think I'm intelligent; I just don't believe it. I guess I don't want to believe it. I don't know why I don't want to believe it—I just don't want to. It should give me confidence, but it doesn't. I think they just really don't know." This individual can perceive and accept only derogatory statements about herself, because they fit in with her self-concept.

A negative self-concept may have many causes, but a prominent one is competitive pressure. When children are subjected too soon to academic comparisons with other children, some of them will inevitably fail the norm. Repeated comparisons that cause a child to appear too often at the "bottom of the heap" are not likely to strengthen his feelings about himself. For some children, achievement may get worse instead of better as a result of competition. As a general principle, competition causes children to perform well in many situations, but there is no way of predicting when it will begin to have adverse effects on the youngster who is not able to cope with ever-rising academic hurdles.

According to the perceptual theory, threat exists when there is a marked difference between what one is expected to do and one's self-concept, what one perceives oneself as *able* to do. This can be a source of vague uneasiness and tension, commonly called "anxiety." When demands on one's self conflict with the perception of the self, the threatening experience is prevented by perceptual distortion or denial from being accurately symbolized.

Chodorkoff (1954) has advanced the following hypothesis regarding the relationship of self-perception, perceptual defense, and personal adjustment:

1. The greater the agreement between the individual's self-description and an objective description of him, the less perceptual defense he will show.

2. The greater the agreement between the individual's self-description and an objective description of him, the more adequate will be his personal adjustment.

3. The more adequate the personal adjustment of the individual, the less perceptual defense he will show.

It is hoped that every individual develops a realistic picture of himself. Yet, many children develop grossly distorted self-concepts. The school has the responsibility to help bring these self-perceptions closer to reality. An important requirement for the healthy growth of the self-concept is steady feedback of knowledge of school achievement and social growth. Every child needs to get correct and frequent information about himself in order to see himself as others see him. Naturally, the more favorable and success-oriented this feedback is, the more it will do for his self-concept.

We might consider the process akin to the focusing mechanism of most modern cameras. The object is to align the two images in the range finder so that the lens is in focus. The child's self-concept and the view others have of him are like two separate images. The farther apart these two images are, the more likely it is that the child is in need of counseling. How much variance in self-image constitutes an adjustment problem is an individual matter. But, if a group of "focused" children are compared with a group of widely "unfocused" children, poor achievement, poor discipline, and personal problems are likely to be characteristic of the "unfocused" group.

The teacher and the school are not necessarily responsible for the adjustment of children's self-concepts. If a child functions well in school, the adequacy of his self-concept is not usually a critical problem. But, if a child is not doing very well in both his schoolwork and his relationships with teachers and other children, how he feels toward himself is an important concern for the teacher and counselor. Unacceptable behavior in the classroom is often a symptom of negative self-concept.

SELF-CONCEPT AND THE TEACHER

A very large part of the effectiveness of a teacher is determined by the quality of his spontaneous response to student behavior. This process has something in common with the functioning of a computer, which absorbs great quantities of information from the outside, combines it with information already stored in its memory bank, and then provides the best possible solution to a given problem almost instantaneously. In the case of the computer, the entire process is, of course, determined in the first place by the program in the computer. In a human being, the "solution" to most problems—especially those relating to affective responses—is largely derived from the individual's perceptual field. How a teacher functions depends on what perceptions he retrieves about the nature of the persons he is working with. For example, Ryans (1960) found that good teachers tend to be extremely generous in their appraisal of the behavior of others.

Stains (1965) tested some concepts concerning the teacher's relation to the students' self-concepts. His data significantly supported the hypothesis that it is possible to distinguish reliably between good and poor teachers in normal classrooms on the basis of the frequency and kinds of comments they make with reference to the learner's self. There are marked differences between teachers in the frequency of their positive or negative comments on the child's performance, status, and self-confidence. The experiments also proved the hypothesis that the teacher can make specific changes in the learner's self-picture while aiming at the subject-matter objectives of teaching. Statistically significant changes were found in two dimensions of the self—certainty and differentiation. Both changes were interpreted as indicating greater psychological security. A control class taught by a teacher having no awareness of the self-concept as an outcome of teaching showed significant decreases in certainty about the self and in differentiation, interpreted as leading to a marked psychological insecurity and poor adjustment.

THE EFFECTS OF PERCEPTION
ON CLASSROOM BEHAVIOR

As we have seen, the closer an event is perceived to be to the individual's self, the greater is its effect on his thought and actions. In other words, the individual tends to react most to ideas and events that have direct significance to him. During an otherwise routine moment in a classroom when the children are working at various tasks, calling out a child's name brings an automatic response from almost everyone—but especially the child himself. He is likely to drop everything and come running. In fact, many children have only partial interest in most activities in the classroom except when these activities draw them in on an individual basis. Motivation tends to be high when the child is doing something that causes him to stand out before others as an individual.

The perceptualists have put their finger on the weakest link in most classroom instruction today: *the lack of personal meaning.* This is especially true in the teaching of the basic skills and understandings necessary to master most fields of knowledge.

By contrast, most children take naturally to play activities, which provide opportunities for them to develop in ways appropriate to their level of physical and emotional maturity. Even the most sedentary activities, such as playing with dolls or small toys, result in far greater spontaneous motivation than much classroom instruction, primarily because the child can pursue these activities on his own terms. He can play as energetically or as quietly as he chooses; he can arrange the activity in any way that promises the most fun and challenge. In fact, he almost *has* to make it a personal thing—that's what play activities are all about.

School subjects, however, typically start out in an intellectual, abstract manner, the appeal being that "It is good for you" or the more aversive "You'd better learn this if you want to get a good grade" approach. Even when school subjects are personally relevant in the early stages, the teacher too quickly "upgrades" the course to purely mental and abstract functions, with only a few opportunities—as occasional reinforcement—for personal involvement of the student with what he is studying.

The self that is growing must feel at all times that it is involved, that it is truly a part of what is going on, that, to some degree, it is helping to shape its own destiny. Perhaps no quality is more important for the developing person than this feeling of involvement in what is taking place. In the antiwar demonstrations of May, 1970, some observers noted instances of young protesters who actually had little real knowledge of the issues for which they were demonstrating so fervently; they admitted that they were turned on by the intense feeling of togetherness and personal involvement of the protest movement, a feeling that they had rarely experienced in college life.

What are some of the practices in the classroom that seem to inhibit involvement, openness, and creativity? The following factors are suggested in *Perceiving, Behaving, Becoming: A New Focus*, the yearbook of the Association for Supervision and Curriculum Development (Combs, 1962, p. 145):

1. A preoccupation with order. Much of our practice seems to worship order, categorization, classifying, description, and pigeonholing of one sort or another. Such a preoccupation is likely to discourage breaking loose and finding new solutions.
2. Overvaluing authority, support, evidence, and the scientific method. Such rigid, tight concepts often permit no question or explanation. They are, by definition, *so*.
3. Exclusive emphasis on the historical point of view. This seems to imply that those things that have been discovered in the past are always good and change in the present is bad.
4. Various "cookbook" approaches—the "filling in the blanks," "color the picture correctly" approach. This is an ever present danger of teaching machines also.
5. The essentially solitary approach to learning emphasized in some classrooms. Creativity is very highly dependent upon communication.
6. The elimination of self from the classroom.
7. The school ruled almost entirely by adult concepts.
8. Emphases on force, threat, and coercion. The use of "guilt" and "badness" as means of control; also, severe forms of punishment, ridicule, and humiliation. Anything that diminishes the self interferes with openness and creativity.
9. The idea that mistakes are sinful and that children are not to be trusted. Where mistakes are not permitted, there can be no experimentation. Teachers who fear youngsters and the possibility that they may get out of hand cannot permit the kind of movement and freedom required by creativity.
10. School organizations that emphasize lock-step approaches, rules and regulations, managerial and administrative considerations, rather than human ones.

LIMITATIONS OF PERCEPTUAL PSYCHOLOGY

The chief limitation of perceptual psychology, with its strong emphasis on the importance of the child's sense of self-worth, is the possibility that the teacher will be inhibited by the fear of hurting a child's feelings and hence his self-concept. Unfortunately, the growing child cannot expect to succeed every day in everything he tries. Unless he is both very capable and very lucky, he is going to have good days and bad days, and there is no way to shield him from every disappointment. It isn't easy for children to perceive a setback such as a low grade or some other academically negative feedback as a personal victory rather than a defeat. Just as children and adolescents rightfully take credit for their triumphs, so they are likely to feel personal responsibility for their defeats.

An automatic concern for the feelings of children should not, in every instance, take precedence over the demands of teaching or the long-range welfare of the child. If it did, grades would be reported only when they were high; no student would be compared to others except when his test score appeared at the top of the distribution; no child would have to account for his time or his use of materials; all young people would be protected from any hurt as a consequence of having misbehaved or made a "mistake," accidental or otherwise; and no teacher could express normal feelings of frustration or exasperation toward children without incurring massive feelings of guilt.

A second limitation of perceptual psychology can be stated quite simply: Perceptualism is much easier said than done. It is much easier to apply perceptual principles in dealing with one student at a time than in a group. Much of the literature of perceptual psychology was written by persons who were not teaching in a public-school classroom and who therefore were not directly involved in the instruction of groups of children in basic skills. In fact, most authorities in perceptual theory derived their assumptions about behavior from training and experience in counseling and psychotherapy with highly verbal, college-age youth and adults. They often worked in educational and therapeutic settings that do not involve the kinds of institutional and societal demands that characterize most public schools.

By definition, perceptual psychology focuses on the individual. But the teacher in the classroom—from kindergarten through senior high school—almost always has to deal with groups, and the behavior of an individual alone can be very different from his behavior when he is with twenty peers (Jackson and Lahaderne, 1967). Teachers are often amazed to note the differences in the behavior of many children out of the classroom and inside the school. The same boy who seems to be consistently rude and willful and uncooperative in social-studies class may be courteous, helpful, and quite mature when his social-studies teacher encounters him bagging groceries at the supermarket on Saturday morning. This, incidentally, is one reason school administrators look favorably upon teacher involvement in extracurricular and community affairs: it affords beneficial out-of-class contacts with young people.

PERCEPTUALISM AND BEHAVIORISM

Perceptual psychology has attracted many followers because of its usefulness in describing reality, as a basis for teaching and counseling techniques, and in the design of curriculum. Insofar as perceptual processes are heavily influenced by relationships with other people, perceptual psychology has much in common with current theories of transactional psychology. Indeed, it is a very "human" psychology, because it attempts to peel away the veneer of behavior that seems to obscure so much of our true selves and provides many principles and techniques to help people to achieve self-actualization.

But perceptualism is not necessarily more "humane" than behaviorism. Perceptual psychology—commendably—places heavy responsibility on the individual himself for his actions. The individual is viewed as having the power to raise himself by his own perceptual bootstraps and change the way he looks at the world and himself. He may need some help in bringing about change, but he himself must be the prime agent. Perceptual psychology says, in effect, that one is not necessarily bound by his past or his environment, or by any habits to which he has been conditioned. Thus, the individual cannot pass responsibility completely to his environment or to others by saying "What I am is what the world and others have made of me." At any time during his life, he was free to choose otherwise, to look honestly at himself and his behavior, to bring about the conditions for his own change and development.

Not so for the behaviorist. According to behaviorism, with its emphasis on external factors in learning and development, our present behavior has been shaped largely by the conditioning we have received. We are the products of our times. There is considerable evidence that much of what we perceive (for example, stereotypes regarding race, social class, sex roles) is so ingrained by the conditioning process as to be virtually impossible to eradicate from our thinking. The teacher who has a strong respect for the effects of environmental conditioning will quite logically have a "humane" attitude toward children, in the sense of believing in the value of intervention. The teacher can account for the behavior of the problem child, in effect, by saying that the child got that way because of the circumstances of his life, that he had little control over these circumstances and is hardly even aware of their effects. The teacher can sincerely believe that it is the school's obligation and responsibility to intervene wherever possible to change these circumstances and begin the counterconditioning process. The teacher, as a behaviorist, acts on the assumption that any child has considerable difficulty breaking the bonds of conditioned habits and therefore needs the enlightened help of the teacher and the school.

Thus, consistent with the theme of this text, neither the behaviorist nor the perceptual position is wholly right or wrong. The teacher must operate on the general behaviorist assumption that children can benefit from changes in their environment effected by school authorities. Nevertheless, the teacher must also regard each child as unique, important, and central to the learning process. Manipulation of the environment is vital, but it won't work unless the teacher takes careful note of the ways in which each child perceives and reacts to these environmental changes.

REFERENCES

AUSUBEL, D. P. 1969. The influences of experience on the development of intelligence. In J. M. Seidman (ed.), *The child: A book of readings.* New York: Holt, Rinehart & Winston.

BAUMRIND, D. 1972. From each according to her ability. *School Review,* February, 80(2), 161–97.

BERETTA, S. 1970. Self-concept in the reading program. *Reading Teacher,* 24, 232–38.

BRIDGMAN, P. W. 1969. *The way things are.* Cambridge, Mass.: Harvard University Press.

CHODORKOFF, B. 1954. Self-perception, perceptual defense, and adjustment. *Journal of Abnormal and Social Psychology,* 49, 508–12.

COMBS, A. W. 1962. A perceptual view of the adequate personality. In A. W. Combs (ed.), *Perceiving, behaving, becoming: A new focus.* Washington, D.C.: Association for Supervision and Curriculum Development, National Education Association, 50–64.

―――. 1967. *The professional education of teachers.* Boston: Allyn & Bacon.

COMBS, A. W., and D. SNYGG. 1959. *Individual behavior.* New York: Harper & Row.

CONNELL, D. M., and J. E. JOHNSON. 1970. Relationship between sex-role identification and self-esteem in early adolescents. *Developmental Psychology,* 3, 268.

ERIKSON, E. H. 1963. *Childhood and society.* New York: W. W. Norton.

GIBSON, E. J. 1969. *Principles of learning and development.* New York: Appleton-Century-Crofts.

JACKSON, P. W., and H. M. LAHADERNE. 1967. Inequalities of teacher-pupil contacts. *Psychology in the Schools*, 4(3), 204–11.

JONES, M. C., and P. H. MUSSEN. 1958. Self-conceptions, motivations, and interpersonal attitudes of early- and late-maturing girls. *Child Development*, 28, 491–501.

LECKY, P. 1945. *Self-consistency: A theory of personality*. New York: Island Press.

ROGERS, C. R. 1961. *On becoming a person*. Boston: Houghton Mifflin.

RYANS, D. G. 1960. *Characteristics of teachers*. Washington, D.C.: American Council on Education.

STAINS, J. W. 1965. The self-picture as a factor in the classroom. In J. W. Stains (ed.), *The self in growth, teaching, and learning: Selected readings*. Englewood Cliffs, N.J.: Prentice-Hall.

STONE, L. J., and J. CHURCH. 1968. *Childhood and adolescence*. New York: Random House.

SUPER, D. E., *et al.* 1957. *Vocational development: A framework for research*. New York: Columbia University Bureau of Publications.

CHAPTER SIX

Intelligence and Creativity

EVERYONE has the potential for developing traits and characteristics that will differentiate him quite sharply from everyone else. Teachers and school administrators are taking a very serious look at the range of individual differences in our school population, for it has a direct bearing on every aspect of education, from school philosophy to daily classroom activity.

Even when the nation's population was much smaller and fewer children attended school, there was a wide range of differences among children in such characteristics as intelligence and personality. The *number* of truly unusual children, however, was very small. With the growing size and heterogeneity of the school population, it became increasingly important to develop ways of measuring differences in interests and abilities both among children and within each child, in order to make education fully "relevant" and to help young people plan their future educational and vocational careers.

Teachers have always been aware of the spread of abilities and aptitudes among children, but only since the turn of the century have systematic attempts been made to measure these differences. Prior to this time, the individual child's ability was estimated on the basis of the observer's beliefs about what children at a particular grade level should be capable of doing. This method may have been helpful for the teacher, but it contributed very little to an objective appraisal of the child.

The three areas of individual differences most important to teachers at all school levels are intelligence, personality, and the values and attitudes associated with social class. These characteristics of children constitute the most important variables in the teaching situation. They determine not only the rate at which each child's motivational gyroscope turns but also how he will adjust to the responsibilities, challenges, and stresses of the school years.

THEORIES OF INTELLIGENCE

One of the most obvious differences among individuals is in mental functioning. One third-grader is clever in arithmetic but only average in verbal skills. Another is a "natural" when working with mechanical gadgets but is a slow reader. A third child has a pleasant personality and is a natural leader but doesn't do especially well in academic subjects. These children function mentally in different ways. By high-school age, they will be far apart in ways of thinking and learning. Who is the more "intelligent"—the child who is clever in math or the one with mechanical ability? Or are social skills the best indicator of intelligence, since they seem to be so important for achieving success in later life?

Intelligence is so complex a subject that there is little agreement even among psychologists on its definition. One set of definitions centers on the effectiveness of the various intellectual processes: memory, reasoning, spatial organization, and imagination. According to this approach, intelligence is the ability to do abstract thinking, to learn, and to respond in terms of truth and fact. But intelligence has also been defined as the ability to adjust to one's environment, and there are numerous other definitions as well.

GENERAL AND SPECIFIC ABILITIES

In general, theories of intelligence have followed one of two theoretical lines. One of these says, in effect, that our minds tend to function in an over-all, integrated way. Just as a small baby tends to laugh or cry "all over," mental functioning, too, tends to be a total operation. Charles Spearman (1904, 1923, 1927) was the first to propose the theory that intelligence involves a very high degree of general ability. He believed that all mental activity was actually the exercise of "mental energy," which he called the "general (g) factor" of intellectual functioning. The strength of this energy varied from individual to individual. Spearman also speculated about the existence of certain other factors (s) that are specific to particular situations, while the g factor is common to all. (See Fig. 6.1.)

For many years, emphasis on the g factor in intelligence was popular

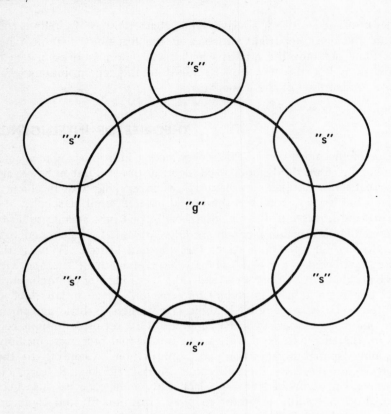

Fig. 6.1. Spearman's concept of the relationship of the $"g"$ factor to specific $"s"$ factors.

in theory and in the construction of intelligence tests. More recently, however, there has been increasing interest in the study of specific abilities, especially as they relate to academic success in science and mathematics and in verbal areas. L. L. Thurstone (1946), for example, identified seven primary mental abilities, or "factors": space, number, verbal, word fluency, memory, inductive, and deductive.

Theoretically, these factors were believed by Thurstone to be quite distinct from one another, but in statistical analyses he found some degree of intercorrelation among them. He labeled this intercorrelation a "second-order" factor, but critics viewed it as simply the g factor cropping up. Nevertheless, Thurstone continued to argue that intelligence manifests itself in more or less distinct ways. The intelligence test he developed, the *Primary Mental Abilities Scale* (Thurstone and Thurstone, 1950), reflects this emphasis on specific abilities and has been used quite extensively in primary and elementary schools.

J. P. Guilford (1959) proposed a multifactor theory that identifies 120 or more components of human intelligence. He explains mental functioning as the result of combinations and interactions of these specific abilities. Guilford's theory thus in a sense straddles the issue of general versus specific factors in intelligence. One of the most striking byproducts of Guilford's work is his identification of two important problem-solving processes. According to Guilford, problem situations can be roughly classified as either *convergent*—requiring the choice of the correct solution from two or more alternatives—or *divergent*—requiring the production of many possible approaches as a means of arriving at an original solution or alternative. Guilford's theorizing about intelligence has spawned considerable research on creativity and has stimulated a new emphasis on the need for creative thinking in the classroom.

Another psychologist, H. E. Garrett, proposed another position midway between the models of intelligence as a process of integration (the g factor predominantly) or as one of differentiation (many relatively specific abilities). In one study, he tested nine-, twelve-, and fifteen-year-old children for memory, verbal, and number abilities. The degree to which the general factor was revealed in responses to these tests varied with the age of the children (see Fig. 6.2). On the basis of this and other studies, Garrett postulated the following hypothesis: "Abstract or symbol intelligence changes in organization as age increases, from a fairly unified and general ability to a loosely organized group of abilities or factors" (Garrett, 1946, pp. 372–78).

Since there now appears to be a respectable body of research supporting each of these models of intelligence, the issue at present is deadlocked. A theory of intelligence that emphasizes the g factor provides the conceptual framework for measurement of the individual's total mental capabilities, such as is provided by the *Stanford-Binet Individual Intelligence Scale*. This scale yields an estimate of the subject's general level of mental functioning. It is therefore useful in determining the extent to which a given individual is underachieving academically—i.e., functioning below general level of ability—as well as in other ways.

On the other hand, a multifactor theory of intelligence provides the framework for tests that pinpoint specific areas of abilities and aptitudes, such as the instruments used in vocational counseling.

For the teacher, Garrett's differentiation hypothesis is perhaps the most helpful, since it conforms to common-sense impressions of the way in which children develop intellectually. It provides a developmen-

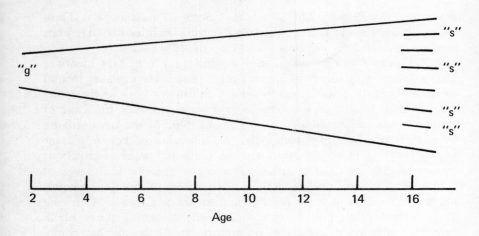

Fig. 6.2.   The differentiation of mental ability from general ("g")
to specific ("s").   Abstract or symbolic intelligence changes in organization
as age increases, from a fairly unified and general ability to a loosely organized
group of abilities or factors.   (From H. E. Garrett, "A Developmental
Theory of Intelligence," *American Psychologist, 1* [1946] , 374.)

tal, rather than a fixed, concept of mental functioning. The very young
child tends to respond "all over"—both mentally and physically—to
environmental stimuli. His learning style tends to be the same whether
he is explaining something in a "show and tell" session or working at a
nonverbal task such as arranging blocks. For example, if a five-year-old
has a careful, methodical work style in one activity, it is highly probable
that he will work in this same way in other activities as well. If he is
attentive in one class, he is likely to be attentive in all classes. If he is a
very active child, his vitality will be apparent in all the situations he is
in.

Since the young child's abilities are "global," it is probably unwise to
look for evidence of specific abilities. If a first- or second-grader, for example, gets along quite well in reading but appears to have difficulty in
working with numbers, this should not necessarily be considered an indication that he has potential ability for reading but not for math. He
may, for example, respond to a different method of teaching math. At
the preschool and primary-school age, a too-literal application of the
multifactor theory of intelligence may result in varying expectations and
perhaps even in denial of responsibility for the child's total development.

As children grow older, they begin to develop variable learning styles.

They usually do well in some subjects and less well in others. By noting these emerging patterns, the teacher can identify the strengths and weaknesses of an older child. Recognizing this gradually differentiating growth will also help the teacher to match the child's learning style to realistic objectives in each individual subject area, a strategy that may lead to greater success.

HEREDITY VERSUS ENVIRONMENT

The relative influence of heredity and environment on intelligence has been the subject of considerable investigation since early in the twentieth century. Traditionally, the weight has been on the side of heredity as the primary influence. Thus, L. M. Terman (1959) found that gifted children were much more likely to come from an intellectually distinguished family than were children in the population at large.

In recent years, however, renewed recognition of the problem of cultural deprivation and its influence on test scores has resulted in new thinking about the issue of heredity *versus* environment. It was always known that environment influences a child's performance on both intelligence and achievement tests, but the social and cultural implications of this form of bias were not fully appreciated until recently. If children from culturally stimulating middle-class homes profited from the cultural bias of schoolwide testing programs, this was not viewed as especially serious, since a spuriously high score was not likely to be a disadvantage either in school or in life. Perhaps the individual might experience some disappointment later, but at least he was not discriminated against by teachers and counselors. In fact, he probably benefited from the positive expectations others held toward him.

But for those who scored lower than they deserved, it was quite another matter. Bloom (1964) has estimated that impoverishment of the environment may lower performance on an intelligence test by as much as twenty IQ points. Furthermore, the evidence suggests that the younger the child, the greater the influence of environment on his intellectual development. A study by Lee (1951) of black children in Philadelphia showed that migration had decreasing effect the older the child was when he moved north.

RACE AND INTELLIGENCE: THE JENSEN CONTROVERSY

Until quite recently, the best thinking held that intelligence is not wholly the result of either heredity or environment (although heredity is the major contributor) but arises from the interaction of a child's genetic inheritance with his life circumstances. A leading authority in the study of intelligence, Ann Anastasi, put the issue this way:

> Two or three decades ago, the so-called heredity-environment question was the center of lively controversy. Today, on the other hand, many psychologists look upon it as a dead issue. It is now generally conceded that both heredity and environmental factors enter into all behavior. The reacting organism is a product of its genes and its past environment, while present environment provides the immediate stimulus for current behavior [1958, p. 197].

But the debate has lately been revived, creating great controversy in both professional and lay circles. The impetus was an article by Berkeley psychologist A. R. Jensen (1969) asserting that there is a relationship between race and mental ability.

Jensen has postulated a two-level model of mental functioning, from associative to conceptual learning. The development of Level I associative abilities is necessary but not sufficient for the development of Level II conceptual-abstract abilities (Jensen, 1970).

Level I involves neural registration and consolidation of stimulus input and the subsequent formation of associations. There is relatively little transformation of the input, so that there is high correspondence between the forms of the stimulus and the forms of the response. Level I ability is tapped mostly by tests of, for example, digit memory, serial rote learning, and selective trial-and-error learning with reinforcement (feedback).

Level II abilities, on the other hand, involve self-initiated elaboration and transformation of the stimulus input before it eventuates in an overt response. Concept learning and problem solving are examples of Level II abilities. Certain neural structures must exist in order for Level II abilities to develop, and these differ from the neural structures that underlie Level I. Jensen hypothesizes that Level I abilities are distributed evenly in all socio-economic classes, and that Level II abilities are distributed disproportionately among social-class groups.

Level I abilities are associated with basic survival skills. Level II apparently corresponds to Spearman's g, the general intelligence factor, as measured by traditional tests of intelligence involving verbal-scholastic abilities. Jensen considers this intellectual level the one that provides the basis for complex technological culture, requiring abstract and symbolic thinking skills. Because Level I functions are necessary but not sufficient for the development of Level II functions, the rate of development of Level II is related to individual differences in Level I, especially if there is impairment in Level I. Lower-social-class children do not lack learning abilities in Level I tasks, but they apparently lack elements of Level II abilities, all of which go to make up what we call intelligence.

One of Jensen's tentative conclusions is that our social and cultural milieu operates in such a way as to maximize the importance of Level II abilities—i.e., the conceptual abilities. It is precisely this level of transferable knowledge and cognitive skills that is needed in order to learn by means of the highly verbal and symbolic medium of the traditional classroom—and it is at this level that culturally disadvantaged children are educationally handicapped, even though they may be average or even superior in basic learning ability.

A much more complex issue raised by Jensen's interpretation of research on IQ and scholastic achievement is the possibility that certain genetic characteristics are associated with Level II ability. Jensen's hypothesis has aroused a storm of controversy because it reinforces old stereotypes regarding race and is therefore perceived as a step backward in social justice. Others regard the entire issue as a tempest in a teapot.

Regardless of the validity of Jensen's research hypotheses and conclusions on the relative effects of race and environment on school achievement, we must contend with the fact that racial bias in one form or another permeates our entire way of life. Surely this must be a contaminating variable in even the best-controlled experimental studies of genetic effects on intellectual functioning.

Even if genetic factors were, however, found to be related to academic ability (and there appears to be little likelihood that this is so beyond any reasonable doubt), this would be justification for redoubled efforts to maximize educational enrichment for deprived children. Height is considered to be even more related to genetics than mental ability—over 90 per cent of variance in height is attributable to genetic inheritance—yet environmental conditions of better nutrition and health habits have caused quite dramatic increases in height in the United States during the past one hundred years or so. There is little question that the potential for raising human capabilities through environmental changes is very great.

THE CONCEPT OF MENTAL AGE

Probably no educational issue has resulted in more confusion, misinformation, and even hostility than the concept of the intelligence quotient, or "IQ." Although widely used in one form or another, it has

come under severe scrutiny in recent years. It is important to understand what has caused this recent shift in attitudes toward the concept
of IQ. But first let us take a look at the rationale for intelligence testing
itself.

Most investigators agree that the growth of intelligence is most rapid
in infancy and early childhood and then tends to taper off. In general,
intelligence is said to increase because the student can solve more
problems as he grows older. The tapering-off process is so gradual that
it is usually difficult to tell when the plateau has been reached. The
best estimates place the age of terminal growth in the early twenties. By
the age of six, when they begin first grade, children show a noticeable
range of differences with respect to mental functioning.

The concept of mental age has provided a useful basis for the construction of intelligence tests because it anchors the entire process to the
idea of mental growth calculated on the months of age. The child who
is "average" in mental ability is, in effect, growing mentally and chronologically at the same rate. The bright child is developing intellectually
faster than chronologically. This is expressed mathematically as follows:

$$IQ = \frac{\text{Mental Age } (\textit{expressed in months})}{\text{Chronological Age } (\textit{expressed in months})} \times 100$$

or

$$IQ = \frac{MA}{CA} \times 100$$

A ten-year-old child with an IQ of 120 has a mental age equivalent to
that of an average-ability child aged twelve. A ten-year-old with a 90 IQ
has a mental age equivalent to that of an average child aged nine. Of
course, unlike chronological age, the mental age of any child proceeds
in a consistent rate only theoretically. His score may fluctuate to some
extent throughout his life. This is largely related to the lack of precision
in existing intelligence tests, but there is also the element of differences in actual mental functioning from one time to another, since mental behavior is closely related to personality characteristics in general. It
is possible that one's rate of intellectual development varies in the
same way as one's physical growth seems to go through fast and slow
periods. Generally, intelligence-test scores have been most valuable for
predicting in what broad category of intellectual functioning a particular individual is likely to be—below average, average, bright average, or
superior.

Intelligence-test results are usually reported either as IQ scores or as point scores. If they are reported as point scores, the test usually provides a table for the conversion of the point values into an equivalent IQ or mental-age score.

INDIVIDUAL INTELLIGENCE TESTS

An individual intelligence test is administered to only one subject at a time. It yields an intelligence quotient (IQ) or standard score for mental age and provides a description of behavioral characteristics. This is especially useful for the diagnosis of reading difficulties or other forms of learning disability. The four best-known and most highly regarded individual intelligence tests are the *Stanford-Binet Intelligence Scale*, the *Wechsler Adult Intelligence Scale* (WAIS), the *Wechsler Intelligence Scale for Children* (WISC), and the *Wechsler Preschool and Primary Scale of Intelligence* (WPPSI).

THE STANFORD-BINET INTELLIGENCE TESTS

The entire concept of intelligence testing began with a brilliant Frenchman named Alfred Binet. In 1904, the French government appointed a commission to study the problem of identifying children who were too mentally retarded for normal classroom instruction. Binet and a collaborator, Théophile Simon, devised a test for measuring general intellectual functioning, the *Binet-Simon Scale*, which they published in 1905.

There were no precedents or guidelines at the time that Binet began the task of devising a means of identifying individual differences in mental functioning. A skilled psychologist, he was familiar with the theoretical approaches developed by others, but he was faced with an unusual problem: the measurement of children who, because of age or impairment, had few or no verbal skills. It was already known that teachers' judgments of children with mental deficiencies were highly unreliable. There was a risk of labeling as deficient and ultimately segregating the able child who was making no effort and the troublemaker the teacher wished to get rid of. School officials also wanted to be able to identify slow children whom teachers might hesitate to rate low because they came from good families or had docile, pleasant personalities.

After considerable experimentation, Binet developed a series of thirty mental tasks ranked from easy to difficult. These were tasks familiar to children, such as tying a knot, cutting out a figure from a piece of paper, identifying objects, stringing beads, and recognizing verbal absurdities. The scale of tasks was linked to age groups, so that at each successive age level about half the children failed a given task and half passed it. Eventually, Binet was able to administer the series to a child of a given age and determine the child's approximate intellectual limit by the place on the scale where the tasks became too difficult for him.

The test items were designed to cover a wide variety of functions with special emphasis on judgment, comprehension, and reasoning, which Binet regarded as essential components of intelligence. That Binet had reasoned logically was proved by the fact that his age-level scale was the first intelligence test that really worked: It succeeded to a considerable degree in differentiating bright and dull pupils. Unfortunately, he died at the prime of his life, before he could perfect his test.

Binet's scale attracted considerable attention, and it was so useful that, for a number of years, other test-makers contented themselves with little more than slight revisions or translations of the original instrument. Many of the tasks in intelligence tests currently in use are essentially the same as in the original Binet version.

The most famous revision of Binet's first scale was that developed under the leadership of L. M. Terman at Stanford University. It was in this test, known as the *Stanford-Binet*, that the "intelligence quotient," or ratio between mental and chronological age, was first established. The concept of the IQ itself was not invented by Binet but by a German psychologist, Wilhelm Stern (Anastasi, 1961).

Terman's first version of the *Stanford-Binet* appeared in 1917. The version that has been most widely used was the first revision, which appeared in 1937. The 1937 revision received some minor alterations in 1960, and it is now rated by many experts as the best measurement of intelligence for individuals aged two years through early adolescence.

The *Stanford-Binet* is administered to one subject at a time. The person taking the test must answer the questions orally—not by writing or marking the answers—and the administrator records the responses. It is essential that the test administrator be well trained and experienced. This is not a test that anyone can administer simply by following the directions in the test manual. In order to get a reasonably valid test score, the test items must be presented in precisely the way decreed by Terman and his associates. Graduate work in test administration is required to become qualified for this procedure. However, every teacher may have occasion to use the information provided by an intelligence-test score and the test report. As we will see, the value of the *Stanford-Binet*, as well as of the Wechsler tests, is in the test report (discussed later in this chapter).

Before administering the test, the examiner must first establish a *basal age* to ensure that the first questions on the test are within the child's capability, yet not so easy that he or she becomes fatigued by answering too many questions before reaching a challenging level of tasks. By spending time with the child in play activities and in conversation, the examiner attempts to establish rapport with the child and perhaps gain a rough estimate of the child's ability. Administering the vocabulary scale first also helps to establish the child's basal age. Once this has been done, testing continues until the child at some age level fails all the tests. This is called his *ceiling age*.

Here is an abbreviated description of the test for the first two age levels:

FIVE-YEAR LEVEL

First test: completing the figure of a man. The scoring is based not on artistic ability but on how well the child can conceptualize the man—that is, how well he adds such significant details as arms, legs, hands, mouth, hair, and so forth.

Second test: folding a 6-inch square of paper into a double triangle after watching a demonstration.

Third test: defining "ball," "hat," and "stove." The child must get two definitions out of three to pass.

Fourth test: copying a square printed on the test booklet. The child must perform at least one out of three trials satisfactorily.

Fifth test: identifying similarities and differences among pictures. The child must get nine out of ten correct.

Sixth test: putting together two triangles in order to form a rectangle. The child gets credit if he is able to perform the task two out of three trials.

SIX-YEAR LEVEL

First test: defining at least five out of a list of forty-five vocabulary words arranged in order of difficulty. Testing stops after six consecutive failures.

Second test: identifying differences between *bird* and *dog*, *slipper* and *boot*, and *wood* and *glass*. The child must succeed in two out of the three.

Third test: identifying what is missing in mutilated pictures of a *wagon, shoe, teapot, rabbit, glove.*

Fourth test: number concepts. The child must correctly count blocks in four out of five trials.

Fifth test: opposite analogies (for example, "A table is made of wood; a window of . . ."). Credit is allowed for three correct out of four.

Sixth test: solving two out of three simple pencil mazes by tracing the proper pathway on the test booklet.

At the higher levels, the child is asked to tell what is foolish or absurd about short statements, to copy a drawing of a diamond, to repeat digits forward or backward, to supply missing words in sentences, and to solve a variety of mathematical and other kinds of problems—to mention just a few of the many types of questions. With increasing age levels, the tasks become more verbal and abstract.

THE WECHSLER INTELLIGENCE TESTS

As widely used as the *Stanford-Binet,* though serving somewhat different purposes, are the various tests developed by David Wechsler and the Psychological Corporation.

David Wechsler was a psychologist at Bellevue Hospital in New York City, working largely with children and adults afflicted with various forms of mental illness. Wechsler felt that current intelligence tests on the market—notably, the *Stanford-Binet*—were verbally and academically biased. He viewed intelligence as a combination of various mental traits. From his experience with the mentally ill, Wechsler concluded that measurement of verbal-scholastic aptitude will not adequately predict one's mental functioning in all the situations one is likely to encounter in life. He noted that many individuals with high academic abilities and skills were often unable to cope with day-to-day problems and stresses of living whereas many who scored quite low on verbal-scholastic tests of intelligence functioned reasonably well in daily living. They had the nonintellectual personality characteristics and social skills that are often characteristic of well-integrated, productive people.

In other words, Wechsler believed that performance on an intelligence test—as in life situations—reflects a complex interaction of inherent and experiential factors. Emotional factors may heighten attention, persistence, and adaptability, or they may impair ability to mobilize intellectual resources. Anxiety, self-confidence, the desire to impress the test administrators, and so on are clearly learned reactions that affect adjustment to testing situations; they are also related to success or failure in real-life situations. Thus, the Wechsler tests attempt to measure intellectual potential in relation to experience and motivational factors.

Wechsler defined intelligence as the "aggregate or global capacity of the individual (a) to act purposefully, (b) to think rationally, and (c) to deal effectively with his environment" (1958, p. 7). In order to measure these abilities, Wechsler's tests use a verbal scale (cognitive) to determine general intelligence and a performance scale (conative) to provide a diagnostic aid in determining how the individual functions in timed, nonverbal testing situations.

Wechsler's original scale, the *Wechsler-Bellevue*, was a promising instrument but needed considerable revision. An independent testing concern, the Psychological Corporation, collaborated with Wechsler on a revision of the *Wechsler-Bellevue* designed especially for children. The WISC, or *Wechsler Intelligence Scale for Children* (aged seven to sixteen), was published in 1949. Several years later (1955), a revised scale for adults came out, called the WAIS—the *Wechsler Adult Intelligence Scale*. In 1967, the *Wechsler Preschool and Primary Scale of Intelligence* (WPPSI) was published for use with children aged four to six and a half.

The following is a description of the subtests on the WISC (for ages seven to sixteen):

VERBAL SCALE

First test: general information. These questions measure general knowledge, such as distances between cities, number of states in the union, names of some eminent people.

Second test: general comprehension. These questions are intended to measure common sense and practical judgment—for example, "What is the thing to do when you cut your finger?"

Third test: arithmetic. This consists of arithmetic problems of the kind found in most elementary-school textbooks.

Fourth test: similarities. The subject is required to tell how two things are alike—for example, a peach and a plum.

Fifth test: digit span. Repeating numbers forwards and backwards.

Sixth test: vocabulary. The subject is asked to define words orally.

PERFORMANCE SCALE

First test: digit symbol. This requires the subject to match symbols with numbers.

Second test: picture completion. The subject must determine what is missing from each picture.

Third test: block design. Colored blocks must be arranged in a specified design.

Fourth test: picture arrangement. A series of pictures must be arranged correctly to make a story.

Fifth test: object assembly. Four jigsaw puzzles.

The *Performance Scale*, which provides a measure of nonverbal abilities, is often used with individuals who have speech impairment or are bilingual. It is also used with the mentally ill in cases where verbal skill is low, such as in certain forms of schizophrenia.

An important difference between the Wechsler and *Stanford-Binet* tests is that answers on the Wechslers are scored by points rather than months of credit. This permits the examiner to give points not only for the correct answer but, in some cases, according to the quality of the answer and the speed of response.

In an extensive study in California, Weise (1960) found that the *Stanford-Binet* is preferred by school psychologists for screening children in the third grade and below for giftedness and mental retardation. The Wechsler tests were most often used for other psychological appraisals, such as emotional problems, neurological dysfunction, and learning problems other than mental retardation, beyond second grade.

THE SLOSSON INTELLIGENCE TEST

Because the *Stanford-Binet* and Wechsler tests require a highly skilled test administrator, they are time-consuming and expensive. Therefore, a strong demand arose for a short-form test of verbal-abstract intelligence. As a consequence, the Psychological Corporation developed the *Slosson Intelligence Test* (1961–63), which has many tasks similar to test items in the *Stanford-Binet* and the Wechsler tests but is much shorter and easier to administer. In fact, it can be administered reliably simply by following directions in the test manual. The *Slosson* provides a close estimate of the child's verbal-scholastic ability, which is especially useful for diagnosing aptitude for reading (Armstrong and Mooney, 1971). It should be noted, however, that children with speech or sensory impairment or cultural deprivation will predictably score low. For these children, diagnosis of learning disability requires much more extensive testing and observation.

Test validity is best for children aged four years to adulthood. Because of the verbal nature of the test items, IQs for children under four years of age must be regarded as only tentative.

THE TEST REPORT

When the examiner completes an individual intelligence test, he scores the responses in the test booklet and computes the subject's IQ. In addition, he prepares a test report that contains important information regarding the child's behavior during the testing situation (Fig. 6.3). This diagnostic information is often more useful to a teacher, counselor, or psychologist than the test score. In addition to knowing

```
              PSYCHOLOGICAL REPORT:  STANFORD-BINET (1960 Form L-M)


    Name:                                 School:  Washington Elementary School
    Age:    5-8                           Grade:   Kindergarten
    Birthdate:                            Examiner:
    Test date:    12-30-67
```

SUMMARY

The subject's I.Q. (107) places her in the average range of mental ability and at the 67th percentile compared to other children in the general population. At the time of testing her chronological age was 5-8 while her mental age, as determined by this test, was 6-0. The results of the test are considered to be a reasonably valid estimate of the subject's general intellectual functioning. Scores for children at this age are not the most reliable. However, the chances are that two out of three times this subject's "true" score would fall between about 101 and 113. On this basis, it may be predicted that the subject will be able to compete adequately with other children in a school setting.

CHARACTERISTICS OF THE SUBJECT AND TESTING SITUATION

The subject is a girl of average height and weight for her age. She appeared to be in good health at the time of testing. She constantly talked to the examiner during testing, considerably lengthening the time of testing. She was quite eager at first, but became very bored and began asking if she could quit. It is difficult to determine whether the sudden and consistent drop off of successes in the last two age levels resulted from her lack of interest and restlessness or if she had really reached her ceiling in the areas of abilities assessed.

The test was administered at the subject's home. Heating, lighting, and ventilation were good. However, there were constant distractions such as telephone calls and people walking past.

The subject is the youngest of four girls, but she has an even younger brother. She is quite domineering over him. She seemed to need constant attention and, if she didn't get it, would start to cause trouble.

TEST DISCUSSION AND ANALYSIS

The examiner began testing at 4-6 level based on subject's chronological age. She passed all tests at this level and at the age 5 level, establishing this as her basal age. She continued passing tests until the 9-year level, establishing this as her ceiling level.

Perhaps the most prominent feature of the test results for this subject is the consistency of her performance. Of twelve subtests administered to her at or below her mental-age score, she passed ten. The two tests failed were at her mental age. Beyond her mental age she passed only two of twelve tests.

An examination of her performance on the various tests shows a possible weakness in vocabulary. She wasn't able to pass this test at her MA.

Her strongest area is memory ability. The only tests she passed beyond her MA were tests of memory ability.

It is difficult to evaluate her verbal reasoning in that the only tests of this kind were administered beyond her MA level. Suffice it to say, this is probably not her strongest area.

In summary, the subject shows average ability with strength in memory ability and a possible weakness in vocabulary. If this is true, she may experience a little difficulty in a school setting. Otherwise, she should be able to compete adequately.

Fig. 6.3 A typical Stanford-Binet psychological report.

whether the child gets right or wrong answers, it is important to know how the child adjusts to the testing situation. Is he attentive? Does he answer decisively or does he tend to labor at it, even when he makes a correct response? Is his attention span long or short? Is he anxious or agitated? These are only a few of the behavioral characteristics a subject might exhibit while being tested. The observant examiner, having tested and watched many subjects in this situation, has a standard of performance in his mind that helps him to evaluate a particular child's problem-solving style. This can be important in making recommendations for academic placement and remedial help, or in understanding classroom learning problems.

As an example, consider two boys—Mark and Fred. Both are given the *Stanford-Binet* and both achieve an IQ of 80. But their performances may differ considerably in quality, and this will be revealed by the narrative part of the test report. Mark is slow with his answers, but he is attentive and diligent. He wants to please the examiner, expresses interest in, and curiosity about, the test itself, and persists at the tasks even when he has great difficulty finding the right answer. In other words, his verbal-abstract powers appear to be quite limited, yet he demonstrates considerable nonintellectual qualities—concentration, persistence, positive attitude, and so on—personality characteristics that are essential in almost all learning situations. Although academic subjects may be difficult for him, Mark should remain in normal classes, with specific remedial help given if he falls behind.

Fred performs quite differently. He, like Mark, has difficulty getting correct answers, but he also is restless, interrupting the test frequently by reaching for the test equipment, asking irrelevant questions, occasionally taking a walk around the room, and so on. He takes longer than Mark to arrive at an answer and usually provides little elaboration in his responses. His attention span is so short that the examiner must administer the test in two or three segments at different times.

Fred's score is the same as Mark's, yet his poorer adjustment to the test situation (as explained in the test report) could result in a recommendation that he be assigned to a special class where he can receive more individual help from the teacher. Usually, further testing and diagnosis are necessary before so important a decision is made, but Fred's test behavior strongly suggests that he will not profit very much from instruction in a normal classroom.

For the subject who is of average or above-average ability but who has a severe speech handicap, is extremely shy, or has some other personality characteristic that masks or inhibits his true ability, the test report may provide valuable insight into potential learning capacity.

Nonverbal mental tests such as the Wechsler "Performance Scale" can yield a rough estimate of the effects of cultural deprivation. The deprived child or the bilingual child with poor skills in standard English may show more ability in solving problems of a nonverbal nature, such as putting together a jigsaw puzzle or arranging colored blocks in a pattern. Again, this requires careful observation by a trained and experienced test administrator.

GROUP INTELLIGENCE TESTS

Since individual intelligence tests such as the *Stanford-Binet* require either oral responses from the subject or manipulation of materials, such tests are not suitable for group administration. Like the first Binet scale, group testing was developed to meet a pressing practical need. When America entered World War I in 1917, 1.5 million army recruits had to be classified with respect to general intellectual level. As a result, the first group intelligence tests were developed—the *Army Alpha* and the *Army Beta*. The *Alpha* was a test of general ability; the *Beta* was a nonverbal scale used with illiterates and foreign-born recruits who were unable to take a test that required them to read English.

From this beginning, the use of mass testing underwent rapid expansion in schools and clinics throughout the nation. Group intelligence tests proliferated, and many of them were inferior in quality. Although test-makers cautioned that intelligence tests were still in their infancy, schools began nevertheless to rely heavily on them for vocational-educational advisement. In spite of recurring attacks by some educators and segments of the public, the use of group intelligence tests became accepted practice throughout the educational system.

Group intelligence tests have many characteristics of individual intelligence tests. In the first place, like the *Stanford-Binet* and the Wechsler scales, they are based on the theory that general ability can be measured by sampling a variety of mental activities. Group-test items, therefore, are usually similar to individual-test items in that they elicit word meanings, verbal analogies, sentence completion, verbal absurdities, arithmetic problems, general information, picture arrangement, and so on. Second, the arrangement of items in both group and individual tests usually runs from easy to difficult so that almost every subject is able to obtain some correct responses. Third, the nature of the test items and their level of difficulty are appropriate to various ages and grade levels of the subjects. For example, at the kindergarten level, the test items are nonverbal. At the senior-high and college level, they are almost entirely verbal and numerical. Finally, the raw score is converted into a mental age, which, in turn, is converted into an IQ score. Unlike individual intelligence tests, however, on which the subject responds orally to many of the test questions or manipulates test objects, all group tests require the subject to make his responses on an answer sheet.

The scoring on group tests is objective and allows for no judgment about quality of response. In fact, most group intelligence tests are scored by computers, which also provide comparative data such as percentiles. Thus, group tests offer little or no means of assessing adjustment behavior on the part of the individuals who are taking the test.

Another important difference between group intelligence tests and many individually administered tests is that group tests usually require considerable reading on the part of the subject; consequently, reading skill correlates highly with mental test scores (Neville, 1965). Some group tests, however, contain nonverbal, quantitative, or spatial-visualization subtests as a means of measuring abilities without relying on verbal skills.

The *California Test of Mental Maturity*, for example, is a widely used paper-and-pencil test that can be administered to large numbers of children or adults at the same time. The "Language Form" covers six levels of grade and age, from preschool to adult. At each level, mental development is measured in terms of logical reasoning, spatial relationships, numerical reasoning, verbal concepts, and memory. These five factors are measured in twelve test units (two for each grade level) grouped in two sections—"Language" and "Nonlanguage"—which differentiate, in general, between responses to stimuli that are primarily verbal in nature and responses to stimuli that are essentially nonverbal or pictorial. According to the test booklet:

> Through analysis of the profile of scores, the teacher or counselor gains insights into the composition and functioning of an examinee's mental abilities. This knowledge may be utilized in individual counseling and guidance, and in planning the most appropriate instructional program for the examinee.

How do individual and group tests of intelligence compare in merit? The individual tests are still preferable in terms of validity and usefulness. The major standard for group tests is how well their scores correlate with scores on the *Stanford-Binet* and, to a lesser degree, the Wechsler tests for comparable age levels. For a case study of an individual student, the individually administered and personally scored test provides much more information than the group test, which usually yields only an IQ number. The number and variety of the student's responses, his resourcefulness, style, and strategy of problem solving, all are revealed and available in the test report on an individual test. Group tests of intelligence provide little insight into these nonintellective factors and therefore must be interpreted with caution in making instructional decisions.

INTELLIGENCE AND ACADEMIC ACHIEVEMENT

There always has been a relationship between IQ scores and future success in school, especially since intelligence tests have tended toward scholastically oriented tasks in their construction. As early as 1927, Kelly found a 90-per-cent overlap between tasks included in intelligence tests and those incorporated in achievement tests. A more recent study found the overlap to be 95 per cent (Coleman and Cureton, 1954).

The relationship between IQ scores and school achievement seems to be strongest during the years from middle childhood to adolescence, becoming less strong during college years. For example, Frandsen (1950) found that the *Wechsler Adult Intelligence Scale* provides a highly accurate prediction of academic achievement for above-average adolescents who intend to go on to post-high-school education. Taken as a whole, IQ scores provide fairly accurate prediction of school achievement within broad categories of below-average, average, high-average, and superior (Bolton, 1947). These facts notwithstanding, any prediction of academic achievement from IQ scores must be based on the assumption that the students who have been tested do not differ markedly in social-class characteristics from the dominant social class of the educational system in which they are competing.

As a general rule, the closer the tasks in an intelligence test are to the kinds of activities the individual will actually perform in a future educational or vocational setting, the greater will be the accuracy of prediction. Since most mental tests have high verbal content, they correlate best with future performance in verbal subjects such as English and social studies.

INTELLIGENCE AND SEX

When the first intelligence tests made their appearance between 1910 and 1920, the issue of women's rights was very nearly as controversial as the issue of ethnic-minority rights has been in recent years.

The dominant bias at that time was in the direction of seeking to "prove" the inferiority of women, but the trend of objective research from the beginning surely must have sharply disappointed the male chauvinists of that time. Terman reported in 1916 that the Binet intelligence scales he was using showed only very small differences between boys and girls in average scores. In fact, he found that, up to the age of thirteen, girls showed a small but fairly constant superiority over boys. Thereafter, boys maintained only a small margin.

Since that time, a great quantity of research has accumulated regarding the relationship of sex to measures of intelligence, and the pattern of conclusions indicates only two general areas of differences: First, although there are not consistent differences in *averages* between males and females, there appear to be differences with respect to *variability*. It is clear that males appear oftener at the very high and very low levels of IQ score distributions. This finding is generally interpreted as support for the theory that males are more likely to run to extremes whereas females tend to mediocrity. Although there are more males than females among retardates at birth, the preponderance of eminent males over females is now generally suspected to be due largely to cultural rather than genetic factors (Lynn, 1972).

What is more significant is that there are differences between males and females in specific areas of intellectual functioning, although, again, it is not wholly clear whether these are culturally or genetically based. Males are clearly superior, on the average, on tests of mathematical reasoning, spatial relationships, and science. Females perform better on tests of verbal fluency, rote memory, perceptual speed, and dexterity. Some of these differences develop earlier and appear to be more fundamental than others (Tyler, 1965). A rapidly expanding area of research today is the relationship of cultural roles to intellectual functioning. Thus far, the results have been scanty, primarily because of the difficulty of finding sufficiently large control groups of men and women who have grown up in a totally nonsexist environment.

To summarize, it is generally conceded that there is greater variability among boys, but the issue is not an important one. Of greater importance is whether intellectual style is predetermined by sex or is the result of subtle environmental influences.

INTELLIGENCE AND PERSONAL ADJUSTMENT

A number of stereotypes are commonly associated with such terms as "high IQ," "genius," "dullard," "slow learner," and all the other ways in which we label those whose mental ability falls at the extremes of the distribution. For example, "Ignorance is bliss" is a popular cliché: Children who have limited ability are believed to be happier because their minds apparently are not burdened with the heavy intellectual content that is the "affliction" of the very bright. Also, many believe that the child of very low ability often compensates for his dullness by becoming clever in mechanical skills, and that this helps him to be better adjusted emotionally. Another widespread belief is that genius is but a short step from insanity and that the highly gifted child is often physically frail, introspective, moody, and emotionally unstable.

Research refutes these and other stereotypes. High intellectual ability is associated with better adjustment and emotional stability, while instability and anxiety are likely to be characteristics of those for whom schoolwork is difficult—regardless of their mechanical skills. Unfortunately for the below-average child, not only does he have the problem of tough competition from his brighter peers, but he is much more prone to worrying about his difficulties in learning than the average or above-average child. Resnick (1951) investigated the relationship between school marks and various factors related to mental health. He found that, for the most part, pupils who earned higher grades also made higher mean scores on personality measures, indicating more satisfactory personal adjustment.

INTELLIGENCE AND SOCIO-ECONOMIC STATUS

Since Terman formally introduced the Binet scales in 1916, many people, including test builders themselves, have warned about the limitations of intelligence tests; yet the public has had far more faith in them than the tests have warranted. The intelligence-test movement grew largely because of the public's fascination with "genius" and with attempts to predict the future.

By the late 1950's, intelligence tests (and many other forms of mental and psychological testing as well) began to arouse severe criticism on the ground that they are biased against three types of individuals: (1) the bright but unorthodox person, (2) the person who lacks experience in taking standardized tests, and (3) the culturally deprived (Holtzman, 1971). Of the three, the problem of bias against the culturally deprived stands out as the most serious, because it involves a considerable proportion of the population.

It was always known that children from poverty-stricken rural or slum areas functioned less well on educational tests because of their poor experiential background, but the pervasive nature of this social-class bias was not taken very seriously except by psychologists and the test builders. Binet himself recognized quite early that differences in test scores were related to differences in the social-class backgrounds of the respondents. Later, Terman (1916) reported that children of "superior social class" scored fourteen points higher on the average than did those of "inferior social class." Davis (1948) was one of the first to point out that tests of mental ability do not accurately measure the intelligence quotients of black children because the tests are culture-laden in a way that favors middle-class, white children. Test publishers early pointed to the confounding effects of social-class deprivation on test scores and emphasized the importance of using tests wisely. But school administrators and counselors went ahead and administered the tests anyway, probably because it was expected that a large proportion of low-social-class children would drop out of school.

Leaving school early was acceptable and useful several decades ago and, in fact, was often encouraged by teachers and administrators. Now it is generally believed that the educated person is likely to achieve status and economic advantages as well as to have enhanced self-esteem and personal development, while the premature dropout is cast in an inferior role. Further, it is recognized that school dropouts, in the words of James Bryant Conant (1961), are "social dynamite," in that their resentment, boredom, and frustration may cause them to lash out destructively at the institutions of society. It is hardly surprising that members of minority groups and other nonaffluent individuals have raised angry cries at any screening device that could deprive them of entrance to better schools, jobs, and social positions. These critics have as their goals the elimination of mental testing, except when its value is fully substantiated and acceptable, and the development of "culture-fair" tests.

Drastic cutbacks in the use of all forms of mental tests do not appear likely. To begin with, elimination of bias-prone tests would be like the ancient practice of slaying the bearer of bad tidings. After the mental tests have gone, the effects of injustice and deprivation and their social and environmental causes will still be with us. Nevertheless, the threat of cutbacks will undoubtedly result in more responsible use of tests. In fact, many inner-city school districts have curtailed or eliminated mass testing and are concentrating primarily on selective use of individual tests for clinical purposes.

The development of "culture-fair" tests is a much more complex problem. Since intelligence is a socially valued characteristic and therefore, to some extent, is defined in social-cultural terms, a truly culture-fair intelligence test seems only remotely possible. Any intelligence test assesses past experience—behaviors that have been shaped by the culture. A "pure" measure of genetically determined ability (one not influenced in any way by environmental circumstances) assuredly would be a just assessment of the individual, but it would reveal nothing about his capacity to adapt to his environment, a crucial trait.

At this writing, attempts to develop bias-free tests have been largely unsuccessful. For example, the *Davis-Eells Games* is a pictorial test that is administered orally and is intended to be an unbiased test for lower-social-class children in American society. The results of almost thirty research studies indicate that the test has not correlated as high with achievement tests and teachers' grades as conventional tests have, and that lower-social-class children perform just about as poorly on this test as on the more traditional tests (Anastasi, 1961).

Nevertheless, many psychologists have been fascinated by the notion of observing mental processes directly—a "pure" measure of ability—by means of instrumentation and computers. One method is to measure the efficiency and speed with which information is transmitted from one neuron to another. The so-called neural efficiency score is expected to reflect an individual's "true" ability, regardless of environmental factors (Tracy, 1972). But, at the moment, the measurement of neural activity is still in the research stage.

Obviously, social-class bias in mental testing involves serious moral issues. The use of biased tests is not only unfair to potentially high-achieving individuals, but it is shortchanging our society. Genetically, intelligence is randomly distributed among all children, regardless of social-class status. It follows that there are potentially more "geniuses" among the lower-social-classes because that is where most of the children are! Talent is a valuable national resource. It is doubtful that a society can continue to grow and prosper if it fails to identify and develop its gifted children.

INTELLIGENCE TESTS AND THE EXCEPTIONAL CHILD

The gifted are usually defined as those whose IQ scores are about 125 to 140 and up, depending on the test used. Combining the intelligence-test score with additional measures of achievement has provided a fairly reliable prediction of giftedness—usually in over 90 per cent of the cases. Often, however, very bright children have been identified by teachers without the help of test scores. In a few spectacular instances, an IQ score and test report have alerted teachers and administrators to a child who is uninterested and noncompetitive but extremely capable intellectually. Identification of the "gifted underachiever" has been one of the most valuable spin-offs from the development of intelligence tests. The identification of unusual talent in young children continues to be one reason for the continued use of intelligence tests, both individual and group.

On the other hand, the "discovery" value of intelligence tests rarely, if ever, works to the benefit of the slow learner. An intelligence test seldom reveals a student who performs extremely well in all phases of school to have a "true" IQ that is low. If such an "overachiever" is discovered, it is usually the result of a large measurement error in the intelligence test itself. Of course, as in all areas of educational practice, spectacular exceptions do occur, but the consequences of such an error for slow learners are quite different from the consequences of errors in identifying the "gifted underachiever." With the latter, the school usually makes strenuous efforts to get the child to perform closer to his mental potential. The child is at least informed of his potential and urged to live up to it.

Thus, educational decisions based on intelligence tests have usually been of greatest benefit to the truly bright child. For the truly dull child, intelligence-test scores have not had equally beneficial effects. Too many teachers and counselors still feel it necessary to inform the child that he is not capable intellectually.

THE VALUE OF INTELLIGENCE TESTS FOR TEACHER AND STUDENT

For many years, information about IQs was considered to be confidential; even teachers were frequently not supposed to know a child's score. At present, there is no definite pattern regarding the use of mental-test scores in public schools. In some cases, score data are controlled by the guidance staff, who may discourage access to them by teachers on the ground that what is involved is highly sensitive information that only a test expert can properly understand and interpret to others. But many schools allow both teachers and parents unrestricted access to all data on students, so that they can have more than guesswork to guide them in the diagnosis of learning problems, and so that parents especially will know better what to expect from a child and how to help him.

Unfortunately, however, most teachers and many school administrators lack the expertise to understand the complexities of measurement error, validity and reliability coefficients, and other characteristics of mental tests, although this is not intended to mean that school person-nel should ignore the information mental tests provide. As general indications of where children are with respect to broad areas of mental ability, intelligence-test scores and diagnostic data can be very helpful for teachers in planning classroom objectives as well as for school counselors in educational and vocational advisement. For these pur-poses, most mental-test and achievement-test data are reported in percentiles.

COMMUNICATING THE IQ TO PARENTS

An IQ score derived from a carefully administered and interpreted mental test such as the *Stanford-Binet* may be easier to convey to parents than the subjective judgment of a teacher, which is often based on an inadequate sample of the child's performance. When a child is "dull" to "dull-normal," with an IQ score of around 76–89, parents may have to accept the child's placement in a "slow-learner" class. If the child's IQ is 75 or below, it is quite likely that they must accept his placement in a class for the retarded. All this is on the assumption that the test score reflects true ability and is not unduly affected by cultural deprivation or physical handicaps.

For children whose scores are in the average range (approximately 84–116 on the basis of the *Stanford-Binet*), and for those whose scores are in the "high average" or "superior" category, interpretations of IQ must be made with great care.

An ever present danger of reporting mental-test scores arises from the very ease with which the term "IQ" can be communicated. Since it is a number, it is often assumed by parents to be more accurate than it is. Thus, an IQ of 90 can, in a sense, be considered below average. But, in terms of general intellectual functioning, 90 IQ is within the broad range of "average." In fact—again using the *Stanford-Binet* as the basis—children with measured IQs of from 84 to 116 should be regarded as "average" to "bright-average." This IQ band comprises about 68 per cent of all children. For those whose score is above or below this range, any discussion of an IQ, or its equivalent percentile, must always be accompanied by information regarding the nature of the test, its validity, and the probable error of measurement (see Chapter 10).

Almost every teacher knows of at least one student whose intelligence-test score is high, but who is not doing well in schoolwork. One reason for this discrepancy might be that the test score is inaccurate. This is quite possible, but it is seldom the only reason. We know that in-tellectual aptitude is only one of the many factors that contribute to success in school. Even bright children have difficulty in schoolwork if they are not appropriately motivated or have poor study skills. Test scores are helpful in predicting the student's probable achievement, but the prediction may be in error because of failure to take into account factors other than intellectual-aptitude scores. In other words, personality characteristics (the nonintellective factors) must play a prominent part in educational and personal diagnosis. For example, at the adolescent level many youth are underachievers; they "go to sleep" mentally for several years. They simply are not very much interested in academic activities. A mental test taken at this time may be an unreliable measure of intelligence because it reflects a temporary motivational state rather than optimal mental functioning.

CONSTANCY OF THE IQ

The most valuable attribute of any predictive instrument is the accuracy of its prediction over a long period of time. Intelligence tests have usually provided dependable measures of ability only for short-run diagnosis and prediction. Also, intelligence tests have worked best for elementary-age children. The predictive validity of an IQ for preschool-age children is not very high. Bayley (1955) found correlations for preschoolers averaging .82 between successive tests administered only a month apart. Correlations over intervals of a year or more were very low, however, and were virtually zero between infancy and adulthood. According to Bayley, "It is now well established that we cannot predict later intelligence from scores in infancy" (1955, p. 805). In fact, if major educational decisions are to be made on the basis of IQ-test scores, the child should be retested at intervals of no greater than three or four years until adulthood (*Encyclopedia of Educational Research*, 1969).

The risks rise sharply when intelligence-test scores are used for the prediction of success in academic work more than several years or so in the future and especially for prediction of general success in adult life (McClelland, 1973). There are just too many ways in which a child can spoil an intelligence-test performance—particularly in taking a group test. For teachers and counselors to look at a test score and make pronouncements that could affect a child quite significantly in the future is a practice that can be justified only when mental-test scores are combined with measures of academic achievement, teachers' judgments and anecdotal records, course grades, a measure of reading ability and performance, and some knowledge and understanding of the child as a person.

The appraisal of human learning and abilities is complicated by the fact that these qualities cannot, at this time, be measured directly. If scientists ever find an organic basis for mental behavior, it may become possible to measure general learning ability through the use of an X-ray, an EEG, or some as yet undeveloped electronic device or chemical analysis. Until such time, measurement efforts must be confined to the external manifestations of intellectual functioning and will therefore be subject to varying interpretations. It is a characteristic of research in psychology that there are several equally valid and respectable explanations for any given phenomenon of behavior, and in this respect theories of intelligence are no exception. These theories—which often appear to be almost contradictory—nevertheless maintain equal popularity, because each offers some unique advantages.

Every child has the right to develop his potential fully—social, physical, emotional, and intellectual. But, because most behavioral characteristics are learned, and because each child learns them in unique ways, the range of individual differences in mental ability and achievement among children is the most significant and basic fact in the process of planning and implementing an instructional program. Mental tests—wisely used—can be a valuable tool in this vital process.

CREATIVITY AND INTELLIGENCE

According to F. Barron, who studied creative thinking in adults over a period of several years, the making of thoughts is the most common instance of psychic creation, as the making of a baby is the most common instance of material creation. Both thoughts and babies are unique and yet are typical products of mankind generally. Thus, a man may generate an idea that is totally new for him but is commonly known when all human beings are taken into account.

All of us are both creatures and creators, but we vary both in our quality as a creation and in our power to create.

Great original thoughts or ideas are those which are not only new to the person who thinks them but new to almost everyone. These rare contributions are creative in perhaps a stronger sense of the term; they not only are the results of a creative act, but they themselves in turn create new conditions of human existence. The theory of relativity was such a creative act; so was the invention of the wheel. Both resulted in new forms of power, and human life was changed thereby.

Creative power of an outstanding order is marked by the voluminous production of acts which can claim a notable degree of originality, and the occasional production of acts of radical originality. It is instructive to read in a good encyclopedia the history of the basic scientific disciplines; one soon finds the same names cropping up in field after field, for it is the nature of genius to range with fresh interest over the whole of natural phenomena and to see relations which others do not notice. [Barron, 1969, p. 19.]

One of the most extensive studies made of creativity is reported by Getzels and Jackson (1962). Subjects' intelligence was measured by three conventional intelligence tests: the *Stanford-Binet,* the *Wechsler Intelligence Scale for Children,* and a verbal-scholastic group test. Getzels and Jackson also designed and administered a series of tasks to measure creative thinking:

Word association. The subject is asked to give as many definitions as possible for common words (e.g., bolt, bark, sack).

Uses for things. The subject is asked to state as many different ways as he can to use common objects (e.g., bricks, paper clips, toothpicks).

Hidden shapes. The subject is asked to locate geometric figures hidden in complex figures.

Fables. The subject is presented with four short fables in which the last lines are missing, and he is asked to compose a "moralistic," "humorous," and "sad" ending for each fable.

Make-up problems. The subject is presented with four complex paragraphs, each containing many numerical statements. He is asked to make up as many mathematical problems as he can with the information given.

On the basis of their intelligence- and creativity-test scores, twenty-six students were selected for a high-intelligence, low-creativity group and twenty-eight students for a low-intelligence, high-creativity group. The two groups were then compared in terms of school achievement (both groups were superior), motivation for achievement (no differences), and perception by teachers (the high-IQ students were regarded as more desirable and enjoyable than the average student; the high-creativity students were not). Apparently, the chief difference between the two groups was that the teachers preferred the high-IQ students, despite the fact that the creative students were achieving at a level higher than their IQ scores indicated they should achieve.

Getzels and Jackson made some inferences about the values held by hypothetical children.

In effect, the high I.Q. is saying, "I know what makes for success and what teachers like, and I want these qualities too"; the high creative is saying, "I know as well as the high I.Q. what makes for conventional success and what teachers like but these are not necessarily the qualities I want for myself." [1962, p. 36.]

Other studies have confirmed the main conclusion of Getzels and Jackson—namely, that high-IQ students appear to be teacher-oriented and stimulus-bound, and that they structure tasks in terms of what the teacher wants. High-creative students, on the other hand, are relatively stimulus-free—they structure tasks largely on their own terms.

There is a consistent tendency for creative males to score higher on femininity measures than do their less-creative peers on tests of the relative strength of the masculine and feminine components of personality. This finding suggests that creative males conform less rigidly to stereotyped masculine behavior than the average male. Apparently, the creative male is able to develop and express intellectual and cultural interests that are either male or female without feeling personally threatened. He doesn't allow his male identification to interfere with his inclination to express both masculine and feminine traits. He is more likely to be more independent than his more rigidly sex-typed male peers.

It must be borne in mind that creative students—and adults as well—tend to *know* a lot; they predictably score high on achievement tests in the areas that interest them. It should be added, also, that being "stimulus-free" does not necessarily mean that one is also "creative." Many people are "stimulus-free"—including psychotics—but relatively few are very creative. What is now apparent from research on creativity is that the creative person not only is basically bright but has "something else." This "something else" seems to be a factor related to both intellectual ability and certain nonintellective qualities such as courage, independence, and nonconformity.

Creativity in the classroom involves elements of risk, a factor that discourages some timid and conservative school administrators and teachers from fostering it in the school. Most authorities agree that real creativity is independent, original thinking, and in school settings this could result in such disruptive behavior as strikes or boycotts against teachers and administrators, critical questions about the free-enterprise system, race, and other controversial issues, or any number of other provocative questions or explorations that might disrupt the security and complacency of adults. In other words, creativity sometimes has negative as well as positive outcomes. Rather than try to avoid this possibility, school authorities must consider it as part of the price to be paid. Unquestionably, those children who possess the "divine spark" deserve to be identified and encouraged, as well as tolerated.

Conventional goals and forms of measurement and reward for creative effort should be abandoned. Creative students usually generate their own goals, and measurement, too, should be self-regulating. Rewards for these gifted youth should come in the form of public recognition—at science fairs, art exhibits, and forums, or in literary publications. Ideally, these events should occur as often as report cards (Mueller, 1964).

There has also been growing interest in the idea of bringing creative people from the community into the classroom to function as "sponsors" for small groups of imaginative students and as resource people for teachers and curriculum directors. Perhaps the experience gained from interacting with productive, creative adults may contribute to the enhancement of creativity in the public-school classroom.

REFERENCES

ANASTASI, A. 1958. Heredity, environment, and the question how? *Psychological Review, 65,* 197–208.

———. 1961. *Psychological testing.* New York: Macmillan.

ARMSTRONG, R. J., and R. F. MOONEY. 1971. The Slosson Intelligence Test: Implications for reading specialists. *Reading Teacher, 24,* 336–40, 368.

BARRON, F. 1969. *Creative person and creative process.* New York: Holt, Rinehart & Winston.

BAYLEY, N. 1955. On the growth of intelligence. *American Journal of Psychology, 10,* 805–18.

BLOOM, B. S. 1964. *Stability and change in human characteristics.* New York: Wiley.

BOLTON, F. B. 1947. Value of several intelligence tests for predicting scholastic achievement. *Journal of Educational Research, 41,* 133–41.

COLEMAN, W., and E. E. CURETON. 1954. Intelligence and achievement: The "jangle fallacy" again. *Educational and Psychological Measurement, 14,* 347–51.

CONANT, J. B. 1961. *Slums and suburbs.* New York: McGraw-Hill.

DAVIS, A. 1948. *Social class influences upon learning.* Cambridge, Mass.: Harvard University Press.

Encyclopedia of Educational Research. 1969. New York: Macmillan.

FRANDSEN, A. 1950. The Wechsler-Bellevue Intelligence Scale and high school achievement. *Journal of Applied Psychology, 34,* 406–11.

GARRETT, H. E. 1946. A developmental theory of intelligence. *American Psychologist, 1,* 372–78.

GETZELS, J. W., and P. W. JACKSON. 1962. *Creativity and intelligence.* New York: Wiley.

GUILFORD, J. P. 1959. Three faces of intellect. *American Psychologist, 14,* 469–79.

HOLTZMAN, W. H. 1971. The changing world of mental measurement and its social significance. *American Psychologist,* 26(6), 546–53.

JENSEN, A. R. 1969. How much can we boost I.Q. and scholastic achievement? *Harvard Educational Review, 39,* 1–123.

———. 1970. Learning ability, intelligence, and educability. In V. A. Allen (ed.), *Psychological factors in poverty.* Chicago: Markham.

KELLY, T. L. 1927. *Interpretation of educational measurement.* New York: Harcourt, Brace & World.

LEE, E. S. 1951. Negro intelligence and selective migration: A Philadelphia test of the Klineberg hypothesis. *American Sociological Review, 16,* 227–33.

LYNN, D. B. 1972. Determinants of intellectual growth in women. *School Review,* February, 80(2), 241–60.

McCLELLAND, D. 1973. Testing for competence rather than for "intelligence." *American Psychologist,* 28(1), 1–14.

———, J. W. ATKINSON, R. A. CLARK, and E. L. LOWELL. 1953. *The The achievement motive.* New York: Appleton-Century-Crofts.

MUELLER, R. J. 1964. Can the public school foster creativity? *The Saturday Review,* December 19, 48–49, 64.

NEVILLE, D. 1965. The relationship between reading skills and intelligence test scores. *Reading Teacher, 18,* 257–62.

RESNICK, J. 1951. A study of some relationships between high school grades and certain aspects of adjustment. *Journal of Educational Research, 44,* 321–40.

SPEARMAN, C. 1904. 'General Intelligence' objectively determined and measured. *American Journal of Psychology,* Vol. 15.

SPEARMAN, C. 1923. *The Nature of Intelligence and the Principles of Cognition.* London: Macmillan.

SPEARMAN, C. 1927. *The abilities of man.* New York: Macmillan.

TERMAN, L. M. 1916. *The measurement of intelligence.* Boston: Houghton Mifflin.

———. 1965. *The psychology of human differences.* New York: Appleton-Century-Crofts.

TERMAN, L. M., and M. A. MERRILL. 1960. *Stanford-Binet Intelligence Scale: Manual for the Third Revision.* Boston: Houghton Mifflin.

TERMAN, L. M., *et al.* 1925, 1926, 1930, 1947, 1959. *Genetic studies of genius.* Stanford: Stanford University Press.

THURSTONE, L. L. 1946. Theories of intelligence. *Scientific Monthly, 62,* 101–12.

THURSTONE, L. L., and T. G. THURSTONE. 1950. *Primary Mental Abilities Scales: Primary, Elementary, and Intermediate.* Chicago: Science Research Associates.

TRACY, W. 1972. Goodbye IQ, hello EL (Ertl Index). *Phi Delta Kappan,* 54(2), 89–94.

TYLER, L. E. 1965. The psychology of human differences. New York: Appleton-Century-Crofts.

WECHSLER, D. 1949. *Wechsler Intelligence Scale for Children, Manual.* New York: The Psychological Corporation.

———— 1958. *The measurement and appraisal of adult intelligence.* Baltimore: Williams & Wilkins.

WEISE, P. 1960. Current uses of Binet and Wechsler scales by school psychologists in California. *California Journal of Educational Research,* 21, 73–77.

CHAPTER SEVEN

The Dynamics of
School Adjustment

OF ALL THE FORMS of human tragedy, none is more heart-rending than the plight of the poorly adjusted child. The *Final Report of the Joint Commission on Mental Health of Children* (National Institute of Mental Health, 1971) poignantly reveals the magnitude of mental-health problems among our nation's youth.

In 1969, more than 900,000 of our children in the age group 10 to 17 were brought before juvenile courts. In 1968, 437,000 children were seen in outpatient psychiatric clinics, 33,000 were patients in public and private mental hospitals, 26,000 were in residential treatment centers, 13,000 [were] in day/night services, and 52,000 were patients in community mental health centers. Almost 10 per cent of our young people will have at least one psychiatric contact by the time they reach 25 years of age. Thirty thousand children were battered or neglected in 1969, and those were only the ones we know about. Twenty thousand children were admitted to public and private mental hospitals and many of them, unfortunately, will spend years there. Not only have admissions to public mental hospitals doubled for persons under 25 years of age in the last 10 years but also the number of resident patients in this age group has continued to increase annually in spite of the fact that for older age groups the number of resident patients has continued to decline. Teachers of elementary school children feel that, on the average, 10 per cent of the children they teach are "severely maladjusted" and "in need of professional" help.

The report flatly declares that our claim to being a child-centered society is a myth. Not only do we as a nation devote "miniscule" resources to services for children but we fail to offer adequate help to families rearing children.

The idea that a "mentally healthy" person is "well adjusted" originally derived from the biological concept of adaptation, a cornerstone of Darwin's theory of evolution. Animal species and biological structures that best met environmental demands were the well-adapted organisms, structures, or processes. Similarly, human behavior that adequately met the demands of the environment was adaptive, and the individual who adequately dealt with the demands and expectancies of his physical and social world was well adjusted. In the rural society of the nineteenth century, most people were engaged most of the time in a struggle against the uncertainties of the physical environment—weather, crop conditions, food shortages. In today's society, much of our time and energy is spent coping with other people and the demands made by human institutions. Thus, we tend to be concerned more with psychological survival and adaptation to a social world than with physical survival and adaptation to a physical world. Shaffer and Shoben (1956, p. 4) point out the "critical difference between adjusting to your physiological needs and adjusting to your social needs":

> The only successful adjustments to want, hunger, or thirst are to breathe, eat, or drink. Compromises are impossible, and the only outcome of complete deprivation is death. But when a man fails to achieve social adjustment he remains alive and keeps on trying, even though he may be ineffective and unhappy. Inadequate adjustments therefore present a continuing and challenging social problem.

In the context of the school, a mentally healthy child is one who makes gradual but steady improvement in both intellectual and social skills—in the ability to perform effectively in and out of school, in work, play, interpersonal relationships. In other words, mental health means a growth in competence in all areas of living, as evidenced by objective measures of achievement and by feelings of self-worth and well-being as an outcome of learning.

The Association for Supervision and Curriculum Development of the National Education Association (1966) defines the mentally healthy child as one who is able to adapt to a changing environment, who perceives reality accurately, manages stress, stands on his own feet, wants to learn, and possesses feelings of adequacy and well-being.

SCHOOL FACTORS IN MENTAL HEALTH

To understand the forces that contribute to mental-health problems in childhood, it is necessary to understand the impact of the school upon the child. Life in the classroom is a steady press of competition and struggle to meet standards. The child is "on stage" most of the time he is in school, and he must develop appropriate ways of coping. Most children accomplish this task successfully, but many learn failure and avoidance behavior instead.

Many of the mental-health problems of children are related to school work. Studies have shown a strong relationship between school achievement and personality characteristics. As Bloom (1972) put it:

Repeated success in coping with the academic demands of the school appears to confer upon a high proportion of such students a type of immunization against emotional illness. Similarly, repeated failure in coping with the demands of the school appears to be a source of emotional difficulties and mental illness [p. 338].

Stedman and Adams (1972) studied teachers' ratings of children's behavior as a predictor of achievement for lower-social-class Mexican-American children in a San Antonio, Texas, Head Start program. The findings indicated that the ratings of student adjustment constituted the strongest predictor of all achievement measures, including language skills.

There is also evidence of a relationship between social and academic pressures in the school environment and suicide. In his analysis of students who committed suicide during the 1963–64 and 1964–65 academic years, Reese (1968) found two major causes: inadequate social identification in the school environment, and a history of academic failure. These students had few personal relationships with peers or teachers. Half of them were failing or nearly failing their school work, and one-quarter scored below the fifteenth percentile in intelligence tests.

Reese concluded:

Research clearly indicates that social isolation is associated with the act of self-destruction. Educators must direct more effort toward creating the opportunity for all students to achieve meaningful social relationships. Such involvement must not be left to chance, but must be

structured if it is to help rectify maladaptive social behavior. It is suspected that the benefits of a structured social program would also carry
over into the academic realm. The student who has a satisfying social
life is better able to employ his energies in the classroom [p. 11].

The influence that anxiety exerts on school work is difficult to assess
directly. Evidence from clinical studies, however, points clearly and
consistently to the disruptive and distracting effects of high anxiety on
most kinds of thinking (Hewett and Blake, 1973).

It is the child with limited ability for school work who is the most
susceptible to emotional problems. The below-average child has trouble
finding the correct intellectual response to a problem. He is forced to
fall back on an emotional solution instead, and this becomes a part of
his entire pattern of personality. In an intensive study of 45 girls and 60
boys who were about to drop out of school, Lichter and his associates
(1962) found that the primary reason was not any specific learning
failure but a broad educational disability resulting in increased anxiety
and stress. To the child, dropping out was a positive action; to the
school, it was a turning away and an escape.

Lack of ability for school subjects is not in itself an emotional handicap, but the stress of competing with academically superior students
may be. Often, however, the self-concept of a slow learner can be
strengthened in subjects in which he can succeed.

None of this is intended to suggest that the academically able student
is totally immune to severe, debilitating anxiety. His strong academic
capabilities may encourage his parents and teachers to increase their
expectations for him far beyond what he is able or willing to attain
comfortably. Neither intellectual brilliance nor mental deficiency is in
itself a causal factor in childhood behavioral or neurotic disorders. It is
the environment in which these ability levels operate that is significant
(Rutter, 1964).

MENTAL HEALTH AND EMOTION

The word "emotion" is difficult to define precisely. In general, emotions involve feelings and impulses toward action as well as the subjective element of perception that produces the feelings and impulses
(Jersild, 1960).

A child under one month of age expresses a generally vague and
undifferentiated emotion of excitement and possibly distress. The
presentation of strong stimuli—the reflection of bright sunlight on his

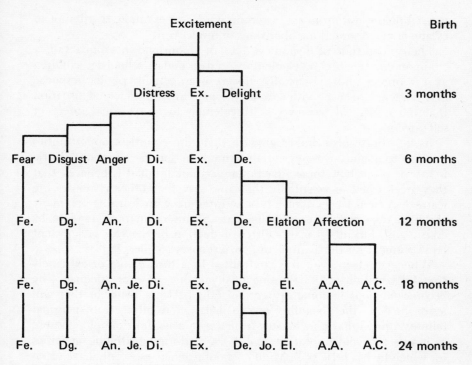

Key: A.A., affection for adults; A.C., affection for children; An., anger; De., delight; Dg., disgust; Di., distress; El., elation; Ex., excitement; Fe., fear; Je., jealousy; Jo., joy.

Fig. 7.1. The approximate ages of differentiation of the various emotions during the first two years of life. (After K. M. Bridges, "Emotional Development in Early Infancy," *Child Development, 3* [1932] , 340. Reproduced by permission of the Society for Research in Child Development.)

eyes, being suddenly picked up, loud noise, being touched with an ice cube—causes him to become agitated; his arm and hand muscles tense, and his legs make jerky, kicking movements. Some time during the early weeks following birth, the general emotion of delight becomes apparent, and thereafter the child expresses increasingly differentiated emotional behavior (see Fig. 7.1).

As children grow older, they develop a range of feelings from extreme annoyance or discomfort to strong satisfaction or pleasure, accompanied by measurable, observable physiological changes such as increased perspiration, respiration, heartbeat, and circulation. They also develop a general predisposition to act in certain ways—for example, to attempt to escape or avoid something obnoxious or unpleasant.

The general state of uneasiness, fear, or gloom known as *anxiety* is a common emotion among elementary- and secondary-school-age children as it is among adults. Generally, anxiety is an actually phobic response or a tendency to react with fear to any present or anticipated situation that the individual perceives as threatening to his personal safety or self-esteem.

In the course of a child's growth, there are countless opportunities for him to acquire fears of certain stimuli in specific situations. Little is known about how these anxieties are acquired, but it is believed that they are learned in essentially the same way that other responses are learned. A high level of anxiety may interfere with learning for many children; responses become ineffectual and discriminations tend to be erratic and difficult to make. Often, reduction of the fear is sufficient reinforcement for the learning of new responses (Miller, 1948).

Whenever an individual is confronted by a threatening or extremely stressful situation—especially one involving his sense of adequacy—he becomes anxious to some degree and falls back on behavior that will lessen or deny the possibility of ego deflation resulting from personal failure. A pupil may play hookey from a gym class, for example, because he wants to avoid appearing foolish by performing athletic activities for which he has little skill. Middle-school teachers especially have often noted that absences tend to increase on announced test days.

Anxiety differs from ordinary fear in that the threat need not be current in nature; it may be anticipated. A person is fearful when an aroused dog lunges at him; he is anxious when he reflects on the possibility of loss of self-esteem resulting from the failing course grade he expects. The situation eliciting anxiety is an impending threat, but one directed primarily against the individual's self-esteem rather than his physical safety. Sometimes insecurity and anxiety occur together. The threat of possible vocational failure, for example, not only is damaging to one's self-esteem but also can result in genuine concern regarding one's chances for survival.

In 1926, in his book *The Problem of Anxiety*, Sigmund Freud wrote that anxiety was the "fundamental phenomenon and the central problem of neurosis." It appears that anxiety is basic to all neurotic behavior, but some anxiety is essentially "normal" or "situational."

In "normal" anxiety, a threat to self-esteem objectively exists. This threat may arise from an external situation—as, for example, an important achievement test used as a basis for college scholarships—or from a need for recognition from peers in athletic or academic competition. Or the source of the threat may be within the individual—for example, the awkwardness and uncertainties that often accompany the rapid physical changes of adolescence. In all cases, the threat comes from a source distinct from the entity that is being threatened; in no case does the threat to self-esteem arise from impaired self-esteem itself.

In neurotic, or "free-floating," anxiety, the essential source of the threat to self-esteem seems to be the individual's impaired self-concept itself. The individual may overreact to a perceived threat, or he may feel a sense of depression and foreboding for no discernible reason at all. The anxiety is usually accompanied by a negative self-appraisal. Highly anxious children generally manifest more self-dissatisfaction and self-disparagement than less anxious children.

According to Kelly (1955), the anxious person has difficulty in making sense out of his environment or certain aspects of it. He is overwhelmed by events in his life that he cannot understand or anticipate. From this perspective, neurotic anxiety is a feeling of helplessness or alienation in the presence of troubling events.

ADJUSTMENT TO STRESS

Much of the current literature on emotional problems of children points to the social and psychological pressures they experience. Perhaps these stresses are no heavier today than those experienced by youth in past generations, but there is no question that today's youth are encountering different kinds of pressures.

The response to stress, which may be defined as actual or potential danger, either physiological or psychological in nature, appears to be a function of the interaction between characteristics of the demand itself (intensity, multiplicity, and duration of stress; importance of the threatened needs or goals; degree of suddenness and unfamiliarity of the challenge) and characteristics of the individual under pressure (general competence; frame of reference; emotional make-up and involvement; and stress tolerance) (Coleman, 1960).

When a child is placed under stress, his initial reaction is usually alarm, often accompanied by a reluctance to diagnose the situation accurately and to accept the seriousness of the threat. Next follows any one of a number of possible responses, or combination of responses, that serve as emergency mobilization of personal resources. These may follow definable patterns of adjustment. The child wants to be recognized and approved of by his teachers and his peers. When a teacher criticizes his school work, his need for appreciation is thwarted. The child may "adjust" to this threat to his self-esteem in a positive way: He may act so as to gain favor in the future, by finding out what he did wrong in order to correct his mistakes, or he may resolve to study more and pay attention in class.

On the other hand, the child may fall back on adjustments that are largely negative and nonintegrative: He may belittle his critic or blame his poor work on interference from other students, inability to concentrate, or poor instruction. Any of these responses may reduce his anxiety temporarily, but it won't win any approval from his peers or help him to improve his schoolwork. In fact, it might bring him into further conflict with his teacher or schoolmates. In other words, inadequate adjustment results from activities that bring the child into conflict with his environment or hinder his ability to cope with stress and responsibility.

The strength of an emotion varies with the severity of the stress situation that provokes it, but the emotional reaction one makes to a stress situation provides clues to his personality. A mildly emotional state can be helpful to the child because it will energize him and motivate him to focus on what is most important. A highly diffuse emotional response, however, can interfere with clear thinking. The teacher must try to determine the level of emotional stress at which the child begins to have difficulty.

Classroom stress affects different children in different ways. If the teacher announces a quiz without warning, the children will manifest a variety of emotional responses. Some children will immediately begin to chatter and fuss with their books and pencils. Others will seem stunned and temporarily immobilized. Still others will show no visible signs of emotion but may be reacting viscerally; their stomachs are literally churning. Throughout the room, there will be a general moaning, dropping of pencils, banging of desk tops. Obviously, the overt ways in which the children react will be most noticed by the teacher. But it is important to keep in mind that the child who seems calm and collected in times of stress is not necessarily serene and composed within himself. He may be experiencing strong inner reactions.

John Holt has described some of the school behaviors adopted by highly anxious children:

The strategies of these kids have been consistently self-centered, self-protective, aimed above all else at avoiding trouble, embarrassment, punishment, disapproval, or loss of status. This is particularly true of the ones who have had a tough time in school. When they get a problem, I can read their thoughts on their faces, I can almost hear them: "Am I going to get this right? Probably not; what'll happen to me when I get it wrong? Will the teacher get mad? Will the other kids laugh at me? Will my mother and father hear about it? Will they keep me back this year? Why am I so dumb?" And so on.

Even in the room periods, where I did all I could to make the work non-threatening, I was continually amazed and appalled to see the children hedging their bets, covering their losses in advance, trying to fix things so that whatever happened they could feel they had been right, or if wrong, no more wrong than anyone else. "I think it will sort of balance." They are fence-straddlers, afraid ever to commit themselves—and at the age of ten. . . .

These self-limiting and self-defeating strategies are dictated, above all else, by fear. For many years I have been asking myself why intelligent children act unintelligently at school. The simple answer is, "Because they're scared." . . .

Perhaps most people do not recognize fear in children when they see it. They can read the grossest signs of fear; they know what the trouble is when a child clings howling to his mother, but the subtler signs of fear escape them. It is these signs, in children's faces, noises, and gestures, in their movements and ways of working, that tell me plainly that most children in school are scared most of the time, many of them very scared. Like good soldiers, they control their fears, live with them, and adjust themselves to them. But the trouble is, and here is a vital difference between school and war, that the adjustments children make to their fears are almost wholly bad, destructive of their intelligence and capacity. The scared fighter may be the best fighter, but the scared learner is always a poor learner. [Holt, 1964, pp. 48–49.]

Generally speaking, an individual who confronts an obstacle has three possible choices of behavior: He may succeed in overcoming or solving the problem; he may fail to do so and then withdraw from the field; or he may engage in nonadaptive behavior—scapegoating, projection, rationalization, and other defense mechanisms (as we shall see later in this chapter). Success, of course, is strengthening; it tends to give the individual greater self-confidence and competence to solve the next problem. Failure may cause him to seek some face-saving explanation or behavior.

According to behaviorist theory, the individual will repeat and thus learn responses that are satisfying or tension reducing. Many experiments with both human and animal subjects show that an immediate reward is more psychologically effective than a long-delayed one. The prompt relief of anxiety that may follow an impulsive act of aggression or withdrawal can therefore outweigh the more remote dissatisfying social consequences. Anxiety reduction resulting from an adjustive but unconstructive act comes soon after the response and thus can reinforce it quite strongly (Shaffer and Shoben, 1956).

In most cases, the basic psychological impetus for an adjustment response is that it satisfies a need or drive. Until the need or drive has been satisfied, frustration is the prevailing psychological state. Unfortunately, we cannot readily identify the motives behind much of our behavior. In some cases, the individual will make an adequate, socially responsible adjustment without the apparent satisfaction of a need. School counselors agree with research studies that have found many instances of spontaneous change in students; for example, pupils who are discipline problems during the freshman and sophomore years sometimes improve in personal behavior for no apparent reason (Glavin, 1968; Clarizio, 1968).

Most human frustration and conflict can be solved in more than one way. If a student fails a course in high school, he may seek out his counselor for an objective analysis of his academic shortcomings, he may decide to take other courses in which he thinks he has a greater chance for success, he may seek prestige in extracurricular activities or in other fields, or he may claim that the instructor was biased against him and cite that as the reason for his failing grade. Some of these reactions are more integrative than others, but none of them can be classified as precisely good or bad. Much depends on the *pattern* of adjustment—whether the individual tends to use rationalization constantly, always blaming his plight on bad luck, inadequate time or materials, and the like.

In the competitive struggles of modern living, almost everyone is going to experience severe setbacks at one time or another or will be forced to deal with unavoidable barriers. At such times, one uses whatever means are at hand to protect his self-concept. In general, an individual's pattern of adjustment can be judged by whether it is primarily active and forward-moving (that is, whether he has the habit of facing his problems squarely and being reasonably rational and persistent in trying to solve them) or is characterized mostly by retreat or avoidance. In the context of the school, adjustment refers to the ways by which the child varies his activities or behavior in response to changing conditions. Adequate adjustment is manifested by behavior that helps to solve problems or achieve control or understanding over a situation and thereby reduce anxiety.

DEFENSE MECHANISMS

Sigmund Freud (1938) was largely responsible for formulating the concept of defense mechanisms—the ways in which the individual responds to stress or threats to self-esteem. According to Freud, these mechanisms are, in varying degrees, unconscious defenses against anxiety and are self-deceptive. The ego defense mechanisms were the first aspects of Freudian theory to be generally accepted into American psychology, although there was little acknowledgment of the source of these concepts.

Defense mechanisms are the systematic ways in which the individual handles disturbing events or information in order to maintain an acceptable self-concept. Because so many defense mechanisms depend upon denial and disguise, they can, over the long run, become more debilitating to the individual than the conflicts over motives that caused them in the first place. The individual personality is caught in a dilemma between anxiety and guilt, on the one hand, and crippling defense mechanisms, on the other. All people use these mechanisms to some degree, but usually the less the individual depends on defense mechanisms, the more likely he is to have a strong self-concept and an integrated personality.

When a child physically attacks another child who is threatening him, he may be making a conscious attempt to solve a problem. He is aware of what he is doing and why. He is acting directly and authentically, and no defense mechanism is involved in his behavior. But when such a child directs his aggression toward an innocent third party and justifies the attack as having been provoked by the innocent party, a defense mechanism is involved. Any attempt to shift the blame for one's own actions to someone else is a defensive measure.

Defense mechanisms involve the partial or complete rejection or distortion of thoughts, motives, or behaviors that are self-belittling, self-degrading, or otherwise unacceptable. Since defense mechanisms are largely unconscious, they are always to a corresponding degree self-deceptive. If the individual were not taken in by them, they would not serve to defend his self-esteem against the feeling of inadequacy. Self-deception is one means of protecting the self-esteem from damage. The poor-achieving, anxious student has a tendency to be self-deceptive in his vocational aspirations. A low-achieving girl, for example, stated in her autobiography: "I want to study to become a surgical nurse; but if I can't do that, I'd just like to be a housewife." She chooses an unrealistically high goal because it sounds important and ego inflating, and then, in order to protect her self-esteem, she chooses as an alternative a goal that she is unlikely to fail at.

SOME COMMON DEFENSE MECHANISMS

Projection means attributing one's own unacceptable and disturbing impulses or strivings to someone else. Under stress, we often tend to see in others precisely those characteristics that we abhor in ourselves. Scapegoating is a form of projection.

Identification is a method of reducing tension through the achievement of another person or group of people. Many desirable traits of personality are learned through identification with others, and in this sense it is one of the basic factors in character formation. Identification is often a desirable behavior, but if a person is fawningly imitative of others who have prestige or is too eager to join groups and support causes in order to "shine by reflected light," it becomes a tension-reduction device similar to compensation or attention-getting.

Displaced aggression refers to the tendency to pass blame or punishment on to someone else. When there is a warm and friendly atmosphere in the classroom and the children like the teacher, they also tend to like each other. But when the atmosphere is punitive, the children show much more aggression toward each other. The teacher is threatening to them, but they can't attack him directly because he is perceived as too powerful, so they tend to direct this aggression against each other. Another example, school vandalism, is often an expression of displaced aggression against teachers or school administrators. Interestingly, some school administrators have noted that children often tend to commit destructive acts in the specific area of the school building where they have experienced failure or punishment.

Reaction formation characterizes the behavior of people who really desire one thing but on the surface seem to want its opposite. A famous example is the minister in Somerset Maugham's *Rain*, who ranted about the wickedness of sex when, in fact, he was so fascinated by it that he eventually succumbed to the very evil he supposedly hated.

Regression is a common method of coping with frustration and anxiety by escaping into a way of living reminiscent of a more satisfying, safer time of life. Regressive devices include daydreaming, fingernail biting, smoking, baby talk, and overeating, among others. "Some of these regressions," according to Hall (1955, p. 96), "are so commonplace that they are taken to be signs of maturity."

Compensation is overemphasis on a type of behavior that originally was the source of frustration or conflict. Most commonly the individual overemphasizes the very activity in which he perceives himself to be inferior. Thus a physically frail boy may compensate for his feelings of inadequacy by becoming a bully and troublemaker, hoping to derive some satisfaction from being criticized for being a "tough guy."

Repression is the mechanism whereby an unwanted or guilt-provoking impulse or the thought of unhappy or shameful past events is actively and totally excluded from consciousness. The object is to forget these impulses or thoughts or to remember them in ways that are least threatening or self-incriminating.

Defensive withdrawal is a reaction to weakness or ineptitude that is the opposite of compensation. Defensive withdrawal is a purely mental mechanism, a retreat from what is desired but considered unattainable —a common behavior among children who have difficulty achieving tough standards in school.

Coping, or constructive adjustment, requires that we understand our limitations and not try to reach the unobtainable. Defensive withdrawal, by contrast, is a subtle form of self-deception by which we try to convince ourselves that we don't care much about the loss of something we very much wanted. By saying to myself "I don't care," I protect myself against the devaluating experience of failure, prospective or retrospective. "I *didn't* fail," I say in effect, "because I just didn't try. And I didn't try because it doesn't really matter to me." What makes defensive withdrawal maladjustive is that it prevents further efforts to attain the desired goal or even to assess the situation realistically.

IDENTIFICATION AND BEHAVIOR

There is general agreement that problems of adjustment increase during the adolescent years, in part because of the highly volatile emotions characteristic of this period. Adults may unknowingly bring on emotional disturbances in adolescents by imposing adult expectations on them too harshly or too soon, thus prolonging dependence, or by presenting a poor example. The adolescent is trying to understand what and who he is at the same time that his relationships with adults are the most ambiguous. He occupies a halfway house between childhood and adulthood, where he frantically tries to juggle old fantasy heroes with one hand while trying to hold onto rapidly emerging, reality-oriented identifications with the other.

The processes involved in identifying with and imitating a model are as influential in determining a child's behavior as are the reward and punishment of specific acts. Aggressive, dependent, and sexual behaviors assume different strengths in the child's behavioral pattern according to the extent to which they resemble behaviors of the models the child has chosen for identification (Kagan, 1958). When an act that is consistent with the model's overt behavior is rewarded, the child is likely to practice that action again. For example, a boy is likely to develop a strong achievement drive in school if his father rewards achievement and expresses strong positive attitudes toward the values of an education. The child's behavior is much less predictable, however, when there is inconsistency—for example, if the father rewards his son's aggressiveness toward others but rarely demonstrates aggressiveness himself.

From age three to age six, the child identifies primarily with his parents, for they are the adults he knows best and most respects and admires. But his parents' influence wanes as he grows older and becomes aware of other adults with qualities and skills that surpass those of his parents (Kagan, 1971). It is in the middle-school years and beyond that young people begin to identify with heroes and heroines of fact and fiction. Creatively inclined youth may identify with creative individuals in their favorite subject fields, athletic youth with professional stars, and so on. Some of these identifications are strong, some are weak, but each contributes to the adolescent's image of himself or herself. In a summary of research, Kagan (1971) states that children are most likely to identify with a model who evokes an initial perception of similarity. Psychiatric reports suggest, for example, that sons with unusually powerful and competent fathers often fail to identify with them, perhaps because there is so little apparent similarity that the son is discouraged from drawing such identification.

Erik Erikson's theory of personality development gives central importance to adolescence as a time of "searching for identity" (Erikson, 1963). Maturity begins when identity has been established and an integrated, independent individual has emerged who can stand on his own feet without using others as emotional crutches and without repudiating his past, "when he no longer has at every moment to question his own identity" (Erikson, 1959, p. 336). Researchers in the field of guidance and counseling agree that a primary characteristic of the adolescent is a growing curiosity about himself and his environment. This is evident in his efforts to discover where his special abilities, strengths, and weaknesses lie; in his attempts to reconcile the realities of life with the idealism that characterizes the formal instruction he gets; and in his strong reactions to his own successes and failures. The ganglia of his personality are supremely sensitive to anything in his environment that he can relate in some way to himself or utilize to find out more about himself.

For example, in helping students to choose reading assignments for book reports, merely to suggest that a given book is "interesting" is not likely to turn anyone on; the typical adolescent is too jaded for that. But say to a student, "I think you will enjoy reading *The Diary of Anne Frank*; you remind me a whole lot of the girl in that story," and her interest is going to jump. She will read it avidly in order to find out something about herself.

There are numerous opportunities in the course of a school day for the teacher to use his subject matter or the classroom situation as a way to help the student learn something about himself. The physical-education teacher can challenge the student to find out how well he can perform a given skill. The counselor can suggest that the student elect an art course in order to find out whether he has any talent in art. Later in the semester, in reviewing the student's progress, the emphasis should be primarily on how much he is finding out about his capabilities and not on how well he is doing by objective standards.

IDENTIFYING MENTAL-HEALTH PROBLEMS OF CHILDREN

Most teachers would probably agree that problems of mental health are manifested as behavior that interferes with the process of teaching and learning. Problem behavior may itself cause difficulties by interfering with the effective functioning of the individual or the classroom group or it may reveal the existence of difficulties, indicating that a child or a group is not functioning effectively. Such diverse symptoms as extreme shyness, defiance of teachers and other authority figures, inability to concentrate, habitual tardiness or truancy, and lack of self-control may all be considered varieties of problem behavior.

But these symptoms may be quite adequate coping mechanisms from the child's frame of reference. For example, extreme shyness is one way for a child to become invisible in a classroom situation where he meets mostly frustration and humiliation. The question that must be answered is whether the child really wants to become invisible and whether the shyness helps him in school work and in social situations.

Emotional disturbances, like other ailments in children, should be identified as early as possible. Unlike most other ailments, however, emotional problems manifest themselves over a period of time. The classroom teacher is best able to detect a developing pattern of non-adjustive behavior and to initiate steps to prevent the problem from becoming irremediable.

As a beginning, the teacher should be alert to identify children who show steady resistance toward the subject matter or the teacher. This may be expressed by consistent bewilderment in spite of clear explanations by the teacher, ready promises to cooperate followed by procrastination and "forgetting," dependency on the teacher and/or other students for answers to questions that the student himself could answer with a little thought or independent search, or outright hostility over a period of time (Lighthall, 1964, p. 20).

Bower (1960) suggests five characteristics of children who have potential mental-health problems:

1. An inability to learn that cannot be explained by intellectual, sensory, or health factors. This characteristic is the most significant one in spotting children with mental-health difficulties.
2. An inability to get along well with others.
3. An inability to act or feel appropriately under either normal or stress situations.
4. An inability to shake off the blues. Children who are unhappy most of the time usually reveal such feelings in their artwork, expressive play, or discussion periods.
5. A tendency to develop physical symptoms, pains, or fears associated with personal or school problems. These are sometimes referred to as psychosomatic disorders.

Morse (1969) offers some general guidelines in working with children who manifest undesirable behavior:

Study what the child actually does. Observation of how and to what the pupil responds often shows that much of what the teacher is doing is quite beside his intent. Many disturbed children are adept at controlling teachers by getting them to make inappropriate responses, thus reinforcing just what the teacher wants to eliminate. If the pupil cares more about having *some* kind of relationship with the teacher than he does about *what* kind of relationship he has, he can get teacher attention by misbehavior. Thus, a teacher encourages repeat performances of an undesirable behavior even as he tells a pupil not to behave that way. . . .

Many pupils do not operate on the basis of high-level gratifications, such as love of learning. Teachers must deal with them on their own motivational level. For example, the attention span and motivation of some who need concrete rewards suddenly improves when the teacher recognizes this need. Free time earned for work done or proper behavior may help to get children started who have never had any real success before. They forget their "can't do" attitude to earn free time. Behavior that approximates being acceptable is worth rewarding at first [p. 35].

THE WITHDRAWN CHILD

There has always been a strong tendency among teachers to assume that a child who is quiet, obedient, and passive in the classroom has satisfactory school adjustment. This is probably true if the child is also achieving measurable progress in school work and has at least a few friends. But the withdrawn child who is a loner and also a poor performer in school work is likely to have at least an incipient mental-health problem.

In a widely cited study, Wickman (1928) found that teachers tend to regard as most serious behavior that is outward and aggressive. Psychiatrists and clinical psychologists, however, tend to rate behavior that is inward, withdrawn, and self-incriminating as potentially the most serious.

Stouffer (1959) asked a cross-country sample of five hundred parents to rank the behaviors on Wickman's list and found that they tended to have attitudes similar to the attitudes of teachers in Wickman's study thirty years earlier. For purposes of comparison, the twenty symptoms ranked as most serious by parents, teachers, and psychological workers in Stouffer's study are shown in Table 7.1.

The withdrawn and socially isolated child is less visible than the active, disruptive individual. Yet a number of studies show that a tendency to withdraw from competition and social interaction is predictive of later psychological problems. Barthell and Holmes (1968), for example, found that many high-school graduates who were later diagnosed as schizophrenic and needing to be institutionalized participated in significantly fewer activities during their school years than other students.

Withdrawn behavior can lead to serious consequences for the individual concerned, but it is usually not directly damaging to others unless the withdrawn person also gives up on his responsibilities as a husband, father, and so on. Since the withdrawn child has no one directly dependent on his output, he might limp along for quite a while before anyone perceives his problem as serious.

THE AGGRESSIVE CHILD

By contrast with withdrawn behavior, aggressive, "acting out" behavior toward peers, teachers, or school administrators is quickly noticed. In fact, children with this broad range of symptoms are regarded by teachers as potentially the most pathological and are the group most frequently referred to special services and special classes (Tolor, Scarpetti, and Lane, 1967; Morse, 1969).

Aggression affects society as a whole and therefore has always been an important concern of mankind. One consequence of aggression in school is that it usually antagonizes the very people whose acceptance and recognition the aggressive child seeks. Directing aggression toward members of the peer group results in counteraggression, and conflict between children then begins to escalate. The end result is usually social isolation for the aggressive child.

Aggression also causes interruptions and disturbances in the classroom, which can be annoying to teachers and students alike. Most elementary-school teachers report several fights per day of varying degrees of seriousness. Some of these fights are expressions of normal exuberance and self-seeking behavior, but some are part of a persistent pattern of anxious or possibly disturbed behavior.

Psychologists have been deeply interested in the assessment of conditions leading to the instigation, learning, and performance of aggressive behavior. Studies have indicated the importance of three factors: (1) frustration, experienced as a result of adult punitiveness, restrictiveness, and rejection; (2) imitation of aggressive models in the environment; and (3) reinforcement through norms that endorse aggressive action (Cohen, 1971).

THE TEACHER'S DILEMMA

Most teachers have been inadequately prepared for the identification of mental-health problems among children. Sarason (1960) not only confirmed the finding that teachers were unable to identify the anxiety-prone children in their classrooms but discovered that they often used anxiety-arousing techniques in dealing with those children. Only in recent years have teachers become somewhat more knowledgeable about mental health, but not necessarily about the identification of problems.

It is apparent that there are limits to our power to predict a given child's psychological behavior in the future from classroom observation, his performance on psychological inventories, and personality ratings. As a person grows, he changes. Many factors affect his pattern of adjust-

TABLE 7.1

The Most Serious Behavior Problems of Children, Ranked According to Seriousness by Mental Hygienists, Teachers, and Parents.*

Mental Hygienists	Teachers	Parents
1. Unsocial, withdrawing	1. Unreliableness	1. Stealing
2. Unhappy, depressed	2. Stealing	2. Untruthfulness
3. Fearfulness	3. Unhappy, depressed	3. Heterosexual activity
4. Suspiciousness	4. Cruelty, bullying	4. Destroying school material
5. Cruelty, bullying	5. Untruthfulness	5. Cheating
6. Shyness	6. Unsocial, withdrawing	6. Cruelty, bullying
7. Enuresis	7. Truancy	7. Unreliableness
8. Resentfulness	8. Impertinence, defiance	8. Truancy
9. Stealing	9. Cheating	9. Disobedience
10. Sensitiveness	10. Easily discouraged	10. Impertinence, defiance
11. Dreaminess	11. Resentfulness	11. Obscene notes, talk
12. Nervousness	12. Destroying School materials	12. Impudence
13. Suggestible	13. Suggestible	13. Selfishness
14. Overcritical of others	14. Heterosexual activity	14. Unhappy, depressed
15. Easily discouraged	15. Domineering	15. Masturbation
16. Temper tantrums	16. Temper tantrums	16. Suggestible
17. Domineering	17. Selfishness	17. Domineering
18. Truancy	18. Nervousness	18. Easily discouraged
19. Physical coward	19. Disobedience	19. Profanity
20. Untruthfulness	20. Laziness	20. Lack of interest in work

* From Stouffer (1959). The twenty behaviors specified were taken from Wickman's original list of fifty.

ment. Life makes different demands on different people, and almost everyone is continually seeking new and better ways to cope with these demands. Many of the individual's earlier difficulties get resolved as he encounters new experiences and challenges. For young people, merely leaving the sheltered, dependent world of school and accepting responsibilities in a vocation can bring out positive personality characteristics that never appeared in earlier school and home experiences. Anderson (1970) found that some children who were rated low in adjustment early in life moved up the scale and achieved satisfactory adjustment when they were on their own and away from school and home.

The dilemma faced by the teacher is whether to intervene in a child's emotional world as soon as problems are suspected and set in motion the entire mental-health chain or wait until the child shows unmistakable symptoms. Too early intervention or too eager diagnosis can create a mental-health problem where only a temporary difficulty exists. In fact, psychiatrist Thomas Szasz (1970) asserts that many so-called mental aberrations are "manufactured" by society. On the other hand, the teacher's overcaution about getting involved can also be detrimental to the child, and it has the added danger of putting the teacher in jeopardy. If a child's adjustment problems go too long without identification, the first reaction of the parents is, "Why weren't we notified?"

The teacher should generally operate on the assumption that most children are normal, with the normal, usually temporary, problems of growing up; he should not spend his time searching for sick children. It is understood that a child may, at any time in his life, begin to show a pattern of behavior that could be regarded as symptomatic of a mental-health problem. Before the teacher intervenes, however, the various ways in which the child acts must add up to a clearly definable pattern of problem behavior. Also, there must be clear evidence that the child's emotional problems are the chief reason for his poor academic work. For example, many boys in the fifth, sixth, and seventh grades begin to act quite aggressive physically. They love to run and jump and jostle their classmates. The teacher must recognize this horseplay both in and out of the classroom as the normal vitality of healthy children, even though it can become a source of annoyance for the teacher—especially at the end of a long, hectic school day. Many young and progressive-minded teachers want to encourage informality in the class, but the presence of a handful of physically well-developed, boisterous boys can make this rather risky.

Occasionally, an individual child's vitality is such that it brings him into continual conflict with others. The serious stage is reached when he is subsequently rejected by his peers and he reacts by venting his hostility and defiance on teachers and other authority figures who are trying to channel his energies into constructive activity. This may be the time to consider the possibility that his behavior has crossed over to being a symptom of maladjustment.

If a child has a persistent pattern of nonintegrative behavior, the teacher should first consult with the school counselor, ask him to conduct an exploratory case study, and attempt to bring together all the teachers who are involved in the student's schedule to identify the causal factors in the behavior. In most cases, the sharing of perceptions and experiences will be very helpful, especially to the new and inexperienced teacher.

One of the insights the teacher may gain is that, although the child behaves or achieves poorly in one class, he does well in other classes. The case study will help the teacher to look more carefully at his own relationship with the student. He need not be afraid to have this problem formally aired before other teachers. Even experienced teachers occasionally have difficulties with a student who is successful in other classes.

THE SCHOOL AS A SOCIAL SYSTEM

The school is the most important setting in the child's social world. The typical child enters this world the moment he steps into the school bus. He enters a social system as complex as society itself. The way this system "works" affects the mental health of every child in it—and every teacher, as well.

The school is a community where children and teachers live and work in equilibrium with all the forces that have positive or negative effects on mental health. Teachers and administrators responsible for mental health can to some extent manipulate these forces so as to maintain the right balance between concern for the intellectual development of each child and concern for his emotional and social development. We know from experience in the classroom that the affective (feeling) aspect of the child is interwoven with his cognitive (intellectual) nature. Biber (1961) puts it this way:

> It is no longer feasible to dichotomize the learning functions (mastery of symbol system, process of reasoning, judging and problem solving, acquisition and ordering of information, etc.) on one hand, and the processes of personality formation (self-feeling and identity relatedness potential, autonomy, integration, creativity, etc.) on the other. It is no longer an open question as to whether or not the school has an impact on developing personality; nor is there any logic in engaging in controversy as to whether or not the school is over-extending its function when it concerns itself in personality issues [pp. 323–24].

This is self-evident. Yet school systems need periodic rededication to this ideal, for a kind of Gresham's Law operates by which the cognitive, subject-matter goals, when left uncontrolled in the academic marketplace, drive out the affective ones. For example, in their understandable zeal for quality and prestige (and community approval), music and theater directors and athletic coaches sometimes overemphasize the production of a handful of stars at the expense of providing educational experiences for as many students as possible.

THE TEACHER'S ROLE IN MENTAL HEALTH

It must once again be emphasized that it is not the teacher's responsibility to identify problem behavior in the classroom in order to "treat" children in some way. Teachers are not trained as therapists and should not try to play the therapist role. An understanding of basic principles of mental health should help the teacher to identify the 2 or 3 per cent of the children who are too disturbed to profit from normal classroom instruction and who should be referred for treatment by a psychiatrist, psychiatric social worker, clinical psychologist, or, in some cases, school counselors; and to create a more livable, supportive atmosphere in the classroom. The classroom atmosphere should function not simply as medication to "cure" maladjusted children but as a vitamin shot for the stimulation of maximal learning and healthy social interaction. The teacher and the entire system—principal, guidance staff, custodians, teacher aides, clerks, lunchroom personnel, bus drivers—all can facilitate learning by rearranging the environment in positive ways and thus promoting intellectual and emotional development.

As Torrance (1965) stated:

A society's concept of the meaning of mental health and personality adjustment determines in a large measure its child-rearing procedures, its educational practices and most of its institutions. A classroom teacher's concept of the meaning of mental health strongly influences his relationship with his students, his disciplinary procedures, his evaluation procedures, and the content of his curriculum. Similarly, the activities of school administrators, counselors, psychologists, social workers, ministers, physicians, psychiatrists, nurses, and others are determined in a large measure by their concepts of mental health.

By the very nature of his intervention in the early life experiences of the child, the teacher is in a highly strategic position to provide services that contribute directly to mental health. In order to further this aim, it might be helpful to bear in mind the following propositions:

1. The school must educate the child regardless of the nature of his home life. In fact, success in school can do much to help a child to cope more effectively with the guilt and anxiety that are so often the by-products of families beset by personal problems or problems resulting from poverty or minority-group status.

2. Learning school subjects and general mental health are interwoven. The school must accept responsibility if large numbers of children are not learning and are not responding constructively to stress and change.

3. An important goal of education is to prepare individuals to live in a world of accelerating change. "Since we can't know what knowledge will be most needed in the future, it is senseless to try to teach it in advance. Instead, we should try to turn out people who love learning so much and learn so well that they will be able to learn whatever needs to be learned" (Holt, 1964).

SELF-DIRECTION AS MENTAL HEALTH

Socialization in young children begins with reliance on other people, and this reliance becomes a means for later social learning. Therefore, it would not seem useful to teach a preschool child to inhibit his need for dependence in order to foster self-reliance. No child is totally dependent or totally independent. Instead, a child vacillates between self-reliant striving for mastery, on the one hand, and dependency, on the other. The young child learns to accept the help of others at the same time that he learns how to help himself. Cross-cultural studies suggest that severe repression of independence in early childhood is associated with anxiety about social relationships and personal insecurity in adult life (Whiting and Child, 1953).

More important, however, is the fact that early, direct training and encouragement of self-reliance and assertiveness seem to increase such behaviors on the part of the child. Studies of preschool children indicate that independence is increased both by reinforcing independent effort and by providing the child with experiences that increase his proficiency in the task at hand. For example, Fales (1955) trained nursery-school children to take off their coats, but he praised only some of them for their efforts. The group that was both trained and reinforced refused assistance far more frequently than did the untrained and unreinforced group.

As independent, self-reliant behavior begins to emerge and to become a stable part of the child's personality, inappropriate forms of dependency can be discouraged. But the weakening of dependency should be induced by the withdrawal of reinforcement rather than by the application of criticism or punishment. Studies in behavior modification conducted at the Laboratory of Developmental Psychology at the University of Washington suggest that careful withdrawal of reinforcement for inappropriate behavior is a necessary component of training for more desirable activity (Harris, Wolf, and Baer, 1964).

THE HAPPY CLASSROOM

In the opening lines of *Anna Karenina*, Tolstoy says, "Happy families are all alike; every unhappy family is unhappy in its own way." This applies to classrooms as well. The most common characteristic of happy classrooms is a "can do" atmosphere. Each child feels that he is accomplishing something worthwhile. The teacher makes it possible for every child to meet most of his school requirements and also to exercise individual control and judgment.

Few people enjoy living under rigid rules and restrictions—children included. Yet, beyond the days of infancy, rules and restrictions become an inevitable part of life. Some are obviously necessary in school. Children are not damaged by knowing what adults expect them to do, and what peers expect of them as well. To the contrary: it is as unpleasant to be ignored by adults as to have them nag you all the time. A teacher who lets children do everything they want to do will make them every bit as unhappy as one who rules them with an iron hand.

But the normally developing child naturally wants a maximum of self-determination. Like adults—and sovereign nations—he wants to do what he thinks will serve his own needs and interests, and he does not want to be thwarted. Yet, whether he realizes it or not, any control he has over his own destiny during his growing years is largely a state of mind. Most of his activities both in and out of school are supervised and monitored by adults.

The dilemma arises in that broad area where effective group functioning requires easing the restrictions on individual children. Here, the teacher must make decision after decision about whether it is better to allow one child greater freedom of action or to restrict particular bits of conduct in order to achieve more efficiency in group learning.

Good classroom management requires some basic rules that children understand and accept, but also as many opportunities as possible for them to do things by themselves under minimal restrictions. When the teacher finds himself saying no most of the time and yes only rarely, this is a first step toward a punitive classroom atmosphere. The teacher should not spend a great deal of time discussing rules, regulations, and restrictions, for this has a depressing effect on many children. In the absence of really good reasons for imposing restrictions, it is preferable to allow children to work on activities and problems that are important to them and that they can perform on their own terms. Rules of conduct can then be discussed on an individual basis as occasions arise.

Children rarely remember the rules anyway, and the existence of too many rules encourages them to look for the loopholes and then initiate debate with the teacher over whether the rules apply. Even if the teacher wins the argument, debate of this kind is counterproductive.

The teacher might find it profitable to take time out occasionally for freewheeling discussion with the class about matters of personal interest to them and to allow children to ventilate their feelings in class, being careful to avoid the temptation to make a negative response to unpleasant statements or occurrences unless the situation is unusually serious. Throughout a school day, children will say and do a lot of things that can be easily interpreted as deliberately rude or challenging to the teacher's authority. How the teacher responds to these events will determine the atmosphere of his room. When a child stumbles over a chair during a quiet study session, the beginning teacher especially tends to react with consternation and begins to bark commands instead of finding some way to handle the situation more lightly. The effective teacher tries to bend with the antics of children. Then, when something really serious happens that is unmistakably deliberate and that must be corrected, the teacher's decisiveness will be clear to the students.

In his highly controversial study of inequality, Christopher Jencks (1972) contends that the acquisition of cognitive skills does not seem to have as much effect on adult income and socio-economic status as is commonly believed. In addition, he points out that there is very little "hard" evidence that curricular and other changes in elementary and secondary schools, increased financial support, or desegregation efforts have resulted in measurable socio-economic gains in adult life. He does not oppose equalizing educational quality and opportunity in the schools; he simply insists that we must change our reasons for wanting such changes. He believes that the schools should exist as an end in themselves—like the institution of the family—rather than as a means to some other end. "The primary basis for evaluating a school," Jencks asserts, should be "whether the students and teachers find it a satisfying place to be."

TRANSCENDENTAL MEDITATION: THE SCIENCE OF CREATIVE INTELLIGENCE

At the beginning of this chapter, we defined mental health as growth in the ability to perform effectively in and out of school, in work, in play, and in interpersonal relations, as evidenced by objective measures of achievement and increased feelings of self-worth and well-being as an outcome of learning. But "effective" performance may not reflect an individual's full development of his "creative" potential. Should the student learn simply to "cope" and "adjust," or should the school attempt to bring out all his resources for creative intelligence—with or without subject-matter mastery? Can and should the school help each child to achieve a sense of fulfillment apart from getting good grades? Educators have always taken it for granted that children will reach self-actualization as they master subject matter or succeed in social interaction. It is one of the realities of school life that, sooner or later, every child has to achieve something in competition with others in order to gain full acceptance and recognition.

True fulfillment means the full expression of one's creative intelligence. Some believe that this state—nebulous though it may seem—can be achieved through the technique of transcendental meditation (TM) —going to the wellsprings of our creative natures in much the same way as a gardener treats the deficiencies in the development of the many separate leaves of a plant by simply watering the root. The technique of transcendental meditation is a procedure of "turning the attention inward toward the subtler levels of a thought until the mind transcends the experience of the subtlest state of the thought and arrives at the source of the thought. This expands the conscious mind and at the same time brings it in contact with the creative intelligence that gives rise to every thought" (Yogi, 1969, p. 470).

The technique of meditation can be learned easily in about six hours of instruction (spread out over four consecutive days) from a Maharishi-trained teacher. Once learned, it is practiced individually every morning and evening for fifteen to twenty minutes at a sitting. It requires no changes in one's life-style or daily routine and is not related to any specific religious or philosophical dogma. It can be done by individuals as young as five years old.

Objective research studies show that participants experience marked reductions in tension and moodiness. Other reported outcomes are increased creativity, perceptiveness, self-confidence, productivity, reading speed, psychomotor facility, and learning ability. But perhaps the most startling outcome is evidence that TM results in significant reduction in the use of tranquilizers, stimulants, and other drugs, both prescribed and nonsubscriptive (Levine, 1972).

Driscoll (1972, p. 237) reported that the introduction of TM in a New York State secondary-school system provided aid to students: "Scholastic grades improve, relationships with family, teachers, and peers are better, and, very significantly, drug abuse disappears or does not begin."

The positive evidence for transcendental meditation has been so strong that many colleges and universities have formed classes to promote it on a systematic basis. In 1972, the National Institute of Mental Health awarded an initial grant of $21,540 to train secondary-school teachers to teach meditation techniques in U.S. high schools.

Transcendental meditation, sometimes referred to as the Science of Creative Intelligence, reflects the search for alternative or additional solutions to current mental-health problems. Many educators believe that, if the objective of the school is not simply the inculcation of subject matter but the fulfillment of each child's potential, then all promising avenues to that goal should be carefully studied and tested. At this writing, TM promises to be an important approach in efforts to help young people learn and grow in the classroom.

REFERENCES

ANDERSON, G. J. 1970. Effects of classroom social climate on individual learning. *American Education Resource Journal, 7,* 135–52.

Association for Supervision and Curriculum Development. 1966. *Learning and mental health in the classroom.* Washington, D.C.: National Education Association.

BARTHELL, C. N., and D. S. HOLMES. 1968. High school yearbooks: A non-reactive measure of social isolation in graduates who later became schizophrenic. *Journal of Abnormal Psychology, 73,* 313–16.

BIBER, B. 1961. Integration of mental health principles in the school setting. In G. Caplan (ed.), *Prevention of mental health disorders in children.* New York: Basic Books.

BLOOM, B. S. 1972. Innocence in education. *School Review, 80,* 333–53.

BOWER, E. M. 1960. *Early identification of emotionally handicapped children in school.* Springfield, Ill.: Thomas.

BRIDGES, K. M. 1932. Emotional development in early infancy. *Child Development, 3,* 324–41.

CLARIZIO, H. 1968. Stability of deviant behavior through time. *Mental Hygiene, 52,* 288–93.

COHEN, S. 1971. The development of aggression. *Review of Educational Research, 41,* 71–85.

COLEMAN, J. C. 1960. *Personality dynamics and effective behavior.* Chicago: Scott, Foresman.

DRISCOLL, F. G. 1972. TM as a secondary school subject. *Phi Delta Kappan, 54*(4), 236–38.

ERIKSON, E. 1959. Identity and the life cycle: Selected papers. *Psycho-*

logical issues monograph series, I, No. 15. New York: International Universities Press.

————. 1963. *Childhood and society*. New York: W. W. Norton.

FALES, E. 1955. Genesis of aspiration in children from one and one-half to three years of age. Reported in K. Lewin *et al.*, Level of aspiration. In J. McV. Hunt (ed.), *Personality and the behavior disorders*. New York: Ronald Press.

FREUD, S. 1926. *The problem of anxiety*. New York: W. W. Norton.

————. 1938. *The basic writings of Sigmund Freud*. New York: Modern Library.

GLAVIN, J. P. 1968. "Spontaneous" improvement in emotional disturbed children. Doctoral dissertation, George Peabody College for Teachers. *Dissertation Abstracts*, 28, 3503A.

HALL, C. S. 1955. *A primer of Freudian psychology*. New York: New American Library.

HARRIS, F. R., M. M. WOLF, and D. M. BAER. 1964. Effects of adult reinforcement on child behavior. *Young Children*, 20, 8–17.

HEWETT, F. M., and P. R. BLAKE. 1973. Teaching the emotionally disturbed. In R. M. W. Travers (ed.), *Second handbook of research on teaching*. Chicago: Rand McNally.

HOLT, J. 1964. *How children fail*. New York: Pitman.

JENCKS, C., *et al.* 1972. *Inequality: A reassessment of the effect of family and schooling in America*. New York: Basic Books.

JERSILD, A. 1960. *Child psychology*. Englewood Cliffs, N.J.: Prentice-Hall.

KAGAN, J. 1958. The concept of identification. *Psychological Review*, 65, 296–305.

————. 1971. *Personality development*. New York: Harcourt Brace & Jovanovich.

KELLY, G. A. 1955. *The psychology of personal constructs*. New York: W. W. Norton.

LEVINE, P. H. 1972. Transcendental meditation and the Science of Creative Intelligence. *Phi Delta Kappan*, 54(4), 231–36.

LICHTER, S. O., *et al.* 1962. *The dropouts*. Glencoe, Ill.: Free Press.

LIGHTHALL, F. F. 1964. *Anxiety as related to thinking and forgetting*. Washington, D. C.: National Education Association.

MILLER, N. E. 1948. Studies of fear as an acquirable drive: I. Fear as motivation and fear-reduction as reinforcement in the learning of new responses. *Journal of Experimental Psychology*, 38, 89–101.

MORSE, W. C. 1969. Disturbed youngsters in the classroom. *Today's Education*, 58(4), 30–37.

National Institute of Mental Health. 1971. *Report to the Director*. Washington, D.C.: U.S. Government Printing Office, Public Health Service Publication #2184.

REESE, F. D. 1968. School-age suicide and the educational environment. *Theory Into Practice*, 7, 10–13.

RUTTER, M. 1964. Intelligence and childhood psychiatric disorders. *British Journal of Social and Clinical Psychology*, 3, 120–29.

SARASON, S. B. 1960. *Anxiety in elementary school children*. New York: Wiley.

SHAFFER, L. F., and E. J. SHOBEN. 1956. *The psychology of adjustment*. Boston: Houghton Mifflin.

STEDMAN, J. M., and R. L. ADAMS. 1972. Achievement as a function of language competence, behavior adjustment, and sex in young, disadvantaged Mexican American children. *Journal of Educational Research*, 63, 411–17.

STOUFFER, G. A. 1959. The attitudes of parents toward certain behavior problems of children. *Research for the teaching profession*. Indiana, Penn.: State Teachers College.

SZASZ, T. S. 1970. *The manufacture of madness*. New York: Harper & Row.

TANNER, L. N., and H. C. LINDGREN. 1971. *Classroom teaching and learning*. New York: Holt, Rinehart & Winston.

TOLOR, A., W. L. SCARPETTI, and P. A. LANE. 1967. Teachers' attitudes toward children's behavior revisited. *Journal of Educational Psychology*, 58(8), 175–80.

TORRANCE, E. P. 1965. *Mental health and constructive behavior*. Belmont, Calif.: Wadsworth.

WHITING, J. W. M., and I. CHILD. 1953. *Child training and personality*. New Haven: Yale University Press.

WICKMAN, E. K. 1928. *Children's behavior and teachers' attitudes*. New York: Commonwealth Fund.

YOGI, M. M. 1969. *Maharishi Mahesh Yogi on the Bhagavad-Gita: A new translation and commentary*. Baltimore: Penguin Books.

PART 3

Factors in Classroom Learning

CHAPTER EIGHT

The Motivational Gyroscope

YOU ARE A NEW TEACHER entering your own classroom for the first time. As most experienced teachers will attest, this first encounter is an awesome event. The children are ready and eager—more or less. It is this "more or less" that is the rub of teaching.

Imagine that each youngster has a wheel within him that spins at the velocity of his individual drive toward work and achievement—a motivational gyroscope. As you stand before the class, you must recognize and deal with the fact that each child's gyroscope turns at a unique rate of speed and that there are as many speeds in the room as there are individuals. Some gyroscopes spin very rapidly and evenly and have been spinning this way for a long time, probably since early childhood. For the fortunate few, achievement is already an established pattern of behavior. They have a highly developed, self-directing, and self-rewarding motivational mechanism that propels them toward any goal to which they address themselves.

But there are other children—usually the largest proportion of the class—whose gyroscopes seem to spin at variable rates of speed, depending largely on what they are doing and for what purpose. These children tend to be highly reactive to many influences—teachers, friends, and classroom activities.

Another, much smaller group of children has a gyroscopic pace that spins very slowly in the classroom and sometimes doesn't seem to spin at all. Some of these youngsters (in the lower grades they tend to be boys) have limited ability, but quite a few have average or above-average capabilities. Young Johnny, for example, a typical "slow learner" problem, has great potential for speed and endurance. In fact, *before* the school bell rings, his gyroscope is likely to be humming at a terrific pace—he runs and jumps, badgers the girls, and jabbers to his friends. But as soon as he walks into the classroom, the wheel begins to grind down . . . slower . . . slower . . . until it comes to a creaking halt. School "turns him off." Only the strongest of stimuli—reprimands, threats, highly interesting or novel activities— are likely to rev up his gyroscope. "Johnny, sit up straight!" A rapid spin for about five minutes, and then . . . slower . . . slower . . . stop! "Johnny, if you don't finish those arithmetic problems you will have to do them for homework tonight!" A rapid, anxious spin . . . then slower and slower . . . to a bumpy, uneven pace as Johnny ponders unhappily the prospect of having to do homework during what might otherwise be a fun-packed evening.

THREE CONCEPTIONS OF MOTIVATION

What accounts for these differences in motivation? Are they inherent in the genetic nature of the children and largely fixed? Or do gyroscopes spin mainly because of environmental influences? Three major explanations for basic human motivation have been advanced. They are vitalism; behaviorism, or stimulus-response psychology; and perceptual, or field psychology.

VITALISM

To a vitalist, the center of man is mind. According to this conception, mind is a substance or entity that is totally unlike the obvious, material objects of experience. The mind possesses certain powers, such as willing, reflecting, imagining, and remembering. Although mind has no physical dimensions or substance, it is entirely real because it is the essential nature or reality of man. The essential nature of man is unchanging, and it is presumed to be the same for all men.

Plato is usually regarded as the first person to conceive of the mind as the only true reality. All material things, according to Plato, are but pale reflections of the true object that exists in a perfect state in the mind, or spirit. If the true essence of the person is his mind, then we must look to the individual "state of mind," or level of mental energy, or vitality, as the source of motivation. The drive to achieve, the will to survive and triumph, is largely a matter of individual initiative and will power. Motivation results from "mind over matter"; the child must exploit his own sources of drive. He can spin his gyroscope at almost any speed he chooses.

This hypothesis or explanation is attractive to some because it appears to provide an answer to the creeping mechanization and depersonalization of our society by putting primary emphasis on the dynamic, all-pervasive nature of the mind. If the mind is the center of man and is solely responsible for the activation of will power, then the individual cannot be "programmed" or manipulated in any way by technological, dehumanizing forces in society—unless he allows them to do so. He is his own master.

The simplicity of the theory of vitalism makes it difficult to inquire into its nature objectively; its proponents must embrace it on the basis of faith alone, with an assist from the writings of Plato, Descartes, Bergson, and others. Ascribing mystic qualities to vitalism reduces the necessity to provide scientific validation.

The value of vitalism is that it puts primary responsibility on the individual for the consequences of his acts and choices. This, of course, is highly desirable—as far as it goes. When applied in practice to the education of the child, however, this perspective seems to justify schools and teachers in rejecting responsibility for a child's lack of academic motivation and achievement. In fact, vitalism carried to an extreme could result in the contention that it does not matter very much what kinds of teachers, books, learning activities, school facilities, or background experiences are involved. After all, if the child wills it, he can learn and succeed no matter what the obstacles!

Although vitalism is among the oldest theories of motivation, it is much less favored today than in the past.

BEHAVIORISM

Behaviorism, or stimulus-response psychology, attempts to explain the whole of life in terms of the operation of scientific laws of movement and change. This is largely a materialistic approach, one that views man as a highly complex but basically machinelike creature who operates in ways as potentially predictable as the physical forces around us. The mind, in this view, is regarded only as a part of the entire mechanism, subject also to basic physical laws.

A dramatic new invention, the telephone, supplied early behaviorists with a mechanical model for the brain's role in relation to motivation. Man was considered to be much like a highly complex telephone switchboard, with his life processes largely a matter of electrical energy flowing through neurons. Early behaviorist psychologists favored a reflex-arc theory of human behavior. A reflex arc is defined as a circuit consisting of a sense organ, such as the ear, a nerve leading from the sense organ to a central "switchboard" (the spinal cord or brain), and a nerve leading outward from the switching area to a muscle or gland. When the sense organ receives a stimulus, the "message" travels along the circuit and ultimately produces a muscular or glandular response. These reflexes were thought to be either inborn or learned. Learning consisted of "stamping in" new connections between specific afferent (incoming) and efferent (outgoing) nerves. The source of human motivation was contained in this process.

Although the mechanical nature of this process was consistent with what was then known about physiology and anatomy, this conception has since fallen into disrepute.

In recent decades, behaviorism has experienced a fresh infusion of ideas as a result of developments in *cybernetics*, the study of electronic-computer processes. According to current theory, the computer is a small, simplified version of the mammalian brain. The operation of advanced computers is considered to be similar to the basic structure of operations that take place in the human brain. But this explanation, although an improvement over the switchboard idea, also leaves largely unanswered the question of what motivates the creative production of the mind.

PERCEPTUALISM, OR FIELD PSYCHOLOGY

Perceptualism, or field psychology, as we have seen, entails a broader view of human endeavor. According to this theory, all behavior involves the total context in which the organism functions. Thus, the emphasis is on wholes and systems rather than on collections of response tendencies. In physical terms, this approach means that each living cell exists within a system of cells that is part of a larger system of organs, which, in turn, is part of an integrated body organization. But the individual also functions within a social system, which is part of larger social and political organizations, and so on. The behavior of each individual affects and is affected by the circumstances and elements of the "field" in which he acts. Basic motivation arises from the effects of the interaction of all the elements and forces in the field.

All organisms tend to maintain the physiological and psychological conditions essential to their well-being. Basically, this involves such necessities as body temperature and supplies of oxygen, water, and food. Cannon (1939) gave the name *homeostasis* to this tendency of organisms to maintain an equilibrium of the "inner environment" in which their tissues live. Like the automatic pilot on an airplane, each of us has a homeostatic system that is alert to changes in what we eat, feel, experience, think about. If any change threatens our physical or mental state, the homeostatic mechanism sends signals through the central nervous system to the appropriate receptors so that the body can adjust to this change.

This concept may be applied to psychological functioning as well. When an individual interacts in reasonable harmony with others around him, he tends to have good mental health. When he is in conflict, or "disequilibrium," with himself or others, he is naturally motivated to restore harmony or defend himself against disintegration.

DRIVES

The simplest explanation for the specific ways in which motivation seems to manifest itself uses the concept of *drives*. This important concept in behaviorist psychology is helpful in understanding the basic life-seeking processes of the body. It is based on the assumption that what lies at the core of our motivational structure is the essential and natural desire to live and grow. For the first several decades of life, most of our vitality is expended in growth and development toward mature status. Thereafter, activity appears to be largely directed toward maintenance of the best level of physical and mental well-being. According to the concept of drives, the beginnings of motivation are readily apparent in the simple drives of the child—for food, water, warmth, affection. Within a few years, these fundamental drives begin to differentiate and diffuse into related needs and wants, which, in turn, splinter into highly complex motivational patterns.

Most early theorizing about drives concentrated on physiological processes, largely because most of the relevant research had been done with lower animals. Little was then known about the most complex psychological drives, because it is difficult to assess psychological behavior in lower animals, such as the laboratory rat. Perhaps one can guess how a rat feels when it runs down a maze and receives an electric shock, but there is usually little measurable evidence other than the animal's manifestations of discomfort. In recent years, more sophisticated research designs have begun to produce insights into the psychologically based drives of both animals and children. Unfortunately, psychologists still disagree over what constitutes a true drive.

White (1959) lists three characteristics of drive: (1) there is a tissue need or deficit external to the nervous system that acts upon that system as a strong, persistent stimulus; (2) this promotes activity, which is terminated by a consumatory response with consequent reduction of need; and (3) the reduction of need brings about the learning that gradually shapes behavior into an economic pursuit of suitable goal objectives. White argues that many so-called drives, such as exploration, activity, curiosity, and variety, fail to meet these criteria.

It is useful to describe drives as primary or secondary. Primary drives are the physiological needs—for food, rest, oxygen, and so on. They are the drives upon which our lives depend. A primary drive may be defined as any tissue need the lack of which leads to death. However, one primary drive—sex—appears to occupy a rather ambiguous position. In the strict sense of the definition, the sex drive is not a primary one, since no one ever died from lack of sexual activity. Many may have suffered from the effects of worrying about having too little or too much sexual activity, but the actual act of sexual union is not necessary to sustain individual life. In fact, many individuals have achieved outstanding goals without it, such as religious ascetics and others who put personal and spiritual goals above sex needs. Sexual deprivation may not even have deleterious psychological effects, as psychologist Abraham Maslow (1954, p. 157) stated:

> It is now well known that many cases are found in which celibacy has no psychopathological effects. In many other cases, however, it has many bad effects. What factor determines which shall be the result? Clinical work with nonneurotic people gives the clear answer that sexual deprivation becomes pathogenic in a severe sense only when it is felt by the individual to represent rejection by the opposite sex, inferiority, lack of worth, lack of respect, isolation, or other thwarting of basic needs. Sexual deprivation can be borne with relative ease by individuals for whom it has no such implication.

Secondary drives are the by-products, so to speak, of the primary drives. The basic need for food, for example, may become closely associated with the desire for money, a means of obtaining food. In a sense, money becomes food, for the acquisition of one means the attainment of the other. Although primary drives are obviously the prepotent ones, secondary drives appear to occupy most of the time and attention of people in affluent societies. A common example is the desire to acquire wealth. What at first is probably desire for an adequate standard of living gradually evolves into a number of secondary drives for more and more material things—far beyond what is required to sustain life.

Even animals develop this trait. Chimpanzees who have been taught to exchange poker chips for food gradually become possessive toward poker chips—even when their hunger is satisfied. They hoard their surplus chips and appear to cast covetous glances at their neighbor's. This is a common phenomenon, of course, with people.

NEEDS

Whereas *drive* is associated with genetically based determinants of behavior, *need* refers to the goals toward which behavior is directed. Needs are not crucial for survival to the same extent as drives are, but psychologists generally agree that all behavior is related to a need in one way or another.

The determinants of human behavior—whether they are called needs, drives, motives, or purposes—serve three important functions. They activate and sensitize the organism toward certain stimuli; they direct its behavior toward certain goals; and they reinforce behavior that is effective in the attainment of the desired goals.

When needs are defined in broad terms, each psychologist's list of needs overlaps with almost every other. When needs are more narrowly defined, however, there tend to be varying emphases. For example, Murray (1938) identifies twenty-eight social (psychogenic) needs. One of the simplest but also most relevant and durable theories of needs was advanced by Thomas in *The Unadjusted Girl*, first published in 1923. According to Thomas, human social needs—"wishes," he called them—can be classified as the desires for (1) new experience, (2) security, (3) response, and (4) recognition (1967, p. 4).

MASLOW'S HIERARCHY OF NEEDS

Probably the best-known conceptual system of needs was developed by Abraham H. Maslow (1943). Although it is a theory, it has the interesting value of being consistent with common sense. Maslow's theory of need gratification is based on a number of assumptions about human nature:

1. People act and think in a wholly integrated way.
2. All human behavior has a cause, and all behavior is purposive.
3. Physiological survival needs are not the principal basis for motivation.
4. Human needs arrange themselves in hierarchical order; that is, success at one level of need usually requires prior satisfaction of another, more prepotent need.

5. Human motivation is affected by biological, cultural, and situational forces, all interacting together.

Figure 8.1 shows Maslow's conception of the hierarchy of needs, starting with the basic physiological needs. He suggests that, under normal conditions, the individual is not "ready" to take on a higher level of need attainment until he has had reasonable success with the one before it. For example, unless a child has had success in meeting his physiological needs, he will not be optimally ready for the next level in the hierarchy—physical safety and security. This means that the chronically undernourished, tired child is likely to be personally fearful as well. As adults, we are not critically aware of this condition, since we learn to inhibit as much as possible needs for personal safety and security. In children, however, this need is not inhibited. "Infants will react in a total fashion and as if they were endangered if they are disturbed or dropped suddenly, startled by loud noises, flashing lights, or other unusual sensory stimulation, by rough handling, by general loss of support in the mother's arms, or by inadequate support" (Maslow,

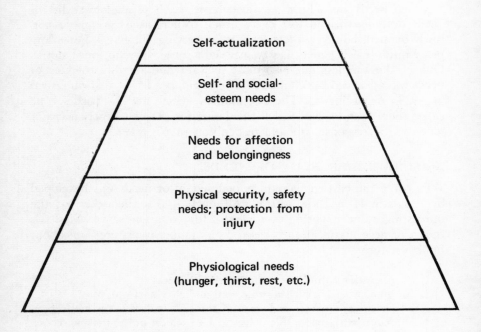

Fig. 8.1. Maslow's hierarchy of needs.

1943, p. 376). Similarly, at the next level, the child who has not developed a sense of personal safety and security is not psychologically ready for close emotional ties with teachers and other children.

One of the ways in which children differ from one another is in their respective "levels" of need. Some first-graders come from emotionally secure homes; they are "ready" to accept the challenge of learning new skills. But, if his home life is characterized by considerable turmoil and conflict, the child may expend much of his vitality in coping with home problems, leaving little to be focused on school tasks. According to Maslow:

> It is such considerations as these that suggest the bold postulation that a man who is thwarted in any of his basic needs may fairly be envisaged simply as a sick man. This is a fair parallel to our designation as "sick" the man who lacks vitamins or minerals. Who is to say that a lack of love is less important than a lack of vitamins? Since we know the pathogenic effects of love starvation, who is to say that we are involving value-questions in an unscientific or illegitimate way, any more than the physician who diagnoses and treats pellagra or scurvy? If I were permitted this usage, I should then say simply that a healthy man is primarily motivated by his needs to develop and actualize his fullest potentialities and capacities. If a man has any other basic needs in any active, chronic sense, then he is simply an unhealthy man. He is as surely sick as if he had suddenly developed a strong salt hunger or calcium hunger [1943, 394].

Maslow's theory of need hierarchy provides a way of looking at personality development. It says, in effect, that we grow from stage to stage, and that growth is dependent on successful experiences at earlier stages. It means, also, that those who have not mastered a particular level but nevertheless have succeeded in moving to the next one have somehow learned to accept their limitations. The requirement is not that all levels must be mastered, but that upward growth be maintained. According to Maslow, the process of growth toward the final level of "self-actualization" is in itself a form of actualization, or realization of potential.

Maslow's theory offers some clues to the determinants of behavior in the elementary- through middle-school years. The child in this general age span should be less concerned with meeting his needs for food, rest, and so on; he should be reasonably free of fear of getting hurt or sick; and he should be at a level where needs for "affection and belongingness" are becoming important in the school setting. Middle-school teachers tend to concentrate on cognitive outcomes in class and to minimize affective outcomes. The middle years are a critical stage between the concrete, sensory experiences of early years and the heavily abstract learning of the senior high school. Children in middle school need teachers who are warm, supportive, and even a bit "corny"—in short, highly interactive with children, yet sufficiently subject-matter oriented so that academic achievement is maintained. It is in the middle-school years that many children begin to "drop out" of the educational stream psychologically, because they still have strong needs for the security generally provided in self-contained elementary classrooms. Meeting their needs for affection and belongingness can help them to build the self-esteem and social esteem so necessary in large, competitive high schools.

THE NEED TO ACHIEVE

An interesting approach to motivation is D. C. McClelland's (1961) theory of motive acquisition, which he refers to simply as the "need to achieve." In effect, the theory says that, when an individual is with a group of people who place a high value on getting ahead, he will feel strong pressure to "conform" in order to be like the others, and hence he will begin to put a higher value on achievement and hard work. This is a restatement of the common-sense principle that we tend to take on the values of the groups in which we have membership. McClelland's system functions like "Achievers Anonymous": When someone in the group falls off the achievement wagon into a state of sloth, his fellow members exert friendly pressure on him to keep up the drive for hard work.

McClelland contends that the values associated with the "Protestant ethic" produce the conditions in childhood that lead to an urge to achieve, and that this achievement motive is passed on as a cultural heritage from generation to generation. Of course, achievement motives exist in all social groups and probably in all societies, but they appear to be more characteristic of some subcultures than of others. This raises the question whether the achievement motive is a new motive or simply another manifestation of primary drives influenced by cultural conditioning. Although its basic nature is still in doubt, McClelland's research provides evidence that the achievement motive is learnable and quite susceptible to peer influence.

McClelland and his associates based their research entirely on men, as have most other investigators of the achievement drive. Matina Horner (1969) undertook to explore the basis for sex differences in achievement. She started with one consistent finding: Women score higher on test anxiety than do men. She began her study with the general hypothesis that whereas for men the achievement motive is socially reinforced, for women the desire to achieve is contaminated by what Horner calls the "motive to avoid success" (p. 38).

Horner's study, like McClelland's, used the *Thematic Apperception Test*. In addition, subjects were asked to read and comment on short stories—in this case, stories about people in success situations. The subjects were 90 girls and 88 boys, all undergraduates at the University of Michigan. Several conclusions emerged very clearly. Girls had strong fears of social rejection as a result of success. Their stories expressed guilt and despair over success, and even doubts about the femininity or normality of highly successful females. Also, girls placed in competitive situations during the experiment performed more poorly than when they worked alone, whereas men were much more likely to achieve better in competition.

A striking finding of the study was the perception, expressed by both males and females, that the highly successful female in medicine, law, science, and other professions was doomed to a life of social rejection, isolation, and personal misery unless she renounced her hard-won success and settled for a life-style closer to the traditional female role.

PEER INFLUENCE ON MOTIVATION

Unfortunately, the effects of peers on students' motivations have never really been tapped in public schools, except in interscholastic sports, which have always relied heavily on student support and enthusiasm. The outstanding academic performer usually has few or no means of bringing glory to himself or to his school. "His victories are always purely personal, often at the expense of his classmates, who are forced to work harder to keep up with him. It is no wonder that his accomplishments gain little reward and are often met by ridiculing remarks, such as 'curve-raiser' or 'grind,' terms of disapprobation which have no analogues in athletics" (Coleman, 1969, p. 280).

Coleman has made the intriguing suggestion that high schools encourage learning by sponsoring citywide or statewide "scholastic fairs" with academic games, tournaments, exhibits, and other forms of competition between schools organized in academic "conferences." "It could be that the mere institution of such games would, just as do the state basketball tournaments in the midwestern United States, have a profound effect upon the educational climate in the participating schools. In fact, by an extension of this analysis, one would predict that an international fair of this sort, a 'Scholastic Olympics,' would generate interscholastic games and tournaments within the participating countries" (1969, p. 281).

A very promising technique being tried on a broad scale is the use of students to tutor other students. Perhaps the most compelling reason for adopting this practice is the possibility that it may help to change the social-psychological climate of the school from one fostering individual competitiveness to concern for each other. In a summary of empirical and experimental research, Elliott (1973) states that the practice not only helps tutors and students but also aids the teacher as well in that it increases the amount of individualized instruction in the school.

OTHER MOTIVATIONAL INFLUENCES

AFFILIATION

Human beings have a strong need to live and work in proximity with others, to share common experiences with others who are not personally threatening to them and who can enter into their activities and purposes as respected equals. This need for affiliation may range from the desire to have friends and to be included in school and community social groups to the intimate relationships of parent and child or husband and wife.

> Affiliation is exhibited in all primates; some form of social contact appears necessary for the normal physical and personality development of the human infant; and total isolation is virtually always an intolerable situation for the human adult—even when physical needs are provided for. [Berelson and Steiner, 1964, p. 252.]

The need for affiliation has both positive and negative value for the growing child. Uniting for mutual protection and profit is usually desirable, but one form of cooperation common among adolescents—"gangism"—frequently does not contribute much to positive social growth or academic achievement.

Anderson (1971) studied the effects of classroom social climate on individual learning. His findings suggest that characteristics of class groups have significant effects on learning, varying widely according to the sex and ability level of the student. Cliques, for example, tend to help low-ability girls, since these girls consider cliques to be school-oriented. On the other hand, boys of below-average ability often form cliques that enable them to escape their school responsibilities and substitute peer-group behavior that does not emphasize academic learning.

French (1956) found that persons with a high affiliation motivation tend to choose people they like as work partners. The achievement-oriented person, however, tends to select as a work partner someone he perceives as being competent in performing the task in question.

MODELING

It is well documented that humans learn much of their behavior by observing and imitating the behavior of other humans (Holt, 1931; Miller and Dollard, 1941; Bandura, 1969).* This phenomenon is called *modeling*. For example, the father demonstrates batting, and his son observes and then imitates him. The father's demonstration serves as a behavioral model. Although the precise nature of the process is still uncertain, modeling accounts for much behavior that is left unexplained by classical- and operant-conditioning theories (MacMillan, 1973).

As Bandura (1965) points out, modeling may lead to: (1) the development of new behavior (modeling effect); (2) the inhibition of present behavior or the elicitation of previously inhibited behavior (inhibitory or disinhibitory effect); or (3) the elicitation of a response that has been inactive, though not as a result of inhibition (response-facilitation effect). Many variables, such as the sex of the model and of the subject, the consequences that follow the model's behavior, and whether the model is on film or *in vivo*, are related to the choice of outcomes. Modeling is often employed in conjunction with reinforcement procedures as a method of bringing about desired behavioral change. Reinforcement can be applied systematically to affect the likelihood that the behavioral change will be maintained in the future.

The perceptive teacher can easily find examples of modeling effects in the school environment. Middle-school and senior-high-school youth especially are very responsive to characteristics of dress and personal mannerisms of entertainment and sports superstars. In the school building also, the behavior of even a small minority of youth with flamboyant life-styles can have noticeable effects on other youth. In this connection, a not-uncommon outcome of allowing students to determine their own dress and behavior codes is that the leadership of the

---

* What constitutes "modeling" or "imitation" in animals is quite another matter. The mother cat shows the kitten some behavior, but much of it is genetic. Very little human behavior is instinctual. Even the sex act is not inherent.

student council may not reflect the broad interests of the student body but may be too responsive to the demands of a vocal minority. The importance of self-government and individual opportunities for self-direction is, of course, paramount. But teachers must carefully observe which individuals emerge as possible behavior models.

Teachers at every grade level have a personal responsibility to "set a good example" for the children: not simply the traditional example of middle-class rectitude, but the more important example of concern for the feelings and worth of each child. Specifically, this means paying attention at all times to the amenities of courtesy toward others. Just as the teacher expects the child to listen attentively while the teacher is talking, so should the teacher listen while a child has the floor. There are innumerable instances throughout the school day when the teacher can demonstrate respect for others. It is always discouraging to note the contrast between the respectful, courteous manner in which teachers address other adults—especially their professional superiors—and their expressed attitude toward the young people in their charge.

When all teachers maintain the example of courtesy and concern for the child's personality at all times—even when the child is openly uncooperative or hostile—the modeling and motivational effects will be very apparent.

SOCIAL CLASS

Research evidence has consistently pointed to the relationship of social class to motivation and achievement—for most youth (Rosen and D'Andrade, 1973). In a comparative study of achieving and under-achieving high-school boys of the same high intellectual ability, Frankel (1960) determined that the achievers came from backgrounds with higher socio-economic status and had better-educated fathers. In another study, Curry (1964) investigated the effects of socio-economic status on the scholastic achievement of sixth-grade children. He found that children with above-average intellectual ability usually overcome the effects of a deprived home environment. For students who are below average in ability, however, deprived social and economic home conditions tend to reduce scholastic achievement.

Much recent research suggests that the single most significant influence on school achievement is the social-class composition of the school (Coleman, 1968; Mosteller and Moynihan, 1972). This is especially noticeable in predominantly black schools, where heavy concentrations of blacks who are poor, of lower-class status, or from fatherless homes result in little stimulation to achievement (Coleman, 1966). Dropping out of school is also inversely related to family social status (Havighurst, 1962).

If the social class of the parents is as important to a child's academic motivation and achievement as these studies indicate, it would seem that greater emphasis should be placed on parent involvement in the child's education. A growing number of educators and other authorities are suggesting that we cannot realistically expect the school to be the sole motivator of the child; parents are going to have to assume greater responsibility (Bloom, 1972; Blum and Coleman, 1972; Mead, 1973; Ward, 1970). Motivation must start in the home and be maintained by parents who are educationally supportive and who set an example by being learners themselves. Parents may have to work at least as hard to bridge the gap between home and school as to provide material necessities for their children. And simply checking a report card every nine weeks won't be enough. They will have to become parastudents at the same school their children attend. Children will have to begin teaching their parents much of what they have learned in school—almost as an educational objective in its own right.

In the early years after the Revolution, Soviet educators and government officials undertook an ambitious plan to eliminate illiteracy. The greatest hurdle they encountered was not poor motivation or a lack of ability of the typical Russian child, but the low educational level of his home. As a result, children were taught to read and write and then told to go home and teach their parents. Only when the family learned together was any progress made.

INTERESTS

There is a widespread belief that children succeed best at subjects in which they have a strong interest. The earliest study of the relationship of interests to achievement was done by E. L. Thorndike in 1917. He found a perfect relationship between expressed interests and the individual's rating of his ability to perform in corresponding areas. These findings probably mean that people tend to say that they like doing what they do well.

Gordon and Alf (1962) studied the value of an interest inventory for predicting grades in fifty-seven Navy training schools involving over fifty thousand recruits. The relationship between interests and subsequent grades in related training was rather small, a finding consistent with those of other studies. In general, predicting success on the basis of expressed interests is exceedingly risky—as many guidance counselors know.

What is more valid, however, is the motivational value of interests. A strong interest often propels the individual to master at least the fundamentals of an activity. The ensuing sense of accomplishment may help him to accept the fact that the activity is (probably) more complex and less glamorous than he had previously thought—and yet to continue to pursue it.

An understanding of students' interests is an important factor in developing classroom objectives and methods. In fact, expressed interests are closely related to the entire issue of "relevancy." What complicates this relationship is, in a sense, a semantic problem. Most teachers today favor the notion of being "relevant" and "tuned in" to youth values, but the teacher himself usually determines what constitutes relevancy, which may or may not relate directly to students' short-run interests. Furthermore, although most parents certainly want school to be interesting for their children—possibly even "relevant"—they are inclined to regard as its chief responsibility the teaching of what will be useful in the long run—regardless of whether or not it is immediately pleasurable or relevant.

In summary, research generally indicates only a slight relationship between measures of interest and measures of ability or achievement. Interests that are strong generally have initial motivational value but may lack staying power. For the teacher, a knowledge of students' interests is most useful as a means of "tuning in" to the opinions and perceptions of young people. This can help to increase communication and understanding between teacher and student.

COMPETITION

There is considerable controversy today about motivational strategies based largely on competition as opposed to strategies that emphasize working together for common goals. There is no question that the quest for status through competition underlies much of the achievement of many students.

Status may be the most important single variable in driving students to one or another adaptation to the school. When it is unavailable in one system, persons shift to systems that will confer it. If competition for status in the school is too stiff for those who are disadvantaged by virtue of home motivation and lower-class manners, they usually find another institution that will reward them. They drop out of school, disavowing the value of education, and invest themselves completely in the values of the deviant peer group. They attempt to find status by their fists, by fast cars, or by sexual exploits. Status is necessary. If the competition system of the school confers status unidimensionally in ways for which some are not equipped, then other dimensions will be found outside of the school. [Weinberg, 1965, p. 110.]

Until the rise of the mental-health movement in recent years, only a few educators and psychologists questioned the value of competition as a motivator. If a student worked hard, he deserved to be rewarded with good grades and high class standing. If the slow student had to work harder to keep up, this was desirable, since it motivated him to over-achieve. Although the bright child often got away with working at a slower pace than his potential, his natural ability brought him the rewards of competition, which maintained his self-concept and prepared him for leadership roles later in life. In terms of society's needs, competition as the basis for school achievement functioned to produce many excellent students. Few teachers and administrators worried very much about those who could not stand the competition and were forced to "throw in the towel," for these people could usually be absorbed in the expanding work force.

Today there is a rising outcry against competitive pressures in elementary schools, secondary schools, and colleges. Many students, teachers, and parents believe that schools should give more emphasis to personal, affective outcomes. According to this view, the chief purpose should be to understand the student as a whole, unique person, with his own goals, his own way of viewing people and the world. We should be concerned less with how much information he can absorb in competition with others and more with how he is organizing subject matter in his subjective world and the relationship between this world and his behavior in all situations (Bloom, 1972).

The potentially harmful effects of competition have been summarized as follows:

1. When success is limited to a few, the losers, in self-defense, withdraw from participation. Generally the weak ones are eliminated or refuse to compete for fear of coming up short, so that competition denies participation to the very ones who need it the most.
2. Competition is harmful when everyone is so busy protecting himself from the threat of the achievements of others that no one can do his best.
3. When the success of others is a source of threat rather than happiness and sincere fellowship, then the need to win at all costs leads to dishonesty, rivalry, bitterness, and reprisals in the event of defeat.
4. The need to excel in competition may interfere with creative social participation.

5. The need to excel in competition can result in little or no development of intrinsic incentives. [Mouly, 1973, p. 352.]

There is a growing belief that the evaluation of a student's performance should be relative to the individual himself—what he has done in the past, or what he is generally capable of doing. The basis for motivation should be the child's natural desire to know and to understand, not simply to win a superior position on a distribution of scores. The advantage claimed for the noncompetitive approach is that it virtually assures at least some degree of "success" for each student, because each has the chance to show improvement relative to his own potential (Glasser, 1969). Because the individual student is not measured against group norms, his anxieties are lessened, and he can focus on his personal improvement.

In theory, this has value for mental health. In practice, however, grading on the basis of individual growth involves problems, particularly in the inability of teachers to make consistently reliable judgments of pupil progress. To some extent, every child ought to be evaluated on the basis of what he has accomplished relative to where he began. Yet, this often involves personality factors and other subjective considerations that can work to the child's disadvantage. Also, at the high-school level there is the problem of determining class rank for post-high-school educational planning.

There is no real consensus on the basic issue. The position that a specific degree of competence need not receive the same grade in different contexts and that more lenient standards should be applied to less capable students, and vice versa, is fairly widely held and is supported on grounds of maintaining motivation and the opportunity for success for the less well endowed. On the other hand, however, concern is frequently expressed at penalizing honors groups by demanding higher accomplishment in them in order to earn the same mark, and this practice has been seen as potentially demoralizing to an honors program. Thus, in the absence of consensus on the desirable policy, often little progress is made toward implementing any policy. [*Encyclopedia of Educational Research*, 1969, p. 764.]

THE INTRINSIC NATURE OF MOTIVATION

We return to the question, "What causes Johnny's motivational gyroscope to spin?" As we have seen, there are many theories. Kelly (1960) claims that theories of motivation in contemporary psychology can be summarized in two ways: "push" theories and "pull" theories. "Under push theories we find such terms as *drive, motive,* or even *stimulus.* Pull theories use such constructs as *purpose, value,* or *need.* In terms of a well-known metaphor, there are the pitchfork theories, on the one hand, and the carrot theories, on the other" [p. 50].

This formulation implies that organisms become quiescent without strong stimulation, the need to achieve homeostasis, or the acquired drives and needs based upon these factors. Yet, recent studies suggest that the response to an absence of such motivating conditions is not quiescence but, rather, boredom. Activity deprivation appears to have consequences similar to those resulting from food deprivation. Humans —and animals, too, under certain conditions—appear to have a psychological need for excitement, novelty, even danger (Ausubel, 1971). We see this phenomenon in the myriad examples of human derring-do, where individuals deliberately seek to raise, rather than lower, their drive states by climbing mountains, stunt-flying, performing with dangerous animals, and so on. Even animals exhibit this need to be "turned on." In several experiments (Hill, 1956; Kagan and Berkun, 1954), it has been found that rats will run on a treadmill just to escape boredom —a behavioral phenomenon that has long been known to be characteristic of children. Bored, repressed children in a classroom will do almost anything—drum fingers, drop pencils, sky-write, tap feet, whistle—to relieve the tedium.

According to Torrance (1965), lack of opportunities for children to be self-directed results in a drop in creative development, accompanied by loss of interest in learning, an increase in behavioral problems, and an increase in emotional disturbance at about the kindergarten, fourth-grade, and seventh-grade levels. At these points in their school careers, children tend to perform less well than children at the next-lower educational level on tests of imagination, originality, creativity, and divergent thinking. They exhibit less curiosity, manipulativeness, and general excitement about learning. Torrance also reports indications that these are peak periods in psychiatric referrals, remedial instruction, and behavior problems. Evidence is also piling up from other fields that any marked reduction in activity level over a substantial period of time realigns the functions of the organism and may be more disturbing than the disorder that brought about the reduction. Immobility, prolonged rest, nonuse of parts or functions bring their own particular type of deterioration (Anderson, 1971).

Fowler (1965) believes that organisms respond, not only to a change in stimulation, but to change for its own sake, which he calls "incentive motivation." Animals will learn some responses in order to experience novel and unfamiliar stimuli. For example, monkeys will repeatedly press a button that opens shutters and gives them the opportunity to see other monkeys playing. The anticipated change in stimulation is the incentive for the monkeys' behavior.

> Striving for stimulation, information, knowledge, or understanding—depending on the level of animal and the kind of activity—appears to be a universal motive among the primates, and especially man.
> Lower animals as well as people actively seek stimulation of various kinds. Sights, sounds, smells, and other sensations that have not led to or been associated with physical satisfaction seem to be interesting, attractive, and sometimes demonstrably rewarding in themselves. [Berelson and Steiner, 1964, p. 245.]

Research on sensory and activity deprivation, then, suggests that a child's motivational gyroscope is not simply turned on or off by various sources of drive and need but functions as an intrinsically powered system of information processing and action. Current theories tend to regard the individual as an "internally active processor of information who sorts through and modifies a multitude of cognitive elements in an attempt to achieve some type of cognitive coherence" (Tedeschi, Schlenker, and Bonoma, 1971, p. 685). According to this view, dissonance between cognitive elements, once discovered or aroused, is noxious to the individual and creates tensions causing actions to be taken to reduce the dissonance. This conception of motivation is based on the affective-arousal potential inherent in a child's cognitive system. So long as the reflex arc was considered to be the fundamental functional unit of behavior, all activity was presumed to be in response to a drive or need stimulus. In the affective-arousal model of motivation, the reflex hypothesis is replaced by the notion of an internal "feedback" mechanism, in which behavior is influenced primarily by incongruity between the input from a set of circumstances and some standard within the organism. This incongruity, or dissonance, may be a discrepancy between the level of complexity encountered and the level of complexity to which an organism has become accustomed (Hunt, 1964). Hebb (1949) first recognized this idea in his theory of pleasure, noting that in any situation organisms tend to be preoccupied with "what is new but not *too* new."

The motivational effects of incongruity appear to be greater as we go higher up the phylogenetic scale. In other words, the energizing effects of expectancies appear to be very much more important to human beings than to animals.

Cognitive-dissonance theory remains a provocative and useful theory of human motivation, but the mechanism by which the individual is aroused to activity in order to reduce dissonance is not clearly understood. The theory appears to explain behavior best after it has occurred, but it is not yet adequate for prediction. The underlying assumptions of dissonance theory are that a "person is genetically endowed with some type of mysterious mechanism, like a gyroscope that [is] automatically activated by illogically paired cognitions" or that there is a "pervasive socially acquired drive that functions to attach unpleasant consequences to psychologically consistent cognitions" [Tedeschi, Schlenker, and Bonoma, 1971, p. 689].

We might say, then, that a child's motivational gyroscope spins because it is intrinsically satisfying to him for it to do so. The psychologically normal child wants to be active intellectually as well as physically. All children engage in a rich cognitive life—imagining and processing symbolic representation. This cognitive process is continually fed with information and perceptions from many internal and external sources, all of which are capable of activating behavior. It is this interaction between the child's cognitive and perceptual world and his environmental experiences that seems to be the basic motivator.

Some schools have attempted to meet the child's intrinsic need for stimulation by allowing free time for personal exploration. A few middle schools have established so-called creativity rooms where children may go during study periods or at other intervals during the school day. These rooms contain art supplies, science equipment, photography, printing, and other hobby apparatus, as well as reading and visual materials. Students go individually or in small groups to work on self-selected projects, or for freewheeling discussions.

At the elementary-school level, where children are usually more closely supervised, some teachers have experimented with allowing brief periods of "open time" each day. As the pupils learn to utilize these short sessions, the time intervals are increased. This technique appears to work best in school buildings with open spaces.

Unfortunately, current strategies to allow time for exploratory activities tend to favor the better students—especially at the secondary-school level. Also, there is little agreement on the age at which children can profitably use substantial amounts of exploratory time, and there is ever-present concern about behavioral problems that are thought to be the by-product of unsupervised activity. In spite of these difficulties, however, many classroom teachers are moving slowly—but moving nevertheless—to provide opportunities for personal exploratory activities. Surely, on the basis of experimental evidence, the need for stimulating activity appears to be basic for *all* children.

SUCCESS AND FAILURE

In a sense, the term "ego drive" can be substituted for "motivation." In kindergarten and first grade, for example, ego needs are expressed quite directly. The child likes attention and praise, and he dislikes censure and punishment. If he receives enough rewards to satisfy his needs, his motivational level will tend to remain high—his gyroscope will really hum! Because he likes praise, and because this is what he gets when he demonstrates the right behavior, he learns very quickly what he must do to gain recognition. This generalized state of motivation then gradually differentiates into various specific motives—the desire to read, solve arithmetic problems, paint, and so on.

An important principle is that success and failure are cumulative. The more successful the child is, the more opportunity he gets to practice the skill or behavior he is involved in, which, in turn, causes him to improve more and therefore merit even greater reward. For example, if the child starts off fairly well in reading in first grade, he receives various kinds of reinforcement—the teacher's approval, the respect of his peers, favorable regard from parents, and personal satisfaction as well. Since he is developing a basic tool, he is able to take on reading material that is more and more difficult and challenging. The teacher will be inclined to let him spend more time on reading and perhaps less time on activities he does not like. Therefore, he gets further opportunity to practice and improve in reading, which, in turn, results in further success and positive feedback.

Unfortunately, failure is cumulative, too. The child begins with the very normal need for approval. Suppose that when he begins to read in first grade he experiences difficulty, for any of various reasons: poor eyesight, social-class deprivation, an unskilled teacher, or frequent illness during the first months of his reading experience. Thus, as he stumbles along, he does not get much praise—he really doesn't deserve it. Soon the teacher decides that he requires "special help," and he finds himself grouped or identified with other unsuccessful readers. He notices that this is a low-achieving group where there are often considerable commotion and distractions that make it hard for him to concentrate and where the teacher, instead of being approving and relaxed, is likely to be serious and a little anxious toward the halting efforts of these unfortunate pupils.

If the child makes only slow progress, he soon discovers that learning to read is not very much fun. In fact, the most rewarding moment seems to be when the reading session comes to an end and he can switch to a more pleasurable activity. Soon, *not* reading, or *escape* from reading, is the most rewarding event of all. Because the child is learning to dislike reading, he will read as little as possible—thus preventing himself from getting the practice necessary to overcome his difficulty. The less he reads, the slower is his progress. Now the development of his reading begins to move in a downward direction.

OVERCOMING THE EFFECTS OF FAILURE

Usually, knowledge of results—feedback—helps to maintain motivation, especially if it is knowledge of good work or a good grade or guidance suggestions that will lead to better performance. Less satisfying is news about a *lack* of success or a failing grade.

It is generally agreed that children learn better and feel better about school work in general when they know where they stand at all times in their studies and behavior. This principle breaks down somewhat, however, in the case of the low-ability or low-achieving student. Constant reminders of poor performance may function to rigidify an already defeatist self-concept. The older low-achieving student, in particular, often interprets a low grade or an unfavorable teacher evaluation as a personal attack, especially if it is accompanied by insidious remarks on the part of the teacher. The teacher's objective should be to provide sufficient guidance to alter the trend of a poor student performance and then to reinforce the better performance with a higher grade and warm approval and recognition.

With the high-achieving student, knowledge of success helps to maintain motivation. Yet, at times, it is good practice to lower a grade or drop a sharply disapproving word to a generally good student who seems to be taking his class work too casually. In these instances—and they must not occur too often—a low grade can have a dramatic effect, unlike a low grade for the low-achiever, which usually has little motivational value.

RAISING THE PROBABILITY OF SUCCESS

There are two general approaches to helping children to be successful. One uses behaviorist psychology—primarily the reinforcement principle. This approach says, in effect, that the child has developed the habit of behaving in a certain way for which he is usually punished (with a low grade, disapproving remarks from the teacher, or other forms of censure). Perhaps the child is a poor reader—for example, he tends to read one word at a time slowly and laboriously. How can the teacher induce him to look at groups of words instead and to move more quickly over the sentences in order to string ideas together? Just *telling* him to do it probably will not change his behavior, since his reading habits and attitudes are already well formed. One possibility might be to have him read material with a tachistoscope, which forces him to maintain a faster pace and see larger clusters of words. Applying the reinforcement principle, the teacher "rewards" the child after the first trial. Even if he has not improved very much, the teacher can at least compliment him for trying and for showing interest in this new procedure. Thus, he is motivated to run down a different "maze," for which he gets positive feedback.

From this initial trial, the teacher needs to make careful note of any opportunities to give him knowledge of progress, or at least a few words of encouragement. In this way, the teacher can increase the probability that the child will persist at the task. Of course, the more rigid are the child's ineffective reading habits, the longer it will take to change his behavior. Above all, the teacher must concentrate on success and, if possible, de-emphasize temporary setbacks. As the pupil shows evidence of reading with somewhat greater speed and power, the teacher may then compliment or grade him favorably a little less often. The teacher's change to an intermittent feedback routine shows the child that the rewards are not automatic but a bit uncertain, and thus his motivation is maintained.

The perceptual approach involves almost the same procedure as is outlined above, but it can be described in different terms. This approach involves, not a change in the child's behavior through reinforcement, but a change in his perception as a result of a reorganization of the way in which the child regards what he is doing. The perceptualist explains the process in this way: The child has developed a habit of reading slowly and haltingly, for which he usually receives some form of censure, or nonreward. For him, the act of reading is mechanical and external. It doesn't affect him in a "gut" way, as when he reads, say, the instructions accompanying his dad's new snowmobile. That's something else! The prospect of piloting a new snowmobile is tremendously exciting, and he knows, as he reads the manual, that he'd better get it right. In the classroom, there usually is not such a sense of urgency or excitement; the reading materials are often remote from a child's personal experience. The function of the teacher, therefore, is to convince him that he has something to gain from reading. Though, perhaps, a classroom reading assignment will not be as exciting as the snowmobile manual, it still could be interesting and enjoyable, in its own way. So to the tachistoscope—and the opportunity to give reading another try under different conditions. Whereas the feedback from the teacher continues to function as a reward, this time, according to the perceptualist, the experience "tells" the child that learning to read will be good for him; indeed, it may give him the exhilarating feeling that he is finally getting on top of his reading problem, a feeling akin to what he experiences as he careens over the fields in a roaring snowmobile.

Thus, we have two different explanations for the same chain of events, which can result in improved reading. Whether the teacher prefers to view the process from the behaviorist or the perceptualist position is probably not important here. What *is* important is the necessity for changing in some way what the child is doing. Get him off on another foot, so to speak. The second requirement is that there be an opportunity for positive feedback, knowledge of progress, reward, and guidance in learning, because this helps to give him the feeling that reading is worthwhile and that he will personally profit and grow from the experience.

THE TEACHER AS PRIME MOTIVATOR

The chief instructional problem in schools today is underachievement: academic performance below what could be expected on the basis of a student's measured ability. A great deal of teacher time and effort is spent motivating students to learn and achieve at their ability levels. Underachievement, a condition widespread at all grade levels, is wasteful because it often results in the neglect of the very good students if teachers have to spend a disproportionate amount of time working with reluctant learners. Further, underachieving students require expenditures of school funds for remedial reading, remedial math, and other corrective activities in order to bring them up to their grade levels. Finally, underachieving students have the effect of causing teachers to be underachievers as well, in the sense that large amounts of time must be spent on essentially uncreative activities—repetitive basic skills, review and drill, and the supervision of slow students. They often have little time and vitality left for enrichment experiences in the classroom. Although basic skills must be taught, the moments in class when students get involved and excited over issues related to subject matter are the icing on the cake for the teacher. Helping students to bring everything together is the best that teachers can do for them. When young people are stimulated to go beyond the exercise of basic skills to the use of imagination and insight, they are beginning to grasp what learning is all about. These are the golden moments in the class-room.

Any attempt to stimulate the child's will to learn must involve recognition by the child that school learning leads to some worthwhile outcome; that learning is, under certain circumstances, as pleasurable an activity as an arduous sport like baseball; and that such learning can *modelling* make the child more like the adult he most admires (Zacharias, 1964). The child is most likely to gain these realizations when the objectives of instruction and classroom activities reflect the teacher's sensitivity to his needs and interests, and when he is consulted, at least to some extent, in the planning of classroom activities. There really is not much one can do to alter markedly the pattern of a child's wants and desires, but they can be modified at least enough to help the child feel better about doing schoolwork. A useful general principle for the teacher to follow is to attempt to give something positive to every child each day. This might mean simply *listening* to the child without judging or evaluating what he says. Psychotherapist Theodore Reik (1948) called this "listening with the third ear." Classrooms often tend to become one-way communication streets. Teachers always express strong personal concern for children, but, in the hurly-burly of daily activities, the school environment sometimes becomes like a factory, with people and materials mechanically moved around and manipulated. Teachers and school administrators often do not notice this; they are so busy directing activities and events that they grow accustomed to the frenetic atmosphere. To the students, however, who are at the receiving end of these activities, the impersonality and chaotic pace are much more apparent. Too often, a child's need to talk to a teacher—to "relate" for a few moments on a personal level—seems unimportant to adults. The formal requirements of teaching often shut out opportunities for informal contact. Perhaps "listening with the third ear" may not produce immediate benefits, but, in the long run, young people will begin to see that the teacher who listens does so because he is aware of each child, and they will no longer feel "invisible" in his presence. This perception is reinforced when the teacher deliberately takes time and effort to receive and accept a child's thoughts. Human contact of this kind is the most motivating force of all.

REFERENCES

ANDERSON, J. E. 1971. Dynamics of development: System in process. In J. Eliot (ed.), *Human development and cognitive processes*. New York: Holt, Rinehart & Winston.

AUSUBEL, D. P. 1971. Motivation and classroom learning. In H. D. Funk and R. T. Olberg (eds.), *Learning to teach in the elementary school.* New York: Dodd, Mead, 187–91.

BANDURA, A. 1965. Behavior modification through modeling procedures. In L. P. Ullman and L. Krasner (eds.), *Research in behavior modification.* New York: Holt, Rinehart & Winston.

———. 1969. *Principles of behavior modification.* New York: Holt, Rinehart & Winston.

BERELSON, B., and G. A. STEINER. 1964. *Human behavior: An inventory of scientific findings.* New York: Harcourt, Brace & World.

BLOOM, B. S. 1972. Innocence in education. *School Review,* 80(3), 333–52.

BLUM, Z. D., and J. S. COLEMAN. 1972. *Longitudinal effects of education on the incomes and occupational prestige of blacks and whites.* Report No. 70, Center for the Study of Social Organization of Schools. Baltimore: Johns Hopkins University.

CANNON, W. B. 1939. *The wisdom of the body.* New York: W. W. Norton.

COLEMAN, J. S. 1968. The concept of equality of educational opportunity. *Harvard Educational Review,* 38(1), 7–22.

———. 1969. The adolescent subculture and academic achievement. In S. H. Frey and E. S. Haugen (eds.), *Readings in classroom learning.* New York: American Book.

COLEMAN, J. S., et al. 1966. *Equality of educational opportunity.* Washington, D.C.: U.S. Government Printing Office.

CURRY, R. L. 1964. The effects of socioeconomic status on the scholastic achievement of sixth grade children. *British Journal of Educational Psychology,* 32, 46–49.

ELLIOTT, A. 1973. Student tutoring helps everyone. *Phi Delta Kappan,* 54 (8), 535–38.

Encyclopedia of Educational Research. 1969. New York: Macmillan.

FLANAGAN, J. C. 1973. Education: How and for what? *American Psychologist,* 28(7), 551–56.

FOWLER, H. 1965. *Curiosity and exploratory behavior.* New York: Macmillan.

FRANKEL, E. 1960. Comparative study of achieving and underachieving high school boys of high intellectual ability. *Journal of Educational Research,* 53, 172–80.

FRENCH, E. G. 1956. Motivation as a variable in work-partner selection. *Journal of Abnormal and Social Psychology,* 53, 96–99.

GLASSER, W. D. 1969. *Schools without failure.* New York: Harper & Row.

GORDON, L. V., and E. F. ALF. 1962. The predictive validity of measured interest for Navy vocational training. *Journal of Applied Psychology,* 46, 212–19.

HAVIGHURST, R. J. 1962. *Growing up in River City.* New York: Wiley.

HEBB, D. O. 1949. On the nature of fear. *Psychological Review,* 53, 259–76.

HILL, W. F. 1956. Activity as an autonomous drive. *Journal of Comparative and Physiological Psychology, 49,* 15–19.

HOLT, E. B. 1931. *Animal drive and the learning process,* Vol. I. New York: Holt.

HORNER, M. 1969. A bright woman is caught in a double bind. In achievement-oriented situations she worries not only about failure but also about success. *Psychology Today, 3*(6), 36, 38, 62.

HUNT, J. McV. 1964. The psychological basis for using preschool enrichment as an antidote in cultural deprivation. *Merrill-Palmer Quarterly, 10,* 233.

KAGAN, J., and M. BERKUN. 1954. The reward value of running activity. *Journal of Comparative and Physiological Psychology, 47,* 108.

KELLY, G. A. 1960. Man's constructions of his alternatives. In G. Lindzey (ed.), *Assessment of human motives.* New York: Grove Press.

McCLELLAND, D. C. 1961. Toward a theory of motive acquisition. In D. C. McClelland (ed.), *The achieving society.* Princeton, N.J.: Van Nostrand.

MACMILLAN, D. L. 1973. *Behavior modification in education.* New York: Macmillan.

MASLOW, A. H. 1943. A theory of human motivation. *Psychological Review, 50,* 370–79.

————. 1954. *Motivation and personality.* New York: Harper & Row.

MEAD, M. 1973. The effects of changing family patterns on American schooling. *Report on Education Research.* Washington, D.C.: Capitol Publications, p. 9.

MILLER, N. E., and J. DOLLARD. 1941. *Social learning and imitation.* New Haven: Yale University Press.

MOSTELLER, F., and D. P. MOYNIHAN. 1972. *On equality of educational opportunity.* New York: Vintage Books.

MOULY, G. J. 1973. *Psychology for effective teaching.* New York: Holt, Rinehart & Winston.

MURRAY, H. A. (ed.). 1938. *Explorations in personality: A clinical study of fifty men of college age.* New York: Oxford University Press.

REIK, T. 1948. *Listening with the third ear; inner experiences of a psychoanalyst.* New York: Farrar, Strauss.

ROSEN, B. C., and R. D. D'ANDRADE. 1973. The psychological origins of achievement motivation. In E. Zigler and I. L. Childs (eds.), *Socialization and personality development.* Reading, Mass.: Addison-Wesley.

TEDESCHI, J. T., B. R. SCHLENKER, and T. V. BONOMA. 1971. Cognitive dissonance: Private ratiocination or public spectacle? *American Psychologist, 26,* 685–95.

THOMAS, W. I. 1967. *The unadjusted girl.* New York: Harper & Row.

THORNDIKE, E. L. 1917. Interests and abilities. *School and Society, 5,* 178–79.

TORRANCE, E. P. 1965. Continuity in the creative development of young children. In E. P. Torrance and R. D. Strom (eds.), *Mental health and achievement.* New York: Wiley.

WARD, E. 1970. A child's first reading teacher: His parents. *Reading Teacher,* 23, 756–60.

WEINBERG, C. 1965. The price of competition. *Teachers College Record,* 67(2), 106–14.

WHITE, R. W. 1959. Motivation reconsidered: The concept of competence. *Psychological Review,* 66, 297–333.

ZACHARIAS, J. R. 1964. *Innovation and experiment in education.* Washington, D.C.: U.S. Government Printing Office.

CHAPTER NINE

The Management of Learning

IN SPITE OF the ebb and flow of controversy in American education, schools have remained fairly consistent in their stated educational goals, which reflect our society's values and attitudes. According to the Educational Policies Commission:

> The purpose which runs through and strengthens all other educational purposes—the common thread of education—is the development of the ability to think. This is the central purpose to which the school must be oriented if it is to accomplish its traditional tasks or those newly accentuated by recent changes in the world. To say that it is central is not to say that it is the sole purpose or in all circumstances the most important purpose, but that it must be a pervasive concern in the work of the school [1961, p. 12].

A more detailed set of goals was presented in the 1956 report of the Committee for the White House Conference on Education:

1. A general education as good as, or better than, that offered in the past, with increased emphasis on the physical and social sciences
2. Programs designed to develop patriotism and good citizenship
3. Programs designed to foster moral, ethical, and spiritual values
4. Vocational education tailored to the abilities of each pupil and to the needs of the community and nation
5. Courses designed to teach domestic skills
6. Training in leisure-time activities such as music, dancing, avocational reading, and hobbies
7. A variety of health services for all children, including both physical

and dental inspection, aimed at bettering health knowledge and habits

8. Special treatment for children with speech or reading difficulties and other handicaps
9. Physical education, ranging from systematic exercises, physical therapy, and intramural sports to interscholastic competition
10. Instruction to meet the needs of abler students
11. Programs designed to acquaint students with countries other than their own in an effort to help them understand the problems America faces in international relations
12. Programs designed to foster mental health
13. Programs designed to foster wholesome family life
14. Organized recreational and social activities
15. Courses designed to promote safety, including instruction in driving automobiles, swimming, civil defense, and the like.

The school system's statement of general philosophy and objectives establishes the broad purposes of instruction. On the basis of these broad goals, the school administration then develops course outlines, audiovisual materials, textbooks, and tests. But it is the responsibility of the individual teacher to translate the goals set by the system and the materials provided by the school into day-to-day instructional activities yielding measurable results in terms of the specific behaviors students acquire, which presumably reflect instructional objectives. The school's course of study for a given grade level may require the mastery and appreciation of certain literary classics, for example, but the specific nature of mastery or appreciation must still be defined by the teacher, and he must select or devise appropriate learning activities to bring about these goals. Does "mastery" mean the ability to memorize plots and retain information about authors or to be able to describe or analyze writing styles? Does "appreciation" mean repeating what scholars have said about Shakespeare or learning to express one's own feelings about a given work? Does the teacher test the students' personal response to a work, or their knowledge of his own preferences? Does the teacher emphasize intellectual training exclusively, or does he recognize the values of developing citizenship skills, vocational competencies, and self-actualization? Without a clear definition of desired student behaviors and the means to determine whether they have been attained, the teacher has no basis for judging the success or failure of his teaching efforts.

The first step toward shaping instructional objectives is to identify the main components of an instructional program. The simplest instructional model contains three components (Popham, 1972). This may appear self-evident, but, in fact, many teachers have a tendency to lump together the instructional-objectives and instructional-procedures components. Subject matter and learning activities become the general goal rather than the means to achieve clearly stated objectives.

Instructional	Instructional	Performance
Objectives	Activities	Assessment

The three-component instructional design.

The three-components model incorporates the main features of a *systems* approach, which is a shift from a subject-matter–based curriculum to a logical organization of an instructional program. Each component specifies teacher and student roles and responsibilities and reflects both accepted psychological principles of learning and human development and our social and cultural aspirations.

THE INSTRUCTIONAL-OBJECTIVES COMPONENT

According to behaviorist psychology, learning means experiencing a change of behavior that can be described in terms of observable performance. If the individual, as a consequence of instruction or experience, can do something he could not do before, he has learned something. He is now a slightly different person, one who makes new responses, chooses differently, and perceives environmental situations in a new way.

There is a growing interest in defining the objectives of classroom teaching in terms of observable performances (Gagne, 1964). These may be specific, such as learning to respond to a traffic signal; or they may be highly abstract and generalizable behavior, such as logical thinking with numbers. In any case, the process of proceeding from ignorance of some fact or concept to knowledge or understanding of it, or from inability to perform some specified act to ability to perform it, should be stated as a behavioral objective that describes in measurable, observable terms the behavioral outcomes the student is supposed to demonstrate at the end of a period of instruction. Examples of behavioral outcomes are a completed experiment, a performance in athletics, a painting, a cake, any written materials.

Usually, an instructionally usable objective must state the intended outcome in terms of terminal behavior (that is, behavior following instruction); the activities and conditions that the student is to follow in order to achieve the objective; and the minimal, required standards of performance. An erroneous statement of instructional objectives refers to what the teacher does—for example, "to instill in the student an understanding of matter and energy." Once the teacher has done the "instilling" (by lecturing, assigning chapters, performing experiments), it is expected that the student will "know" about matter and energy. It is preferable, of course, to focus on learning outcomes to be achieved by the student himself. This reformulation will usually result in a more measurable achievement. For example, "to demonstrate the knowledge that all living things are composed of cells." This objective might be measured by the student's performance of the following tasks:

1. Given a diagram of a cell, the student can identify the four basic parts (nucleus, cytoplasm, vacuoles, and cell membranes) and explain the purpose of each part in the cell.
2. Given a microscope and slides of plant, animal, and protein specimens, the student can draw conclusions and explain the one characteristic that can describe all three types of living things.

When instructional objectives are stated in this manner, they direct attention to the student rather than the teacher and to the learning outcomes rather than the learning process. This clarifies the purposes of instruction and prepares the way for evaluation of that instruction. Statements of student-centered objectives must use verbs that denote activity rather than implying acquisition of knowledge only. For example, compare the two statements of expected learning outcomes below. Which is preferable?

The student has an appreciation of the power of mathematics as well as of the role mathematics plays in the development of civilization.

The student can state some of the basic reasoning patterns in logic, make truth tables for them, and demonstrate that he understands them by stating reasons for a step-by-step proof of some problems.

By directing attention to terminal student behaviors, the teacher has already begun to measure and evaluate student achievement. If the statements of outcomes are specific, evaluation becomes more precise.

It should be emphasized, however, that the function of these behavioral objectives is to aid in planning instruction, not in informing others of the teacher's intentions.

These objectives are more detailed than the behavioral objectives used typically for the purpose of communicating goals to others. Several types of extremely important objectives are difficult to measure and thus difficult to specify in behavioral terms. As a matter of fact, it seems that the more significant an objective is, the more difficult it is to measure. Examples of objectives which fall into the difficult-to-specify-and-measure category are those in the areas of problem solving, creativity, attitudes, and values. The only solution we see to this problem is for such objectives to be specified as clearly as possible and for the instructor to be as resourceful as he can in developing evaluative measures, including attitude inventories and creativity tests. [Kibler, Barker, and Miles, 1970, p. 5.]

THE LIMITATIONS OF BEHAVIORAL OBJECTIVES

There is no question that approaching teaching by this analytic, operational method generally results in clearer objectives for the student and more precise measurement and evaluation procedures by the teacher. But not always. Good teaching is not entirely dependent on premeditated, specific, and behaviorally defined objectives. It is possible that "the specificity now being demanded of curriculum workers and teachers in the writing of behavioral objectives runs contrary to their values of humanism and intellectualism" (Raths, 1968). An alert teacher senses a "teachable moment" during the course of a routine assignment. This is the time to jettison formal objectives and give the children free rein to pursue an intellectual quest as far as they can. Perhaps this may be simply a spontaneous discussion, or it may be an idea and insight from the personal agendas of the pupils themselves.

Many aspects of the personal relationship between a teacher and a student may have little to do directly with the impartation of knowledge by one and the acquisition of skills by the others, yet they constitute an important element in a child's education. This relationship often becomes the basis for the formation of attitudes and values. These are largely mystical outcomes, because teachers usually cannot guarantee that they will ensue. Students are sometimes "hooked" by a charismatic teacher, often to the extent that they subsequently choose his subject as an occupational goal (Broudy, 1970). Although most experienced teachers have the skill to teach the basic content of the curriculum, inspirational powers are difficult to gauge.

Ojemann (1968) noted that student behavior in what he terms "controlled motivation" situations (in the classroom, that is) may be entirely different from behavior in situations where the student is "on his own." In "controlled" situations, behavior may conform to the teacher's expectations whereas behavior in "on his own" situations may better indicate personal feelings about the significance of what has been learned.

Carefully specified behavioral objectives provide the most fruitful means of starting to plan classroom learning activities (Popham, 1972a). But the idea of behavioral objectives is not sacrosanct. Classroom instruction should be expansive, spontaneous, and serendipitous, as well as specific, premeditated, and logical.

THE INSTRUCTIONAL-ACTIVITIES COMPONENT

READINESS TO LEARN

Each child is at a different state of readiness to learn. The teacher must strive to determine each learner's initial level of ability and background in order to provide him with appropriate learning experiences.

> Studies indicate that there is nothing to be gained by starting youngsters on a particular learning task earlier than readiness normally permits. . . . Most children, if started at a task much earlier than it is normally learned in our culture, do not learn it well, if at all. [Bigge and Hunt, 1968, p. 457.]

The most common procedure for assessing readiness is to administer a diagnostic test—either teacher-made or standardized. Teacher-made diagnostic tests tend to lack validity; they reflect what the teacher expects the child to know. Standardized diagnostic tests are much more thorough, but they often test for knowledge and skills that are not developed in the particular classroom.

Garry (1963) suggests another way to determine readiness:

> Generally, a determination of readiness is made by introducing a task, or a sample of it, and checking rate of learning during early practice sessions. A slow rate of gain and low degree of retention indicates either lack of readiness or excessively difficult material, or both. Accelerated rate of gain and high degree of retention indicate material suitable to learning capacity [p. 22].

The concept of "readiness" means that the child's abilities, achievement, interests, and level of emotional development should be taken into account when developing and presenting classroom objectives. But the beginning teacher should be cautioned against a too-literal interpretation of the readiness principle. Both elementary-age children and adolescents are often "readier" than they appear to be. The anxiety and resistance often expressed at the start of an instructional unit—especially by adolescents—can easily be mistaken for lack of readiness.

THE IMPORTANCE OF METHODS

Most of the problems teachers have with their students concern difficulty in learning. Relatively few children behave badly in school if they are succeeding in school work and are getting positive feedback for their efforts. It is a mistake for the prospective teacher to approach the classroom with the view that, if he can just gain "control" of the students, he will be able to "teach" them something. Actually, it works the other way around. If the teacher provides a stimulating and successful learning environment, the students will "control" themselves. Those discipline problems that arise even when learning is going well can almost always be attributed to youthful antics and vitality. Teachers are hardly ever bothered significantly by the capers of high-spirited children, but the disrupting and rejecting behavior of uninterested learners is quite another story.

The more interesting he can make his subject, the more effective will be the teacher's control over the class. If a teacher must choose between being liked personally and organizing an interesting course of study, the latter goal should be the stronger influence on his behavior. Young people are naturally active and will respond to a multitude of stimuli in the classroom—including each other—unless the teacher can channel their curiosity toward goals that are more educational. This implies, also, that not following the lesson plan may sometimes be a wise decision. Getting off the subject can be a temporary excursion, or it can develop into a serious quest of interest and value to students. But it must be admitted that for every teacher—no matter how gifted—there are going to be "good" days and "bad" days. The behavior of children always has a degree of unpredictability, regardless of how exciting the instruction is.

ADVANCE ORGANIZERS

A concern frequently voiced by both elementary and secondary teachers whose objective is increased self-direction in learning is that students have considerable difficulty getting started. They want freedom to learn, but they seem to take an inordinate amount of time just getting off the ground.

Every experienced teacher knows that how effectively he introduces an instructional unit has a lot to do with the students' learning and retention. This is sometimes overlooked by the busy teacher who wants to "get on" with the instruction. Carefully planned introductory and anticipatory activities, called *advance organizers*, can bridge the gap between what the learner already knows and what he needs to learn (Ausubel, 1968, p. 148). They also provide a "learning set," or psychological expectation.

An advance organizer is not simply an outline of the main topics of new material. It may contain concepts and points of view abstracted from the material, or it may point out how previously learned, related concepts are different from, or similar to, the new ideas to be presented. Learning a few new concepts of higher generality or inclusiveness than the new information provides an organizational framework for the new material and facilitates learning. For example, the teacher who is trying to arouse interest in the cotton gin is better advised to begin by describing—or demonstrating—the basic way the cotton gin works instead of by telling the life story of the inventor. The working principles of the cotton gin provide a structure for reading subsequent material.

Using the study of Buddhism as the principal learning task, Wittrock (1963) got slightly poorer original learning and distinctly poorer retention of learning from students who were instructed merely to understand and remember the material being studied than for three groups of students who were instructed to note and remember similarities and differences between Buddhism and the Judeo-Christian tradition.

Another example of an advance organizer is the technique recommended by reading teachers for increasing comprehension in reading a textbook. The reader is advised first to skim the chapter and convert each subheading into a question. He then examines his list of questions carefully and begins reading for answers to these questions. Because he is reading systematically and sequentially, the "answer" to each question provides a contextual scaffold, or advance organizer, for the next question.

Research evidence suggests that advance organizers are especially effective with slow learners and students working in a field that is entirely new to them. They are least effective with students who have high ability or extensive knowledge related to what is to be learned (Ausubel, 1963; Ausubel and Youssef, 1963). Whether the teacher provides advance organizers or the student develops his own system, the point is that "learning set" is an important—perhaps the *most* important—component of any system of study skills. Without it, there is little hope of fostering genuinely self-directed learning.

EXPOSITORY TEACHING VS. INQUIRY

How students should be helped to learn is a matter of controversy today. Should they be helped through direct instruction or inquiry, expository teaching or exploratory learning?

The goal of expository teaching is primarily to prevent errors and focus attention on responses that will bring success, by demonstration, explanation, or criticism. Demonstration may involve putting the individual through the act. In teaching young children to write, for example, the instructor may direct a child's hand through the motions of forming letters. When teaching athletic skills, the instructor may turn the student's shoulders in a certain direction or place his arm in the correct position.

Teaching by demonstration also may involve performing an act in the presence of the learner and requiring him to imitate it. Many skills in physical-education classes and procedures in science, home economics, handwriting, art, and music are presented initially by demonstration. Very young children have been taught to play the violin by a method that initially requires them to watch a violinist on a television screen and imitate the bowing.

Explanation, generally oral, is the most common form of teaching in the classroom. It is flexible and, if done well, can be explicit and complete. Criticism consists of feeding back information on the students' successful performances and suggesting ways of eliminating errors by substitution of the correct response.

In most cases, demonstration, explanation, and criticism should follow each other in the order named, with the first two preceding the learner's attempts.

The method of expository teaching has been both supported and discredited. Many authorities favor learning by directed discovery (not totally independent), which is believed to increase the individual's ability to learn related materials, to create an interest in the task itself rather than in the external rewards associated with it, to develop initiative in attacking other kinds of tasks, to contribute to higher retention, and to make transfer of learning more probable (Bruner, 1961; Ausubel, 1963). Ray (1961) feels that the directed-discovery method can be used most effectively with low-ability students, and that the type and amount of guidance used should vary according to specific teaching situations, regardless of pupil ability.

Inquiry, or exploratory learning, continues to receive favorable attention in most current textbooks in elementary- and secondary-school methods. One argument is that it trains the student in important thinking operations, such as comparing, summarizing, interpreting, and criticizing. In other words, it teaches students how to learn. As one sixth-grade boy said, "We can give our own ideas and if someone thinks up an idea we don't always have to go along with it—we can do it another way." Another sixth-grader added: "You need to be able to look for lots of references and find out what they say. You can't just look at one book and say that's what it is, because I have seen lots of books that have different stories but are based on the same thing" (Hagen and Stansberry, 1969).

A three-year study of children progressing through the fifth, sixth, and seventh grades found that

> . . . the inquiry strategy appears to have had a continuing effect on the verbal behavior of this group of children over the three-year testing period. The children exposed to the technique changed in several measurable ways: verbal fluency and flexibility were increased, attention to detail became more acute, inferences as to invisible attributes showed a strong trend away from the emotional and locational responses and toward the inherent classificatory attributes, and each of these changes can reasonably be traced to a specific emphasis on the inquiry strategy used in this program [Scott, 1970].

Starr (1972), in a review of research, found no significant gains in critical thinking on the part of a heterogeneous group of pupils exposed to inquiry materials for biology. Reviewing another study, however, he found that the use of this same material with high-ability ninth-graders resulted in significant gains in critical thinking in comparison with similar students not using it.

Another summary of research on teaching inquiry techniques states that, although there is probably no single best method, teacher use of higher-level questions, open discussions, Socratic techniques, and analogies has been successful in developing student critical-thinking abilities (Decaroli, 1973).

A cogent argument for discovery learning has to do with transfer and retention, at least long-term retention. According to Slaughter (1969), inquiry skills do transfer, not method per se, but a kind of attitude, a sense of confidence in one's ability to handle data and to build test theories.

In a study of elementary-school pupils, Hendrix (1947–48) investigated two ways of learning a principle: Pupils in one group were encouraged to derive their own principles; pupils in the other were given authoritative statements of the principles they were expected to apply.

The greatest amount of transfer was achieved by those who had been encouraged to derive principles by their own efforts.

An overview of all the research on inquiry, or discovery, learning suggests that it has definite advantages under proper conditions: It improves thinking operations; it can contribute to critical thinking, creativity, and concept formation—especially with some guidance; it is effective in teaching course content; it teaches skills that transfer and results in good long-term retention; it motivates students and imparts self-confidence and enthusiasm; and it has been used effectively with deprived groups. The phrase "under proper conditions" is important, however, for learning by inquiry does require more time than by authoritarian instruction; it is also less effective for immediate recall. In addition, not all youngsters are equally suited for inquiry in terms of mental set or developmental level or background, and there are times when drill is necessary and effective. The perceptive teacher must judge when the "teachable moment" is at hand to stimulate discovery learning in students.

Despite the evidence that goal-directed discovery learning is generally superior to teacher-directed assignments, research suggests that most teachers, rather than use inquiry methods, prefer a pattern of classroom interaction in which they are the dominant speakers with recitation as the usual mode of student expression (Zevin, 1973). Teachers need to understand that the youngster who shares thoughtfully in the development of learning activities and the establishment of intellectual goals will improve his insight into, and attitude toward, the objectives of all instruction. Joint teacher-student planning helps the teacher to understand the different abilities, interests, and needs of students. For example, the teacher should draw on the students' experiences, using a series of thought questions to lead the students toward acquiring concepts and toward gaining insights into the solutions of problems. Encouragingly, research reveals that this type of assignment is superior to the conventional, dictated assignment (Mathis *et al.*, 1970).

Student involvement does not mean young people making decisions that are beyond their level of maturity, nor does it require that every youngster in the class be vocal during every assignment. But, the teacher may reduce his telling and ordering if he motivates the students to begin exploring the nature and the proper procedures of the new work. He might ask the students to draw on immediate as well as past experiences, as a means of helping them to comprehend the purpose, meaning, and usefulness of the confronting activity.

Student involvement also does not mean disengagement on the part of the teacher.

Student-identified involvement in the content of any subject can best be accomplished when the teacher can create an atmosphere in which the students and the teacher mutually identify the most relevant issues and proceed cooperatively to plan how best to investigate the topic. A student-centered approach to learning, as such, should not lead to a laissez-faire attitude on the part of the teacher, for the success of this approach relies heavily on carefully guided student participation in the learning situation. If we agree that man is interactive, not just reactive, the teacher must actively lead, guide, or facilitate structuring of the learning; however, the student's interests within the structure of the course, as well as those of the teacher, become the center of the class. Thus, when the classroom environment allows students to inquire into their perplexities and when students have a significant part to play in the selection and planning of learning experiences, conditions present should allow more meaningful learning to take place. [Wendel, 1970, p. 330.]

INDIVIDUAL "COGNITIVE STYLES"

No two children learn in the same way or at the same rate. Each child is distinctive not only in the speed and ease with which he learns but in cognitive style. The term "cognitive style" here refers to unique patterns of cognitive behavior resulting from the individual's own perceptual and conceptual organization of the external environment. For example, Davis and Klausmeier (1970) found that individuals differ in the way in which they solve a complex, visual problem. In their experiment, some high-school seniors analyzed the *Hidden Figures Test* in terms of its separate components; others tended to solve the problem by analyzing the total visual stimulus.

Kagan (1965), who has done a series of studies on the cognitive style of children, contends that some children are characteristically impulsive, while others are characteristically reflective. Impulsive children place a greater value on attaining quick success than on avoiding failure. They are attracted to high-risk situations. As they have a fast conceptual tempo, they tend to come forth with the first answer they can think of. Reflective children, on the other hand, take their time before they speak. They avoid situations that are potentially dangerous and may cause failure, humiliation, or harm. When tests of reading and inductive reasoning were administered to first- and second-graders, Kagan discovered that impulsive pupils made more errors than reflective pupils. He also found that impulsiveness is a relatively permanent and general trait that appears early in life and reveals itself consistently in a great variety of situations.

Lynn (1972) has advanced the hypothesis that nature combines with the usual process of acquiring feminine identification to produce a style of thinking and learning for females that differs measurably from the style characteristic of males. This hypothesis is based on the assumption that both male and female infants usually establish their initial and principal identification with the mother. Later, males tend to identify with a culturally defined masculine role, whereas females continue to identify with the mother, or with the feminine role in general. The male's task of achieving masculine role identification is considered a rather complex learning *problem*, whereas the female's task of achieving mother identification is a less complex learning *lesson*. According to this theory, the male "problem" stimulates considerable cognitive activity in the male child, and he is aided in his quest by his high energy level, his vigor, and his curiosity, all probably biologically rooted.

For the female child, learning the "lesson" does not constitute a major problem, according to Lynn, because it takes place in the context of a close personal relationship with the mother. One of the consequences of this process is that females are more motivated than males to learn in a social context (McClelland *et al.*, 1953). Another consequence is that females often show greater docility, passive acceptance, and dependence in learning situations.

Lynn emphasizes that whatever differences in cognitive style appear early in life are then considerably influenced by cultural reinforcement. He cites evidence of the success of learning strategies aimed at stimulating females to the same standard of active problem seeking and solving as that of males. Lynn suggests that one of the ways to achieve this is for schools to become more accepting of impulsive, active, and even aggressive intellectual behavior in girls.

Another example of individual differences in cognitive style is the well-known fact that a physical approach to learning is characteristic of the disadvantaged child. Such a child may learn to read better if he has opportunities to act out the words as well as hear them spoken by the teacher.

It may be difficult to classify a particular child in one category or another, but an awareness of differences in cognitive style may help the teacher to understand why a given technique seems to work better with one group of students than with another. For years, teachers and administrators have talked about the identification of individual differences in how children learn, but the tendency has been to blame poor achievement on the student's emotional block or personality conflict. Little attention has been given to how the child's learning could be improved simply by analyzing his learning style and adapting instructional techniques to meet his needs. This is a principle that is psychologically sound and has the ring of common-sense truth. Students *do* learn things in different ways, even when they are in the same classroom under the direction of the same teacher. Even children who have been preselected on the basis of IQ show large differences in learning rate. Yet, the fact that students will differ widely in rates of learning has not been an accepted principle in day-to-day classroom practice (Suppes, 1964).

Some of the major findings regarding individual differences in learning are as follows:

1. Children do not grow and learn at the same rate. As a group, boys mature less rapidly than girls; but, individually, both grow and learn at different rates.
2. Children learn continuously, although at different rates.
3. Children may learn well in one area and poorly in another.
4. Children at any given grade level vary widely in ability and achievement. The term "grade level" is often misinterpreted as implying an arbitrary standard of achievement for all. Parents and teachers must accept the concept of individual differences among children in a class.
5. The term "promotion" is misleading. Children mature naturally from one stage to another, physically, mentally, and educationally. They advance or mature in accordance with their potentialities and the opportunity for growth offered by the school. Each school decides how best to organize its classes so as to meet each child's needs for instruction (Wrightstone, 1969, p. 4).

TEACHING THE SLOW LEARNER

Perhaps one of the most difficult problems facing the teacher is how to deal with the slow learner. Probably 10–20 per cent of the students in a typical comprehensive secondary school are at the low-ability, or "remedial" level (Mueller and Frerichs, 1967). Slow learners in elementary school are more difficult to identify because the range of individual differences is not so great or so apparent as in the middle- and senior-high-school grades.

Wrightstone (1969) summarizes the characteristics of low-ability pupils as follows. While there are always exceptions to generalizations, the summary may serve as a guide to adaptation of instruction.

1. Low-ability pupils learn by simple mental processes. They are confused by too many approaches and by complex associations with a

topic. The instructional approach should be direct and uncomplicated.

2. Low-ability pupils prefer the concrete . . . to the abstract—the specific [to] the general. Instruction should be focused on the concrete and specific phases of a topic.

3. Low-ability pupils prefer brief units and specific assignments. It is wise to avoid long-range, general, and vague assignments that require a high level of organization.

4. Low-ability pupils possess limited powers of self-criticism. They should have systematic opportunities to discover and correct their errors. The learning process should be so organized that such pupils are not constantly overwhelmed but are enabled to proceed with order and certainty [p. 27].

INDIVIDUALIZING INSTRUCTION

The trend toward individualizing instruction is based on the broad study of individual differences from the points of view of biology, psychology, and the needs of society. Whether they reflect differences in genetic disposition, abilities, previously acquired skills, or personal life-style, it is clear that individual patterns of behavior and interests play an important role in learning (Newsom, Eischens, and Looft, 1972). The problem for the teacher is how to shape each child's educational program according to his unique learning needs.

At present, the most popular interpretation of individualized instruction is for the teacher to make specific recommendations and assignments for each pupil rather than teaching all pupils the same skill or concept simultaneously. Pupils progress at a self-determined pace, often studying self-selected subjects, in order to achieve self-established and evaluated goals (MacQueen, 1971). Jackson (1966) adds further details to this ideal conception:

Individualizing instruction, in the educator's sense, means injecting humor into a lesson when a student seems to need it and quickly becoming serious when he is ready to settle down to work; it means thinking of examples that are uniquely relevant to the student's previous experience and offering them at just the right time; it means feeling concerned over whether or not a student is progressing, and communicating that concern in a way that will be helpful; it means offering appropriate praise, not just because positive reinforcers strengthen response tendencies, but because the student's performance is deserving of human admiration; it means, in short, responding *as* an individual *to* an individual.

This objective is hardly ever achieved except in theory, however. Even in highly innovative schools, teachers are rarely able to work with fewer than three of four children at a time. In some cases, though, a student might pursue an objective entirely by himself at times during the school year.

In the typical individualized instructional program, there is a flexible mix of individual, small-group, and large-group activities, involving frequent conferences between the teacher and individual pupils or small groups of pupils. Temporary interest-centered groups develop, disbanding as they complete their plans. At times, the teacher meets the entire class—at his request or that of a student. A wide variety of materials in many media is available, including resources outside the classroom. The significant element in organizing and using resources is the cooperative planning of students and teachers.

The teacher's role in a school where the primary emphasis is on individualized instruction is obviously not exclusively that of transmitting information. The over-all objective is to make some provision for independent learning, and most teachers and school administrators recognize the potential that increased freedom has for enhancing student involvement. The limitation of current individualized programs is that they are usually available only under special conditions. Kreamer (1972) states that individualized programs, especially those operating in schools that have movable walls and large, open spaces, are more costly, because they require more instructional equipment and software. Schools have always allowed the pursuit of objectives on an individual basis by selected students, typically high-achieving students who are mature and responsible enough for unsupervised study. Currently, the hope is that all students can benefit from individualized, possibly independent, study.

How can the teacher individualize instruction when the school system has not yet been organized for that curricular purpose? A number of elementary and secondary schools have adopted the suggestion that ten minutes a day be devoted to "doing something different."

There is never any problem of finding ten minutes to play with, since what the pupils "must cover" is usually padded in order to fill up time. During that ten minutes, present the class with a number of things they can choose to do. Present them with options you feel may interest them. Allow them the option of sitting and doing nothing if they choose. Moreover, make it clear that nothing done during that period will be graded, and nothing need be shown or explained to the teacher. That ten minutes is to be their time and is to be respected as such. Step out of the way and observe the things your pupils choose to do.

Step out of the way, but don't disappear. Make it clear that you won't tell people what to do or how to do it, but that you will be available to help in any way you can, or just to talk. For ten minutes cease to be a teacher and be an adult with young people, a resource available if needed, and possibly a friend, but not a director, a judge, or an executioner. Also try to make it possible for the ten minutes to grow to fifteen, twenty, so long as it makes sense to you and your pupils. . . . Those ten minutes may become the most important part of the day, and after a while may even become the school day.

Some specific hints on the use of the ten minutes:

—in English class it is possible to read, write (set three or four themes and leave it open for students to develop other ones), talk, act.
—in mathematics the students can set problems, solve problems, build computers, compute, design buildings (or other structures or things), talk about money, set problems for each other and the teacher.
—in social studies it is possible to talk about history; about newspapers, events, people; write about them; compose or listen to poems; play songs about them; talk or invite people in to talk about what is happening.
—in all classes students can do nothing, gossip, write, start a newspaper or a newsletter, listen to music, dance, talk about or play games, bring in things that may interest the teacher or other students and talk about them, write about them. [Kohl, 1972, pp. 71–72.]

Another possibility is to adopt one of the available programs that utilize computer technology in scheduling and program feedback for the student. The Westinghouse PLAN (Program for Learning in Accordance with Needs), introduced in 1967, is designed to assist the teacher in assigning appropriate learning tasks to students according to their needs and abilities and in setting up appropriate ways of accomplishing these learning tasks. It is not intended that the student learn in isolation; but, depending on need, he may learn through small- or large-group activities, teacher-led activities, or independent study, whichever is most appropriate.

There were an estimated 40–50,000 children in PLAN during the 1972–73 school year. Westinghouse Learning Corporation estimates a student PLAN population of one million by 1976 (Wilson, 1972).

The other program, Individually Prescribed Instruction (IPI), which is currently used by an estimated 75,000 students in 264 schools in the United States, is based largely on its own curriculum and uses computer assistance extensively (*Education, U.S.A.,* 1970). IPI allows students to cover a prescribed body of knowledge at their own rates.

Under both programs, the student is introduced to new content by a number of approaches—workbooks, small groups, teaching machines, teacher-led discussions, tape recordings, visual projections, and so on— and is allowed to proceed at his own rate of learning. If he does not complete the prescribed body of content within a specific time, the teacher may revise the objectives; but seldom is the student allowed to discontinue the sequence.

These and similar learning systems are individualized in the sense that each student can work independent of every other student of his age and grade. He is active and self-directing only to the extent that the teacher exerts strenuous efforts to help him continually revise and adjust his goals and learning activities to fit his needs closely. The intention of such programs is a teacher-student relationship in which the teacher—and the school system—is supremely responsive to the cognitive and affective needs of the individual. This may be done either formally or informally; but it always centers on the student.

INDEPENDENT LEARNING

The ultimate goal of individualizing instruction is for the student to work toward an instructional goal independent of classroom restrictions or any bureaucratic restraint. In the past, this has rarely been possible, except on an informal basis. High-school seniors—usually the high-achieving, mature students—have always had a lot of freedom around the school building in the months approaching graduation day. But at all other grade levels, the heavily structured, supervised atmosphere of classroom has exerted a chilling effect on student freedom and self-expression. As the principal of an English prep school told a group of incoming students, "Our policy on student behavior is simple—freedom tempered with expulsion!"

How beneficial have the efforts to allow more independent learning been? A review of current research as well as personal reports from teachers and school administrators reveals a mixed bag.

The movement toward nongraded, individual-progression programs at the elementary level is unquestionably gathering momentum throughout the United States. Most elementary schools are trying to do something to meet the individual needs of the children; some schools have developed innovative practices such as independent study and informal learning activities. Research evidence so far suggests that children in these schools learn at least as much as those in traditionally organized, self-contained classrooms (Godde, 1972). No studies have revealed dramatic gains in pupil achievement in skills and knowledge, but teachers and school administrators do report gains in social and emotional behavior (Rookey and Valdes, 1972).

The middle schools are quite literally in the middle on this question. Individualization has been difficult because the children are in a transitional phase as regards mental and emotional readiness for independent learning, and most of them still need considerable work on reading, math, and library skills. Nevertheless, many middle-school authorities fervently believe that children of this age need more opportunities for self-direction.

At present the senior high school poses the most perplexing challenge. Research evidence appears to be quite ambiguous (Patterson, 1973). Congreve (1963, 1965) reported cautious optimism regarding the results of an independent learning experiment at the University of Chicago laboratory school. Students had "satisfactory" achievement in subject matter, yet Congreve admitted that these results were based mostly on subjective evaluations by teachers.

The Secondary Commission of the North Central Association, the major high-school accrediting agency, sponsored a study of the effects of flexible or modular scheduling on high-school students' achievement (Cawelti, 1969). Eleven high schools with flexible time schedules were compared with eleven schools with traditional schedules. The schools varied in the size of the student body from two hundred to two thousand or more. One variable under investigation was the extent to which students' learning was affected by having varying amounts of unscheduled time. The findings suggest that academic achievement is at least as good, and often better, when students are given increased freedom within the school day.

On the other hand, there appears to be a slight trend among innovative high schools toward cutting back on individualized instructional programs. There is evidence that many adolescents—some of them normally high-achieving youth—do not improve their skills under conditions of unsupervised, self-directed learning; some even achieve less than they did in a traditionally organized schedule. But the decision to cut back on the amounts of independent study time apparently is a difficult one, for many students *do* perform quite well under conditions of greater self-determination (Congreve and Rinehart, 1972, p. 20).

The general principle of individualizing instruction in secondary school is widely accepted; the optimal amount of unsupervised learning is vigorously debated. Dr. Gordon L. Cawelti, Executive Secretary

of the Association for Supervision and Curriculum Development of the
National Education Association, offers the following view:

> Adoption of the flexible schedule has made progress in overcoming a
> serious weakness in American high schools—the inability of the tradi-
> tional schedule to accommodate increasing student diversity in inter-
> ests and aptitudes for learning. It has, however, stopped short of the
> fullest development that can be expected. The innovation was designed
> to help individualize the curriculum, yet most schools have only made
> a bare start in developing the self-instructive curriculum materials
> needed when one suddenly turns students loose. To expect that all stu-
> dents will make effective use of their new freedom is nonsense, but
> to expect students to do it without outlining manageable tasks for in-
> dependent study is also not realistic [1969, p. 30].

REFERENCES

AUSUBEL, D. P. 1963. *The psychology of meaningful verbal learning.* New
York: Grune & Stratton.

———. 1968. *Educational psychology: A cognitive view.* New York: Holt,
Rinehart & Winston.

AUSUBEL, D. P., and M. YOUSSEF. 1963. Role of discriminality in meaningful parallel learning. *Journal of Educational Psychology, 54,* 331–36.

BIGGE, M. L., and M. P. HUNT. 1968. *Psychological foundations of education.* New York: Harper & Row.

BLOOM, B. S. (ed.). 1956. *Taxonomy of educational objectives: Handbook
I: Cognitive domain.* New York: David McKay.

BROUDY, H. S. 1970. Can research escape the dogma of behavioral objectives? *School Review, 79(1),* 43–56.

BRUNER, J. S. 1961. The act of discovery. *Harvard Educational Review, 31,*
21–32.

CAWELTI, G. L. 1973. Personal communication to the author. October 29.
Applied Research in Education.

COMMITTEE FOR THE WHITE HOUSE CONFERENCE ON EDUCATION. 1956.
Report to the President. Washington, D.C.: U.S. Government Printing
Office.

CONGREVE, W. J. 1963. Toward independent learning. *North Central Quarterly, 37,* 298–302.

———. 1965. Independent learning. *North Central Quarterly, 40,* 222–28.

CONGREVE, W. J., and G. J. RINEHART (eds.). 1972. *Flexibility in school
programs.* Worthington, Ohio: Jones.

DAVIS, J. K., and H. J. KLAUSMEIER. 1970. Cognitive style and concept
identification as a function of complexity and training procedures. *Journal
of Educational Psychology, 61,* 423–30.

DAVIS, R. A. 1968. *Learning in the schools*. Belmont, Calif.: Wadsworth.

DECAROLI, J. 1973. What research says to the classroom teacher: Critical thinking. *Social Education*, January, 68, 67–69.

Education, U.S.A. 1970. Washington, D.C.: February.

GAGNE, R. M. 1964. The implications of instructional objectives for learning. In C. M. Lindvall (ed.), *Defining educational objectives*. Pittsburgh: University of Pittsburgh Press.

GARRY, R. 1963. *The psychology of learning*. Washington, D.C.: Center for Applied Research in Education.

GODDE, J. 1972. A comparison of young children in achievement of general skills, adjustment, and attitudes, in an individual progression curriculum organization with young children in a traditional curriculum organization. Unpublished doctoral dissertation, Northern Illinois University, De Kalb.

HAGEN, O. A., and S. T. STANSBERRY. 1969. Why inquiry? *Social Education*, May, 33(5), 534–37.

HENDRIX, G. 1947–48. A new clue to transfer of training. *Elementary School Journal*, 48, 197–208.

JACKSON, P. W. 1966. The teacher and the machine: Observations of the impact of educational technology. Mimeographed, University of Chicago.

KAGAN, J. 1965. Impulsive and reflective children: Significance of conceptual tempo. In J. D. Krumboltz (ed.), *Learning and the educational process*. Chicago: Rand McNally, 133–43, 154–56.

KIBLER, R. J., L. L. BARKER, and D. T. MILES. 1970. *Behavioral objectives and instruction*. Boston: Allyn & Bacon.

KOHL, H. R. 1972. *The open classroom*. New York: Vintage Books.

KREAMER, R. 1972. Schools open up. *Education Digest*, October, 38(2), 25–27.

LYNN, D. B. 1972. Determinants of intellectual growth in women. *School Review*, February, 80(2), 241–60.

McCLELLAND, D. C., J. W. ATKINSON, R. A. CLARK, and E. L. LOWELL. 1953. *The achievement motive*. New York: Appleton-Century-Crofts.

MACQUEEN, M. 1971. Individualized instruction. *Education Digest*, 36, 25–28.

MATHIS, A., et al. 1970. College students' attitudes toward computer-assisted instruction. *Journal of Educational Psychology* 61(1), 46–57.

MUELLER, R. J., and A. H. FRERICHS. 1967. Alienation in the low-ability classroom. *School and Society*, 95, 254–56.

NEWSOM, R. S., R. EISCHENS, and W. R. LOOFT. 1972. Intrinsic individual differences: A basis for enhancing instructional programs. *Journal of Educational Research*, 65, 387–93.

OJEMANN, R. H. 1968. Should educational objectives be stated in behavioral terms? *Elementary School Journal*, February, 68(5), 223–31.

PATTERSON, J. L. 1973. Why has nongradedness eluded the high schools? *Clearing House*, March, 47(7), 392–96.

POPHAM, W. J. 1972. Objectives-based management strategies for the large educational systems. *Journal of Educational Research, 66,* 4–9.

————. 1972a. Must all objectives be behavioral? *Educational Leadership, 29,* 605–8.

RATHS, J. D. 1968. Specificity as a threat to curriculum reform. Paper read at the Annual Meeting of the American Educational Research Association, Chicago, February.

RAY, W. E. 1961. Pupil discovery and diverse instruction. *Journal of Experimental Education, 29,* 271–80.

ROOKEY, T. J., and A. L. VALDES. 1972. *A study of individually prescribed instruction and the affective domain.* Philadelphia: Research for Better Schools, Inc.

SCOTT, N. 1970. Strategy of inquiry and styles of categorization: A three-year exploratory study. *Journal of Research in Science Teaching, 2,* 95.

SLAUGHTER, C. H. 1969. Cognitive style: Some implications for curriculum and instructional practices among Negro children. *Journal of Negro Education,* Spring, 38(2), 105–11.

STARR, R. J. 1972. Structured oral inquiry improves thinking. *American Biology Teacher,* October, 34(7), 408–9.

SUPPES, P. 1964. Modern learning theory and the elementary school curriculum. *American Educational Research Journal, 1,* 79–93, 504–5.

WENDEL, R. L. 1970. Developing climates for learning. *Journal of Secondary Education, 45,* 330–31.

WILSON, E. P. 1972. Development of a teacher attitude scale for use with teachers in Program for Learning in Accordance with Needs (P.L.A.N.). Unpublished doctoral dissertation, Northern Illinois University, De Kalb.

WITTROCK, M. C. 1963. Effects of certain sets upon complex verbal learning. *Journal of Educational Psychology, 54,* 85–88.

WRIGHTSTONE, J. W. 1969. Class organization for instruction. In *What research says to the teacher.* Washington, D.C.: Association of Classroom Teachers, National Education Association.

ZEVIN, J. 1973. Training teachers in inquiry. *Social Education, 37,* 310–16.

CHAPTER TEN

Performance Assessment

NATURE has never created two human beings exactly alike. Each is unique, with his own strengths and weaknesses. The basic purpose of performance assessment and other forms of human measurement is to enable us to learn more about ourselves. Today, a multitude of measures is available to help an adult or child to know who he is and how his abilities and competencies compare with those of his fellows. The elementary-school pupil can find out how well he is acquiring the basic tools of learning, such as reading and arithmetic skills. The high-school student can get a reasonable estimate of how likely he is to succeed in various specific endeavors. One student may discover that he is strong in scientific knowledge and logical reasoning, poor in mechanical skills, and average in the use of language. Another may find out that his mechanical-aptitude score puts him in the top .1 per cent of the population.

Industries, the armed forces, and other institutions use various measurement and evaluation procedures to place people in positions in which they are most likely to succeed, to classify people for certification or promotion, to assess the effectiveness of training programs, and for other purposes. Schools use performance assessment and other measures (1) to help students identify their strengths and weaknesses; (2) to guide them toward appropriate course choices or remediation; (3) to place students in sections at appropriate levels; (4) to determine the relative effectiveness of specific courses, teaching procedures, and curriculums; (5) to determine and report to parents the progress of students; (6) to identify the performance level of students for employers, post-high-school education, and other clients; (7) as positive, immediate reinforcement to enhance motivation; and (8) as a learning experience in itself, in which the student is motivated to bring together all that he knows and then exercise thinking skills.

Until the present century, schools attempted to fulfill these functions largely by casual observation, subjective judgment, and random practices. Today, performance assessment is a scientific endeavor within the discipline of education.

Performance assessment involves both measurement, the process by which we quantify the behaviors or characteristics that we have chosen to observe and record, and evaluation, the determination of the meaning of the raw scores. Educational measurement is frequently carried out by means of tests, but it may also be done with rating scales, checklists, and inventories that yield quantitative data. Tests and other instruments may be constructed by teachers or they may be purchased by the school from commercial firms that specialize in developing measurement devices.

An important part of evaluation is assessing how well a student has attained given objectives of instruction—that is, whether the instruction has changed him in any significant way. Evaluation inevitably involves a value judgment in determining, on the basis of a variety of types of relevant information, whether there has been progress toward a goal, the worth of a program, or how to make an appropriate placement decision. In measurement, on the other hand, an effort is made to minimize personal judgment. For example, measurement techniques may reveal that a given student has achieved a performance that represents a percentile rank of 68 in comparison with others in the class who took the same test. Evaluation is the process by which the instructor appraises the adequacy of the performance—e.g., whether it deserves an A, B, C, or a failing grade.

Evaluation may involve comparisons with others or with some predetermined standard ("norms"); it may use the student as his own standard—for example, the change in his performance over a period of time, or his performance as a function of his previously determined aptitude or ability level; or performance may be judged in terms of a standard that the teacher has developed as a result of his own experience and expertise.

Like measurement, evaluation is always based on the designated goals and objectives of instruction. Once the objectives of instruction are defined, the teacher can turn to the development of classroom activities and procedures to bring about the achievement of these goals. For example, a fifth-grade teacher developed an instructional unit designed to help children to understand the significance of the Age of Exploration—the complex religious, economic, and political motivation of the mother countries; the problems of colonizing and, in many cases, exploiting native peoples, and so on. This objective was then broken down into specific tasks or behaviors—knowing the names of the principal explorers, the countries in which they originated, the dates of their voyages, the lands or territories they discovered and claimed, and the importance of each voyage and discovery. The teacher then developed activities corresponding to these behavioral objectives, including a game of charades, tracing voyages on a map, a film, and some readings. Finally, she constructed a test to measure the students' ability to identify significant explorers, dates, and countries, and to understand the general importance of the Age of Exploration. She followed the testing procedure with a general discussion period to determine subjectively whether the children had developed an awareness of the complex issues of exploration and colonization.

Obviously, the example is oversimplified. But it shows that the objective of instruction makes it clear what will need to be measured, and that instructional procedures suggest the specifics of measurement.

Accomplishment of the objective can be measured by the presence of certain indicators or observable behaviors. Such indices are usually correct responses on a test, and their presence is assumed to indicate that the intended learning has taken place. Virtually any unit of course content can probably yield a larger number of potential questions than can be included in an examination. Thus, most tests are composed of a selection of possible questions. The questions chosen must provide an adequate and representative sample of the course content in order to lead to a fair assessment of a student's performance. Both the degree of difficulty and the content of the questions should be representative of what has already occurred in the course. Ideally, a test would be composed of items that vary from easy to difficult and that test a variety of thinking skills, such as basic recall, the ability to synthesize materials, problem solving, and generalization.

Thus, a strategy of performance assessment consists of a number of basic steps: (1) defining the over-all objective; (2) subdividing this objective into specific behaviors; (3) identifying the indicators that will serve as evidence that the student knows the information and can perform the skills involved (i.e., has learned the appropriate behaviors); (4) designing instructional procedures and activities that will lead to these terminal behaviors; and (5) developing an assessment procedure that adequately samples all levels of learning, from basic knowledge to high-level values and attitudes.

FACTORS IN MEASUREMENT

The performance of students on testing measures is a function of many variables, not the least of which is the quality of the measurement instrument itself. Learning that results from clearly stated objectives and well-planned instruction will be unrecorded if the test is inadequate.

There are four essential components of a good measuring instrument for educational purposes—an objective scoring procedure, validity, reliability, and suitability.

OBJECTIVE SCORING

An objective scoring procedure means that the student's score is independent of the personal bias or subjective judgment of the teacher. A test score should not reflect any factors other than the subject's achievement in relation to the stated goals of the course. For example, if the stated objectives omit the requirement of neatness, then the student who is given a low grade because his paper is messy has been unfairly assessed. Standardized procedures for the administration and scoring of tests are intended to lessen the effects of such factors so as to increase the objectivity of the procedure.

VALIDITY

Validity refers to a test's accuracy, or the degree to which it actually measures what it is supposed to measure. Educational tests are generally intended to measure achievement, intelligence, or values and attitudes. The complexity of these traits necessitates a close examination of the validity of assessment procedures. According to Ary and his colleagues (1972), to ensure validity, educators should ask the following questions:

How well do the chemistry tests measure the chemistry achievements of pupils? Can my creativity test really separate the highly creative people from the less creative? Could we make predictions based on scores made on those tests? Does this test measure other qualities as well? Is it an appropriate instrument for use with all pupils, or should it only be used with certain groups? These questions all concern aspects of the validity of the test [p. 191].

Four types of validity are involved in educational and psychological measurement. *Content* validity is the extent to which a test adequately represents the subject-matter content or behavior to be measured. A history teacher might tell his students that the important things to know about the Civil War are its causes and outcomes. But, if he tests them only on recall of specific names and dates, he has given them a test that does not reflect the objectives he designated as important. The teacher should assess the validity of the test in relation to his course objectives and content.

Predictive validity is the accuracy with which the score on a measure can be used to predict an individual's behavior in a specified situation. This type of validity is especially important in selecting and classifying people for future employment or education. Predictive validity is not a function of judgment but can be established empirically by correlating test scores with some measure of future success. If a test is an accurate predictor of future performance in a specific educational or occupational setting, then it is said to have predictive validity.

Concurrent validity represents the extent to which a measure approximates the results of another criterion available at the same time. For example, one might compare the results of a math achievement test with students' concurrent math performance in class. Predictive validity involves future measures, while concurrent validity relates to presently available measures.

Construct validity is the extent to which a test measures the construct, or trait, that is the basis of the test performance. According to Van Dalen, a construct is an "ability, aptitude, trait, or characteristic that is hypothesized to explain some aspect of human behavior, such as mechanical ability, intelligence, or introversion" (1966, pp. 314–15). A construct is thus an abstraction based on particular factors. Its existence is inferred from many behaviors, none of which by itself is sufficient to indicate that a person possesses the construct. For example, a student can be described as "intelligent" as a result of the observation or sampling of his behavior in a wide variety of situations. No single observation of behavior is sufficient basis to infer that he is intelligent.

A construct is usually embedded in a theory that certain specific outcomes will occur if the construct is present. In other words, the construct is defined both theoretically and behaviorally. For example, people who are very intelligent should answer more questions correctly on an intelligence test than people who are less so. In addition, if the construct of intelligence states that the intellectual abilities of children increase with age, then test results should show improved performance with age. A test of intelligence that yields results consistent with these predictions and that reflects the other characteristics of intelligence as described or predicted from the theory would be said to have construct validity.

To take another example: A theory describing the construct "anxiety" might specify that anxious people are characterized by perceptual rigidity, limited involvement with others, minimal tolerance for ambiguity, and infrequent manifestations of divergent, or creative, thinking. The construct validity of a test of anxiety is established when it results in empirical findings that are consistent with these theoretical predictions.

RELIABILITY

Reliability is another qualitative aspect of measurement, referring to the degree to which the results of an instrument are consistent or stable. However, it is not the same as validity. If one were to determine a student's achievement in history on the basis of a measurement of his shoe size, the measure would be reliable but not valid. Reliability in educational measurement is like using a precisely calibrated measuring cup to dole out sugar when cooking. Adding sugar by the "pinch" would be a highly unreliable way of sweetening the batter, although still "valid." Thus, a measure can be reliable (stable) and yet, from the standpoint of validity, way off the mark. A test, however, cannot be valid unless it is also reliable.

One can estimate the degree of reliability in a score by means of the standard error of measurement (SEM) previously established for the measurement instrument that is used. If an individual were to take a given test several times, his scores, assuming no practice effects, would, in theory, fluctuate randomly around the hypothetical "true" score, estimated by averaging the scores he received in the repeated administration of the test. The individual's observed scores will fluctuate above and below his true score.

We can never know an individual's true score for any measurement. We have only the score or scores we observe. The SEM provides a statistical way of estimating the probability that the subject's true score lies within a band of scores. For example, if Jennifer has an observed score of 108 on an intelligence test that has a SEM of 5, it can be stated that there is—on the basis of a normal-curve distribution—a 68-per-cent probability that her true score lies between 103 and 113 (the observed score plus or minus one SEM), or that there is a 95-per-cent probability that her true score lies between 98 and 118 (the observed score plus or minus two SEM). The chances that Jennifer's true score will be greater than 118 or less than 98 are only about 5 in 100. For practical purposes, Jennifer's IQ should be reported as 108 ± 5, in order to indicate both her observed score and the size of the SEM. This provides the basis for an evaluation of the reliability of this particular measure of IQ.

Random score fluctuation may be due to any number of things, including the varying emotional and physical state of the student, the physical conditions of the testing room, chance variations in scoring or administration procedures, and the length of the test. If the test is a reliable measure of the individual's true score, the teacher can have a high degree of confidence in any evaluation based on that measure.

Test data, whether from an IQ test, an achievement test for basic skills, aptitude-test battery, or a personality-characteristics inventory, are usually reported in terms of derived scores or norms. Valid interpretation of norm scores, however, must include consideration of both the accuracy and the consistency of the test instrument.

SUITABILITY

However accurate a test may be in measuring what it is supposed to measure, it must be suitable in terms of the time, energy, skill, and money required to administer it. The practical features of testing require realistic consideration. There can be false economy in educational measurement as elsewhere.

A test must be reasonably inexpensive to administer and score, and suitable for use by teachers who may or may not be skilled in test administration. The value of the information yielded by the test should be carefully weighed. Once it is determined that a test does, in fact, meet the requirements of validity and reliability, the norm scales should be considered just as carefully. Norms are fundamental to the interpretation of any test score; they provide the basic source of meaning.

BASIC STATISTICS

A test result, as we have pointed out, is initially in the form of a raw score—usually the number of items answered correctly. The raw score has meaning, however, only by comparison with a standard of performance, generally called a "norm." The norm is the average or expected score for children at a particular age or grade level.

Norms are developed by measuring a representative group of people. Their performance is then used to establish the expected scores for people in that group who take the test in the future. Future scores are then compared to this expected score value to see where they are in relation to the norm. Tests that have normative-based scoring systems require that a raw score be translated into a norm scale of some type, such as percentiles, standard scores, grade equivalents, or IQs. A derived score indicates the individual's position on the scale relative to the norm or expected score for his group.

Statistics are mathematical tools used for the analysis of data. They allow one to describe and interpret measurement data succinctly; they are one of the ways by which researchers "tease out" the significance of the knowledge conveyed by the data.

MEASURES OF CENTRAL TENDENCY

One way of describing a score is in terms of its relation to the average score for that group of measures. In statistics, there are three measures of central tendency or average: *mode, median,* and *mean.*

The *mode* is the single score that occurs most frequently in the group measured. In the following set of scores on a 10-item spelling quiz taken by 14 students, 7 is the mode because it occurs more frequently than any other score:

Spelling-Quiz Scores: 1, 2, 2, 4, 5, 6, 6, 7, 7, 7, 8, 8, 9, 9, 10

Notice, however, that the mode would be altered greatly if one of the students scored 2 instead of 7. Indeed, one of the disadvantages of the mode is that it is unstable. Also, since it reflects the position of only one score—that which occurs most frequently—it doesn't communicate much information. Its chief value is that it provides a rough estimate of where most of the scores are located.

The *median* is the exact mid-point of a group of scores. Equal to the 50th percentile, it is the point above and below which 50 per cent of the scores are found. It is therefore based on the rank order of scores. It does not, however, reflect the magnitude of scores. Thus, it is not subject to the "pulling" effect of extreme scores. It is useful for indicating the most typical score in a distribution.

The *mean* is the arithmetical average of a group of scores. It is found by adding all the scores and dividing the sum by N, the number of scores summed. The formula for the mean is

$$\overline{X} = \frac{\Sigma X_i}{N}$$

where $\overline{X}$ = the mean

Σ = the process of summing or adding

X_i = the individual scores in a group

N = the total number of scores summed.

The mean takes all the scores in a group into consideration and may be subject to the "pulling" effect of extreme scores. For example, the median income in a small town may be $8,500 while the mean income for the town is $50,000, since two millionaires happen to live there. The median is not "pulled"· up by these extremes and, in fact, indicates the income that is more typical of the townspeople.

MEASURES OF VARIABILITY

Measurement processes communicate not only a score's position relative to the norm or mean for a group but also the manner and extent to which a group of scores are dispersed or scattered around their norm or mean. Indeed, each of the following three sets of scores has a mean of 10, but they differ in their variability around that mean:

Set #1	Set #2	Set #3
25	15	12
7	15	11
12	15	10
7	5	10
4	7	9
5	3	8

$$\overline{X} = \frac{60}{6} = 10 \qquad \overline{X} = \frac{60}{6} = 10 \qquad \overline{X} = \frac{60}{6} = 10$$

Statistics that communicate variability are therefore necessary to obtain more nearly complete information about a group of scores. *Range* and *standard deviation* are measures of variability frequently used in educational and psychological performance assessment.

The *range* is equal to the number of score units between the highest and lowest scores. The formula for the range is

$$R = X_h - X_l$$

where X_h = the highest score

X_l = the lowest score

R = the range.

In the three sets of scores above, the respective ranges would be calculated as follows:

Set #1	Set #2	Set #3
$R = X_h - X_l$	$R = X_h - X_l$	$R = X_h - X_l$
$R = 25 - 4$	$R = 15 - 3$	$R = 12 - 8$
$R = 21$	$R = 12$	$R = 4$

This measure indicates the distance covered by, or the breadth of, a group of scores. Since, however, a major shift in either the highest or the lowest score would cause a considerable shift in the value of the range, this is an unstable measure of variability. It is based on only two scores—the highest and the lowest.

The standard deviation (SD) is probably the most commonly employed measure of variability. Its basic component is the deviation score, which is equal to the difference between each observed score and the mean for the group. The formula for the deviation score is

$$x = X_i - \overline{X}$$

where X_i = observed score(s)

$\overline{X}$ = the mean for the group

x = the deviation score.

In the three sets of scores above, the deviation scores would be calculated as follows:

Set #1			Set #2			Set #3		
X	$\overline{X}$	x	X	$\overline{X}$	x	X	$\overline{X}$	x
25	− 10	= +15	15	− 10	= +5	12	− 10	= +2
7	− 10	= −3	15	− 10	= +5	11	− 10	= +1
12	− 10	= +2	15	− 10	= +5	10	− 10	= 0
7	− 10	= −3	5	− 10	= −5	10	− 10	= 0
4	− 10	= −6	7	− 10	= −3	9	− 10	= −1
5	− 10	= −5	3	− 10	= −7	8	− 10	= −2
	$\Sigma x = 0$			$\Sigma x = 0$			$\Sigma x = 0$	

To compute the standard deviation, one must first square each of the deviation scores, since their sum would otherwise be zero. These squares are then added together, and the resultant sum is divided by the number of scores in the group. This yields the *variance*. The formula for the calculation is

$$V = \frac{\Sigma x^2}{N}$$

where V = the variance
Σ = the process of summing
N = the number of scores in the group
x^2 = each deviation score squared.

The variance for each of our sets of scores is calculated as follows:

Set #1	Set #2	Set #3
$+15^2 = 125$	$+5^2 = 25$	$+2^2 = 4$
$-3^2 = 9$	$+5^2 = 25$	$-1^2 = 1$
$+2^2 = 4$	$+5^2 = 25$	$0^2 = 0$
$-3^2 = 9$	$-5^2 = 25$	$0^2 = 0$
$-6^2 = 36$	$-3^2 = 9$	$-1^2 = 1$
$-5^2 = 25$	$-7^2 = 49$	$-2^2 = 4$
$x^2 = 208$	$x^2 = 158$	$x^2 = 10$
$V_1 = \dfrac{\Sigma x^2}{N}$	$V_2 = \dfrac{\Sigma x^2}{N}$	$V_3 = \dfrac{\Sigma x^2}{N}$
$V_1 = \dfrac{208}{10}$	$V_2 = \dfrac{158}{10}$	$V_3 = \dfrac{10}{10}$
$V_1 = 20.8$	$V_2 = 15.8$	$V_3 = 1$

The variance statistic, thus derived, is in squared units. Extraction of the square root of the variance yields the standard deviation. The formula for the standard deviation is

$$SD = \sqrt{\frac{\Sigma x^2}{N}}$$

where Σ = the process of summing
N = the number of scores in the group
x^2 = each deviation score squared
SD = the standard deviation.

Thus, the standard deviation of the three sets of scores is calculated as follows:

Set #1	Set #2	Set #3
$SD = \sqrt{\dfrac{\Sigma x^2}{N}}$	$SD = \sqrt{\dfrac{\Sigma x^2}{N}}$	$SD = \sqrt{\dfrac{\Sigma x^2}{N}}$
$SD = \sqrt{\dfrac{208}{10}}$	$SD = \sqrt{\dfrac{158}{10}}$	$SD = \sqrt{\dfrac{10}{10}}$
$SD = \sqrt{20.8}$	$SD = \sqrt{15.8}$	$SD = \sqrt{1}$
$SD = 4.55$	$SD = 3.97$	$SD = 1$

The standard deviation is a useful tool, yielding much information. For example, if one knows the mean and the standard deviation of a group of scores, he can easily determine what percentage of scores to expect within any given portion of the distribution. If the mean for a group of scores is 10 and the $SD = 1$, then 95 per cent of the scores will fall between 8 and 12—that is, 10 ± 2 SD. Likewise, one can determine that the score of 12 is located precisely at $+2$ SD, or at about the 98th percentile. Thus, the standard deviation allows one to describe the general distribution of a group of scores and also to indicate the position of specific scores in reference to the mean. Further, it permits one to estimate the percentage of scores that are expected to fall above or below a particular score.

CORRELATION

Correlation refers to the degree of relationship that exists between sets of scores. For example, if we had both the reading scores and the IQs for a class of students, we would expect the scores to be related, or correlated, since students who read well tend also to have high IQs. The relationship can be demonstrated on a bivariate graph as shown in Figure 10.1. The graph shows that there is a tendency for students with high IQ scores to have high reading scores as well; for students with moderate IQs to be in the middle range in reading; and for students with low IQs to have depressed reading scores.

The relationship between two sets of scores can be represented numerically by means of a correlation coefficient, which will range from -1.0 to $+1.0$. A correlation coefficient of $+1.0$ indicates the presence of a perfect positive relationship; as one set of measures increases, so does the other, in perfect unison. The individual who received the

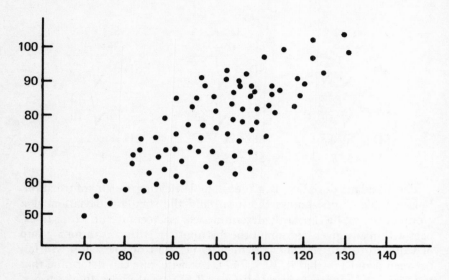

Fig. 10.1. Correlation of reading scores and IQ scores.

highest score on the first measure also received the highest score on the second; the person who received the next highest score on the first measure also received the next highest score on the second measure; and so on. This relationship is shown in Figure 10.2.

A correlation coefficient of -1.0 indicates a perfect negative (or inverse) relationship. That is, the individual who received the highest score on one measure received the lowest score on the other; the individual who received the next highest score on the first measure received the next lowest score on the other measure; and so on. As one set of measures increases, the other decreases in perfect unison. This relationship is represented in Figure 10.3. There are many instances in education of a negative correlation of traits and behaviors. For example, for children as a group, weight correlates negatively with physical agility.

A correlation coefficient of zero indicates that there is no measurable tendency for two sets of scores to be related. That is, there is no tendency for them to vary systematically in relationship to each other.

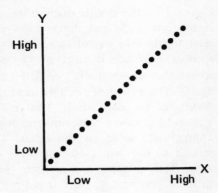

Fig. 10.2. Perfect positive correlation (+1).

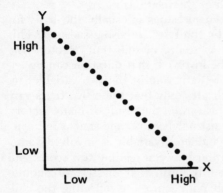

Fig. 10.3. Perfect negative correlation (−1).

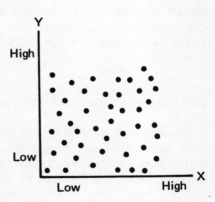

Fig. 10.4. Zero correlation.

Figure 10.4 shows this distribution of scores. The degree to which a correlation coefficient differs from zero indicates the strength of the relationship—the extent to which the varying of the two sets of scores approaches unison in either an inverse or a positive relationship. Sets of scores that are partially correlated are represented in Figures 10.5, 6, and 7. The extent of the relationship is an indication of the predictive powers of the correlation. That is, once the correlation coefficient is known, a person's score on one measure can be used to predict his approximate score on the other. The accuracy of the prediction is related to the degree to which the correlation coefficient differs from zero. Both positive and inverse (negative) correlations can be used to make predictions, since it is the magnitude—not the sign—of a correlation that represents the strength of the relationship.

The degree of correlation between measures is usually the basis for inferring that the traits measured by the tests are also associated. This does not mean, however, that the existence of one trait "causes" the other. Causation may or may not be involved; that question can be answered only by intensive analysis of the nature of the two variables involved. A correlation coefficient indicates only that these two traits vary together in a systematic way, but this can be the result of many factors. For example, the correlation may exist not because one trait is influencing another but because a third, "hidden," variable is involved somewhere. For example, a high correlation between reading test scores and phonics test scores does not necessarily mean that mastery of phonics causes good reading. It may be that *both* scores are reflecting the children's general intelligence and motivation to do well in school. It should be pointed out, also, that perfect correlation almost never occurs in educational and psychological measurement. In fact, correlations in the areas of human traits and achievements rarely exceed ±.90.

RELIABILITY AND VALIDITY COEFFICIENTS

Correlation is a useful tool in assessing the reliability and validity of tests. Correlations can be determined between scores on two halves of a test, between scores from two alternate forms of the same test, or between two scores obtained by the same people on the same test at different times. The reliability coefficient is a statistical means of determining the degree to which test results are consistent and stable. The more consistent the test scores, the higher the reliability coefficient and,

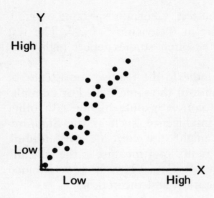

Fig. 10.5. High positive
correlation (+.85).

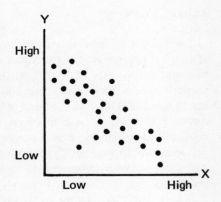

Fig. 10.6. Moderately high
negative correlation (−.70).

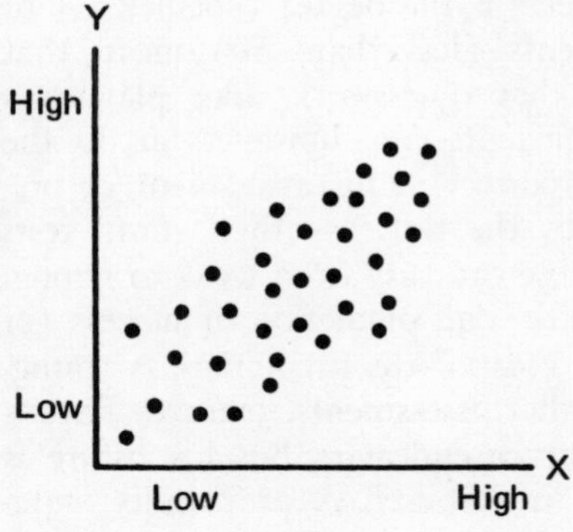

Fig. 10.7. Moderate positive
correlation (+.50).

thus, the greater the reliability of the test. Generally speaking, reliability for a standardized test should be in the vicinity of .90. The test booklet generally indicates whether research studies report high reliability over a period of time.

Validity coefficients also help to indicate the relative consistency of the results of a test and other measures of the same trait. For example, tests of abstract intelligence should correlate quite highly with other tests of abstract manifestations of intelligence, such as the *Stanford-Binet*. Such intelligence-test scores might also correlate with reading scores or grade-point average. The validity of a measure is theoretically enhanced if it correlates with other measures that have been determined to be valid by other means, both empirical and theoretical.

PREDICTION

Coefficients of reliability and validity can be considered "coefficients of risk." They provide a statistical estimate of the strength of prediction and consistency of tests used to assess and advise young people. If properly understood and communicated, coefficients are an aid to teachers, counselors, and school administrators. However, there is always an element of risk involved in trying to predict the future of another individual. No test is perfectly reliable or valid. The element of risk arises when one decides to use a test for some educational purpose and must make a judgment as to how much he can rely on the test results.

A very important factor in this process is the degree (coefficient) of reliability and validity. Low coefficients (less than .50) mean that prediction cannot be much better than guesswork, like playing a long-shot in a horserace. As the coefficients rise, however, so do the odds that the teacher or counselor is correct in his assessment or prediction of performance as measured by the test. In other words, tests provide probability statements, and these can vary from weak to strong.

It must be understood that, even with high prediction of success (or failure), there will be those who will "escape" the prediction. A youngster may, on the basis of tests and other assessments, seem to have a low probability of success in some future endeavor, but his future is not predetermined by this statistical probability. A probability statement does not *cause* future behavior. Perhaps this is an obvious fact, but it needs to be emphasized from time to time that all predictions of

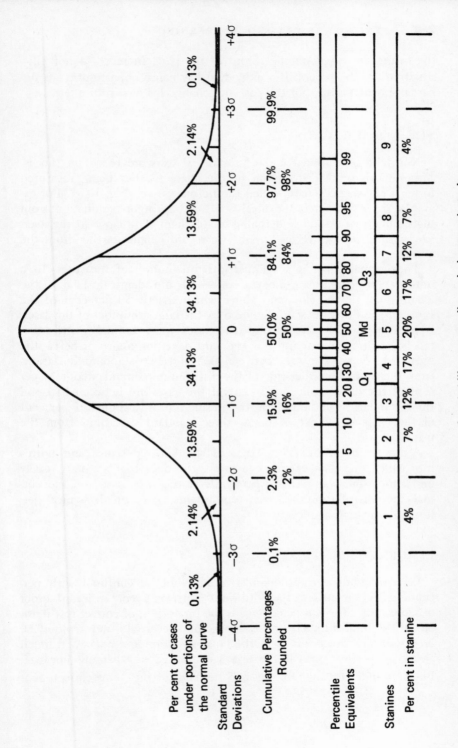

Fig. 10.8. The normal curve of probability, percentile equivalents, and stanines.

Per cent of cases under portions of the normal curve

Standard Deviations
−4σ −3σ −2σ −1σ 0 +1σ +2σ +3σ +4σ

0.13% 2.14% 13.59% 34.13% 34.13% 13.59% 2.14% 0.13%

Cumulative Percentages
0.1% 2.3% 15.9% 50.0% 84.1% 97.7% 99.9%
Rounded
0.1% 2% 16% 50% 84% 98% 99.9%

Percentile Equivalents
1 5 10 20 30 40 50 60 70 80 90 95 99
Q₁ Md Q₃

Stanines
1 2 3 4 5 6 7 8 9

Per cent in stanine
4% 7% 12% 17% 20% 17% 12% 7% 4%

the future are based on the record of the past. In most—if not all—situations in the school, the individual has many opportunities to depart from the patterns of the past and change his own future.

THE NORMAL CURVE

Norms in educational and psychological tests are based on the assumption that the distribution of the characteristics being measured forms a bell-shaped curve, called the *normal curve* (Fig. 10.8). For example, if we measured the heights of all boys upon graduation from high school, we would find that most of them were close to the average, with fewer and fewer boys as we record heights farther from the average.

The normal curve is a symmetrical distribution of measures. In a normal curve, the mean, median, and mode are identical. That is, the mean is the point below and above which exactly 50 per cent of the cases fall, and it is the score achieved by the largest number of the cases. Approximately 34 per cent of the cases in a normal distribution fall between the mean and one standard deviation above or below the mean (± 1 SD). The area between one and two standard deviations from the mean on either side of the distribution contains about 14 per cent of the cases. Only 2 per cent of the cases are between two and three standard deviations from the mean, and only about 0.1 per cent of the cases fall above or below three standard deviations from the mean.

Although there are many types of standardized scores and norms into which raw data can be converted, the ones that are most easily understood are: *stanines* and *percentile equivalents*, based on the normal-curve distribution; and *grade equivalents*, based on the typical performance at each age level.

PERCENTILES

Percentiles, or percentile ranks, should not be confused with percentages. A percentile is the position of a person's score in a rank order of scores (Fig. 10.8); a percentage is the proportion of correct test items out of the total number. For example, John received a raw score of 60 on a multiple-choice test in math. This raw score does not reveal much about his performance. If the test is comprised of 80 items, however, his score indicates that John got 75 per cent of the items correct. It is also possible that his score, or percentage correct, was the best performance in the class. If so, his raw score of 60 is equal to the 99th percentile, or has a percentile rank of 99, indicating that his performance was superior to that of 99 per cent of those measured.

But suppose that on a previous math test John received the highest raw score by correctly solving 95 per cent of the items. Compared to this performance, his score of 60 may appear to represent a drop in quality, but if both scores were the top performance in the class—in the 99th percentile—they represent the same position in the group. In other words, percentiles provide information about one's performance relative to a previous test or the performance of others; it does not provide absolute data. Percentage is a measure of quantity and by itself provides little comparative information.

STANINES

A stanine is a nine-point scale of standard scores, first used by the air force in World War II, when it was developed to meet the need to reduce large amounts of test data to manageable form. This scale is based on the assumption that the distribution of the measured trait approximates a normal curve, or at least that treating the score distribution as if the trait were normally distributed will not result in a serious distortion of fact. The percentage of the total distribution of cases that falls into each of the nine stanine classifications is indicated in Figure 10.8.

Prospective teachers are urged to pursue the subject of stanines and other standard scores in a text that covers educational measurement in depth.* But, as a beginning, it is useful to understand the chief value of stanines: Scores that have been converted to stanines are quantitatively comparable since they indicate a student's standing in a subject in comparison with others of similar grade placement. They convert specific scores into general probability statements containing a built-in norm. For example, it is immediately apparent that a student with a stanine of 7, 8, or 9 in a subject is well above the typical student in his grade in that subject. A stanine of 2 or 3 indicates performance well below average.

---

* E.g., Norman E. Gronlund, *Measurement and Evaluation in Teaching*, 2nd ed. New York: Macmillan, 1971.

GRADE EQUIVALENTS

On many standardized achievement tests, performance is reported in a grade score that (divided by 10) can be read as a grade equivalent. Thus, a grade score of 55 equals a grade equivalent of 5.5. Grade equivalents may be converted to stanines and percentiles.

Grade equivalents are popular because they are relatively easy to communicate. To describe a child's achievement as equivalent to a fifth-grade performance in spelling, a fourth-grade performance in arithmetic, and a sixth-grade performance in reading conveys easily understood information, as does the use of mental age in traditional intelligence tests. Such grade equivalents frequently are used to plot an achievement profile for the child.

A major defect of grade equivalents, however, is that the content of instruction differs from grade to grade. It might be justifiable to measure a fifth-grader against the performance of others in his grade, but it is much less defensible to compare his performance with that of older or younger children in other grades. At each successive age level, varying instructional and developmental factors must be taken into account. Nevertheless, grade equivalents are useful because they provide general estimates of performance.

NORMATIVE-BASED MEASUREMENT

Normative-based examinations, standardized and teacher-made, are typical of the educational system. They are used to assign grades along some kind of continuum, to screen applicants for admission to vocational training and high-level courses, to evaluate a student's strengths and weaknesses for purposes of career guidance and placement, and to assign students to sections within the school program.

National norms are developed by testing a large, nationally representative sample of students. Local norms are based on the measurement of student performance within the local school or school system. The nature of the norm used in interpreting a test score is extremely important. The same score can mean many different things according to the norms cited. For example, a student living in an upper-middle-class suburb might score in the 75th percentile on national norms and in the 50th percentile on local norms. A disadvantaged child might perform quite well on tests that are normed locally but show a low performance when compared to national norms for children of his age and grade. Another such discrepancy can occur, for example, when a large, urban school system compares the reading level of its students to national norms, which often show that students in large, urban school systems are performing below nationwide standards.

A major problem associated with normative-based tests (especially teacher-made tests) is that they are inherently competitive. Since one's score depends on the relative performance of the other individuals in the norm group, the only way to get a good grade is to score well above the average, regardless of one's ability. For this reason, many educational authorities are looking for an alternative to normative-based testing. McClelland (1973) advocates that we assess a wider array of traits and behaviors and that such assessment should be competency-based, rather than tied to averages or norms. This form of assessment, sometimes referred to as *criterion-referenced* testing, requires, first, the development of a list of skills to be mastered. The individual's performance is then assessed on the basis of a predetermined level of competency in each skill, related to the job he is expected to do. The individual either passes or fails the test. Such exams are currently used for entrance into the practices of law, medicine, and nursing and for qualification for a driver's license. Conceivably, similar tests could be developed for use in schools for the same purposes that normative-based tests are now used. At the very least, criterion-referenced tests might be more credible to the public and especially to those whose vocational choices are dependent on test performance. The removal of norms from evaluation might eliminate many of the negative effects of competition and perhaps would stimulate the development of measurement and evaluation procedures more in line with current trends in individualized instruction. Although many school authorities and test builders believe that this is a worthy goal, the development of competency-based assessment would require radical changes in educational testing procedures as well as serious soul-searching on the part of the public on the issue of competition.

PERFORMANCE ASSESSMENT IN THE CLASSROOM

STANDARDIZED ACHIEVEMENT TESTS

For most teachers, the validity of standardized achievement tests poses a more immediate problem than their reliability. It is difficult for commercially produced tests to gain acceptance unless they meet minimal standards of reliability; but validity is not a fixed characteristic independent of the setting in which the test is used. At the elementary-school level, standardized tests of basic skills—the most commonly used tests—are generally close to classroom content. An experienced teacher can usually determine just by inspecting the test items whether they tap knowledge and problem-solving skills similar to what is taught in the classroom. If the standardized test is aimed at high-level thinking skills, it probably serves as an adequate assessment of most classroom versions of the same content. For example, the producers of the *Iowa Tests of Basic Skills* assert that the math subtest items tap problem-solving and conceptual skills at a level sufficiently high to encompass both traditional and modern, or "new," math.

At the middle-school and especially senior-high-school level, however, the validity of standardized achievement tests in the academic areas involves much more complex questions. Subject-matter–oriented teachers choose course content from vast fields of knowledge, and there is considerable likelihood that a nationally standardized test will not accurately reflect what is taught in a given classroom. A standardized test measuring basic thinking skills may reflect course objectives, but even these instructional areas become clouded by variations in terminology and scholarly points of view in the organization and presentation of course content.

It is obviously desirable to have a standardized achievement test at the senior-high-school level that appears to sample quite closely what is emphasized in class. However, such a correlation may mean that someone is "teaching to the test"—that is, that the course objectives are patterned directly after specific items in the standardized test. Although such a practice may lead to impressive test results, it is professionally inappropriate. Assessment should be patterned after objectives, not vice versa.

TEACHER-MADE TESTS

For information about both the quantity and the quality of learning, teachers commonly employ observational procedures and teacher-made tests. Observation of both the processes and the products of learning activities takes place in all the nontesting situations of the classroom—for example, evaluation of student involvement in class discussion or in individualized creative activities. Teacher-made tests include the objective test and the essay examination, each of which has a special function in relation to the goals of teaching.

If the goal of instruction is centered on the student's acquisition of information, the teacher limits his measurement to that outcome. Similarly, if the goal of instruction is broader, including not only a gain in knowledge but also the development of interests, ideals, and mental processes, he employs various means of measuring all these achievements. Thus, the instructional objectives followed by a teacher determine his goals and methods in measurement. In turn, his actual objectives in instructional procedure are revealed by his method of measurement.

Two leaders in educational measurement collected and examined hundreds of teacher-made tests from many school systems (Thorndike and Hagen, 1969). From their study and published studies by others, they concluded that such tests are usually quite deficient means of measurement. They do not cover the range of objectives that many teachers profess to follow. Instead, nearly all the test items require only specific, factual answers, and often they tend toward the trivial. Little or no provision is made for students to relate, organize, or apply and express their knowledge. This suggests that many teachers need to 're-examine and improve their real objectives in both teaching and testing.

Validity. The validity of teacher-made tests is determined partly by the inherent structure of the test. The objective test is designed to measure the specifics, or parts, of learnings; the response to each item is a word or sign. The pattern of this test makes it uniquely suited for measuring recall or recognition of small units of information—terms, facts, and generalizations. It can also be constructed to measure understandings and skills in problem solving. In contrast, the essay examination, consisting of a few broad questions and permitting rather extended answers, is especially appropriate for the measurement of integrated learnings, complex achievement, problem solving, and self-expression. In such a test, a student may be required to show breadth of knowledge and ability to recall and apply facts bearing on the solution of a problem. Within the limits of each task in the test, the examinee is free to recollect, organize, and express what he has learned, and is responsible for doing so.

Objective tests are constructed for testing understanding and thinking. Nevertheless, the components of this kind of test can measure only the separate, specific abilities of problem solving, not the ability to attack a whole problem. Also, in multiple-choice items, the student needs only a recognition level of response. The information required to recognize the correct response is provided in the exercise.

The teacher's skill in constructing either objective or essay tests determines the test's validity. If an objective test is intended to measure understandings and problem-solving skills, it must include items especially designed to that end. Few teacher-made objective tests are so constructed. Likewise, an essay examination does not test organization of thoughts and logical expression unless it requires such intellectual processes. Too many "essay" tests consist mainly of short-answer, factual questions.

Reliability. Consideration of how appropriate a test is in a particular situation—its validity—must be accompanied by consideration of how dependably it does the job—its reliability. Any reasonably well-constructed teacher-made test probably has some reliability. Subjectivity in testing contributes to unreliability. The objective test involves scarcely any subjectivity in scoring but a significant amount in construction. The essay examination is significantly subjective in both construction and scoring.

The reliability of the essay test may be raised by restricting the student clearly and definitely to a prescribed task. Such items as "Tell what you know about grasshoppers" or "Discuss the Fugitive Slave Law" call for vague, indefinite, all-inclusive answers. The teacher who presents a clear problem to the students—for example, "In what ways did the Dred Scott case precipitate the Civil War?"—can hold them to it in scoring the papers. By specifying the goals of the essay test item more narrowly, he clarifies the objective at which he expects them to aim as they write the papers and increases the reliability of the test. Thus, the construction of the essay examination is of basic importance in scoring the papers. Vague objectives and poorly phrased questions, especially in a long essay test, contribute significantly to unreliability of scores. Skill in scoring an essay test cannot compensate for inefficiency in composing it.

In grading, each paper may be rated against the others. Five categories of performance are generally sufficient in classifying students' perceptions of related ideas and organization of thoughts. Reliability in scoring an essay test also requires agreement by the scorers (if more than one) on the chief outcomes they will consider in determining the scores. Ideally, scoring standards should be established by the person who both taught the class and constructed the test.

In testing, the teacher must balance concern for reliability with regard for validity. A high degree of reliability is desirable and, as we have pointed out, must exist to some extent for validity to exist.

Yet, in some testing situations we may be required to choose between high degrees of reliability and validity. For instance, a teacher who aims toward the development of student proficiency in problem solving may use an essay test with superior validity for measuring that result, even though the scores of the test are less reliable than those of an objective test having inferior validity for measurement of that result.

Test Construction. The construction of a good objective test requires considerable time and effort. A test on subject matter taught for a month or a semester cannot be constructed in an hour. A teacher can improve the test by writing items at times throughout the whole month or semester. Of course, he needs considerable creativity and skill in writing and a willingness to apply himself diligently to repeated revision of the items in both content and form.

The composition of a particular form of objective test can be improved with practice if a few requirements are kept in mind. For example, to avoid the possibility that students will stumble on correct responses through the elimination of other responses, a matching test must contain more responses than stimuli. Similarly a multiple-choice test must not include such obviously incorrect alternatives that the correct one is revealed.

Some specific suggestions for constructing any kind of objective test may be helpful (Thorndike and Hagen, 1969, p. 93):

1. Avoid ambiguous items and items that call for obvious or trivial responses.
2. Observe the rules of grammar and rhetoric.
3. Include items the "correct" answer to which all experts will accept.
4. Avoid trick or catch items—that is, items so phrased that the right answer depends on obscure key words to which even good students are unlikely to give sufficient attention.
5. Do not include items that furnish answers to other items.
6. Do not take statements verbatim from the reading material or the lecture.
7. Avoid words that provide irrelevant clues or enable students to respond correctly without knowledge or understanding.
8. For the sake of objectivity, each item should test for only one idea.
9. Be clear in the statement of each item.

A teacher whose aims and practices are focused on complex learnings may prefer suitable essay questions. While he directs students in recalling, relating, and expressing ideas in problematic situations, he grows in the ability to compose thought questions for the class. He can draw on those questions as patterns when he constructs test items.

As we have noted, many so-called essay questions in teacher-made tests, in fact, ask for loosely constructed, informational answers. (E.g., "Tell what you know about the boll weevil"; "What were the principal results of the War of 1812?"; "Discuss John Brown's raid on Harpers Ferry.") What such questions measure, if anything, could be more efficiently measured by objective items. An essay examination should involve the student in reflective expression, requiring him to draw comparisons, to describe cause-and-effect relationships, to support or apply generalizations, to criticize the adequacy or correctness of statements, to describe how to accomplish a task, and so on. This kind of examination consists of one or more precisely expressed problems.

Whatever the phraseology or form of a question, it is not a thought question for a particular group of students unless it provides some degree of novelty. Merely using *why* or *how* in a question will not require students to think if the answer can be expressed in ready-made form by quoting from the textbook, without understanding and thinking. A real thought question presents students with a new, problematic situation—a changed setting, a demand for different facts, a different relationship of the facts. Of course, the question must not be so new as to be completely frustrating.

A few examples of suitable essay questions for some classes may help:

1. Write a paragraph on a topic of your choice. Explain how you followed two rules of good paragraphing.
2. Give and support two generalizations from your reading of *Kon-Tiki*.
3. Compare the writing style of Mark Twain and O. Henry, particularly with respect to characterization. Cite examples.
4. Explain how the principles of the lever provide for relatively easy and swift movement in the bicycle.
5. How does an aviator adjust the wings of his airplane on takeoff? Why does he do this?
6. Explain why cutting a second hole in the top of a can results in a faster flow of liquid from the can.
7. Geographical conditions in Argentina are like and unlike those in the United States. How do the similarity and dissimilarity of conditions in the two countries affect their commercial relations?
8. Discuss the relationship between economic conditions in our coun-

try and increased control of management and labor by the federal government.

Both the objective and the essay test have practical advantages and disadvantages. Adequate preparation of objective test items is difficult and time-consuming, but the scoring is quick and easy. The construction of questions for the essay test is relatively easy, but scoring requires time and effort. If the two tests are appraised solely on the basis of practicality, the objective test has an advantage, but it is not so great as some believe.

The suitability of a test varies with its purpose and structure. Although it is not easy for the classroom teacher to do a good job of constructing any objective test, it is particularly difficult, time-consuming, and somewhat costly to construct such a test for measuring skills in problem solving. Only a few books on educational measurement present samples of objective-test exercises constructed to measure aspects of reflective thinking. Each interpretive exercise, designed to test only one aspect of an act of thought, covers a large part of a page. It typically consists of information to the student in the form of a paragraph, map, graph, or chart, followed by about six multiple-choice questions. This kind of objective item is rare in teacher-made tests, apparently because the process of finding and revising new information and of devising good test items requires much work and skill. The long and difficult process of construction makes such a test low in suitability.

The suitability of the essay examination also must be appraised in relation to its structure and function. This test in any form is unsuitable for obtaining a sample of a student's factual learning over an entire month or semester. This is the special function of the objective test. The essay examination can be so structured that it reveals the student's ability to recall, interpret, relate, and express ideas in complex responses. In terms of covering content, objective tests often have a wide wave band but low fidelity; essay examinations tend to have a narrower wave band but higher fidelity.

Teachers have found that the problems of grading an essay examination can be minimized by stating the questions in the form of clearly structured problems or by prescribing the maximum number of words or pages for the response. Others distribute several relatively short essay tests throughout the semester. A teacher may occasionally use the assignment period to introduce a few thought questions as study guides, using one or more of those questions in an unannounced test on the following day.

The factor of suitability also involves the question of *power* versus *speed*. That is, does the test allow the student sufficient time to make thoughtful, carefully reasoned responses? Or does his test score reflect, not only what he knows, but how fast he can answer the questions? In many tests, quickness of response is an important objective: for example, pressing a brake or other manipulation in a driver-education test. But in most classroom situations, teacher-made tests are intended to measure what a student knows, not how fast he can respond. Beginning teachers (and many experienced teachers, as well) tend to administer tests that are too long and difficult and thus require too much time. A low score may reflect the fact that a student simply did not have the time to answer all the questions, not ignorance of the answers.

But it is entirely understandable that many beginning teachers overlook the time factor in designing tests, having themselves just successfully mastered the highly competitive, accelerated examination requirements of the typical university!

THE PROBLEM OF OBJECTIVITY

Good teachers try to be fair in assigning grades. This is much easier said than done. As a new teacher, you will find that throughout each day you will be forced to judge children's performances, without specific standards to go by. For example, during a class discussion, many factors may enter into your judgment of student responses. If a bright, knowledgeable girl gives a ready answer, does she deserve an A even though you know that the question is easy for her? What about a very shy boy who gets flustered when called upon, so that he appears to stumble with the answer when, in fact, he knows it well? If a particular student is restless and inattentive, does his distracting behavior enter into your evaluation of his achievement? Is it possible that you respond more positively to students who are friendly and outgoing toward you than to those who seem to regard you and your teaching with little enthusiasm?

These are just a few of the factors that can enter into one's judgment of students. Many teachers are sincerely convinced that they evaluate fairly at all times when, in fact, there may be any number of unconscious influences in their judgments, so subtle as to escape their notice entirely.

The *halo effect*, for example, is the tendency to judge all performance according to the general impression, or "image," a student projects. For example, an excellent student may receive high grades all the time—even when he occasionally turns in a less-than-perfect paper—because the teacher already has an expectation of quality from him and, whenever he finds himself in doubt, gives the student the benefit. Conversely, a consistently poor student may be graded lower at times than he deserves because the teacher already has a low level of competence in mind for him. In fact, the teacher may react to an unusually good performance or paper as a fluke, or possibly as plagiarism.

Projection is another all-too-common tendency: to interpret or judge the behavior of others in terms of one's own values and feelings. If a certain student strikes you as "my kind of kid," projection will aid him. If you unconsciously perceive some of your own personal shortcomings mirrored in a student's behavior, you may react negatively to him, even if he is high-achieving and cooperative. Perhaps when we react strongly to a particular trait or behavior in a student we may be revealing something about ourselves.

As Freud pointed out, relatively few of our likes and dislikes can be traced to identifiable causes. Only a small fraction of our memories and experiences are within the scope of our consciousness—that is, capable of being recalled at will. The conscious part of our values and attitudes constitute the tip of the iceberg. Our total attitudes are the result of pleasant and unpleasant associations with myriad forgotten or repressed events of the past. For example, the teacher who places a very high value on neatness in student work may have a rational explanation for this standard, when, in fact, the origins may lie somewhere in his past. One teacher may regard the behavior of highly active boys as uncouth horseplay or excessive roughness while another views it good-naturedly as spirited, Tom Sawyerish pranks—depending on their associations with behavior of this kind.

GRADING: TWO POINTS OF VIEW

Of all aspects of school learning, evaluation exerts the most direct influence on the learner's mental health. Evaluation shapes the child's view of himself as a learner and as a person. Throughout the school day, each child is receiving evaluative feedback of one kind or another—formal and informal. Generally speaking, evaluation contributes to higher levels of performance, although, admittedly, its long-term effects on motivation are as yet unclear (Maehr and Stallings, 1972).

Unfortunately, too much teacher feedback is negative or corrective in nature. In their understandable desire to help students, teachers often concentrate more on diagnosing pupils' weaknesses than on appreciating and building their strengths. Furthermore, much of the evaluation provided by teachers is insufficient, unclear, or inappropriate. Boehm and White (1967) reported on elementary pupils' perception of school marks, suggesting that children are quite sensitive to the teacher's evaluation, even though uncertain of the exact basis for such appraisal.

If evaluation is to be effective, it must be regarded by teacher and learner alike as a continuing and integral part of the learning process. Evaluation is the process of gathering and assessing evidence of how well growth and learning are progressing. If evaluation is to have any value, it must be, as Wilhelms (1967) put it, "converted into genuine feedback to the pupil," leading him "steadily toward sharper, more valid perceptions, and therefore toward wiser decisions and actions."

Students, however, usually take a less sanguine view of grading. The following criticisms are typical:

1. Heavy emphasis on tests and grades limits student creativity and individuality of expression. Thus, grades may discourage rather than encourage learning that is personally relevant to the student.

2. Too much emphasis on tests and grades can result in excessive competitive pressures on students. This can make learning tension filled and unpleasant. Instead of being an enjoyable experience, learning becomes a daily competitive horserace.

3. The need for tests and grades forces teachers to concentrate on what is most easily measured—low-level factual information. Students will forget most of this information after the need to remember it is past.

4. Testing and grading make it difficult for teachers to develop humane relationships with students. Teachers are perceived as too authoritarian, and students feel that they are being pressured to regurgitate the pronouncements of the book and the teacher. Failure to do so results in punishment.

5. Tests tend to reward highly verbal, "testwise" students and to penalize those who are more athletically or vocationally oriented. The student who is not a good reader often fails tests because he doesn't know what the test asks for, rather than because he's unable to produce the answers.

All these criticisms contain both truth and error. It is often difficult for young people to understand how teachers and school administrators can continually profess a desire to be "humane" and "understanding" toward students at the same time that they build competition by means of tests and grades. Many universities have responded to these concerns by instituting "pass-fail" systems or permitting students to elect courses for credit without a grade, in many cases after the course is under way. Some universities allow students to count a certain number of failed courses as "no credit," without the punishment of a lowered grade-point average. Other academic departments have converted conventionally graded courses into seminars where students are evaluated on a personal basis. Here, the student has a major role in determining what he wants from the course, and how he wants to attain his goal. Many students say they would prefer a personal evaluation of their performance to a formal, competitive testing situation.

Because these innovative practices are less threatening to students and teachers alike, they have considerable appeal. But they nevertheless contain hidden drawbacks. To begin with, what is appropriate at the college level may not be appropriate at the elementary- and secondary-school levels, where we are dealing with unselected students who, by law, are required to be in school. With classes of 25 students or more and five or six classes per day, it simply may not be possible for teachers to make a personal evaluation of each student. In fact, often the only students the teacher gets to know well are those whose behavior attracts his attention—slow learners, discipline problems, and the very bright, ambitious, creative students. The majority of low- to high-average students tend to remain relatively anonymous.

As a consequence, it is unlikely that in the foreseeable future most teachers below the college level will be dealing with small, intimate classroom groups, where grading can be done on a pass-fail or letter-of-recommendation basis. In most schools, it is essential to rely on measurements of grade-level performance, subjects, courses, and other areas of achievement. The teacher must determine which students are ready to begin at a given grade level and which are not. Also, in order to expose children to a curriculum that is reasonably appropriate to their achievement capabilities, the teacher and the school need continuous feedback regarding their abilities and performance. Finally, admission to post-high-school vocational and academic programs necessarily requires evidence of the student's ability and achievement.

But the issues of testing and grading cannot be resolved solely in terms of the individual student. We must also consider them in relation to prevailing values and needs of our society. As John Gardner stated:

> It must never be forgotten that ours is one of the few societies in the history of the world in which performance is a primary determinant of status. What the individual can "deliver" in the way of performance is a major factor in how he can rise in the world [1961, p. 68].

Maintenance of our national standard of living depends on our continuing to produce a highly educated populace. The school functions as a preliminary means of sorting out the able and less able individuals. As Gardner points out, this is "very nearly the most delicate and difficult process our society has to face" (p. 71). It places a heavy burden on those who must establish and enforce academic standards. Because they recognize that hostile and anxiety-ridden children usually perform poorly in school, teachers are naturally attracted by philosophies of education that give them a reason to avoid clear-cut evaluations of children. Gardner acknowledges that this aversion to deciding the future of a young person is an understandable reaction, but he goes on to say, "The consequences are all too familiar: the deterioration of standards, the debasement of taste, shoddy education, vulgar art, cheap politics, and the tyranny of the lowest common denominator" (p. 73).

These arguments appear to support society's need for formal evaluation, but what about the welfare of the individual child and his right to equal opportunity for advancement through education? Tests are disliked because they perform the unpopular job of providing detailed and relatively objective comparative information regarding the strengths and deficiencies of students. This process, if successful, ensures that those who have the talent and the skill will receive the rewards of recognition and advancement—*regardless of any personal consideration by the teacher or the institution.* Although it is taken for granted by many young people today, it is necessary from time to time to reaffirm the fact that our society has developed because talent has been able to rise without consideration of financial wealth, family lineage, social connections, or any other artificial means of achieving advancement. As former Presidential adviser Daniel P. Moynihan told a House subcommittee:

One of the achievements of democracy, although it seems not much regarded as such today, is the system of grading and sorting individuals so that young persons of talent born to modest or lowly circumstances can be recognized for their worth. (Similarly, it provides a means for young persons of social status to demonstrate that they have inherited brains as well as money, as it were.) I have not the least doubt that this system is crude, that it is often cruel, and that it measures only a limited number of things. Yet it measures valid things, by and large. To do away with such systems of accreditation may seem like an egalitarian act, but in fact it would be just the opposite. We would be back to a world in which social connections and privilege count for much more than any of us, I believe, would like. If *what* you know doesn't count in the competitions of life, *whom* you know will determine the outcomes [1971, pp. 4–5].

REFERENCES

Ary, D., L. C. Jacobs, and A. Razavieh. 1972. *Introduction to research in education*. New York: Holt, Rinehart & Winston.

Boehm, A. E., and M. A. White. 1967. Pupils' perceptions of school marks. *Elementary School Journal*, 67, 237–40.

Gardner, J. W. 1961. *Excellence*. New York: Harper & Row.

McClelland, D. C. 1973. Testing for competence rather than for intelligence. *American Psychologist*, 28(1), 1–14.

Maehr, M. L., and W. M. Stallings. 1972. Freedom from external evaluation. *Child Development*, 43, 177–85.

Moynihan, D. P. 1971. Speech before a U.S. Senate subcommittee. *Report on Education Research*. Washington, D.C.: Capitol Publications, 3, 4–5.

Thorndike, R. L., and E. Hagen. 1969. *Measurement and evaluation in psychology and education*. New York: Wiley.

Van Dalen, D. B. 1966. *Understanding educational research: An introduction*. New York: McGraw-Hill.

Wilhelms, F. T. 1967. *Evaluation as feedback and guide*. Washington, D.C.: Association for Supervision and Curriculum Development, National Education Association.

CHAPTER ELEVEN

Teaching the
Disadvantaged Child

Something happens to a new teacher the first day he faces a classroom full of children who are of a lower class or of some distinct subculture. That something is called culture shock. Its symptoms are some degree of nausea, a feeling of anxiety or fear, and bewildered alienation from the school and the students.

Oriented to the middle-class way of life through family background or the processes of upward mobility, the teacher is inundated in a sea of children who think, talk, dress, look, and behave differently from those well-scrubbed, respectful, self-controlled, ambitious kids in the lab school. Psychologically unprepared, professionally untrained, and socially disinclined to deal with minority-group children, such teachers lament their ill luck and frantically set about establishing some form of order and structure in their classroom. [Bazeli, 1971, p. 210.]

AS BAZELI POINTS OUT, the first year in the ghetto school is a "purgatory." At the end of that year some teachers are abject failures, some have become dehumanized jailors, but most have arrived at a *modus vivendi* with their pupils in which each plays a role in the game called "school." A few have overcome their shock, established solid personal relationships with their students, created a sound learning environment, and are developing into effective, professional teachers. For the children, however, the "purgatory" continues, for minority-group pupils are never allowed to overcome the culture shock they experience in schools dominated by an alien and threatening life system.

Traditionally, the little red schoolhouse has been an extension of the middle-class way of life—the ideal of rectitude, dignity, cleanliness, achievement, and hope. Poverty was not necessarily a disgrace—the expression "poor but honest" was common in the nineteenth century—but to *remain* poor was not "the American way." The middle-class ideology of American culture held that one must strive to better himself somehow, and in fact no nation in the world has ever offered such opportunities for the poor to enter the middle class. For many, education has provided the route to a better life.

But what of those individuals who did not choose education as the road to economic prosperity? They simply quit school when it no longer met their needs. At the turn of the century, U.S. Commissioner of Education W. T. Harris estimated that only 1.25 per cent of first-grade children would continue in school through to graduation from high school (Wagner, 1909). Today, approximately 75 per cent of the youth across the nation achieve a high-school diploma (*American Education*, 1973).

Almost all schoolchildren, both elementary and secondary, are exposed to a predominantly verbal-scholastic curriculum, although only about 30 per cent of high-school graduates go on to higher education. Yet few have regarded this as a form of educational inequality. At least until recently, the prevailing opinion was that a college-preparatory curriculum was the best of all possible programs. The school should offer only the best, and each student should have the opportunity to enter and succeed in that curriculum.

In one end of the educational cornucopia went the children—bright-eyed, freshly scrubbed, and thoroughly imbued with the conviction that education was the way to a better life. But what came out of this educational process was a highly variable product. Until recent years the primary emphasis was on providing equal *opportunities* for all children. There was little concern with whether the educational system was meeting the *needs* of all the children, not just those who come from privileged middle- and upper-class homes. The growing concern for the effects of education took a quantum leap as a result of the landmark decision of the U.S. Supreme Court in 1954 outlawing racial segregation in public schools.

Following the passage of the Civil Rights Act in 1964, the U.S. Commissioner of Education undertook a survey to assess the "lack of equality of educational opportunity" among minority groups in the United States. Although the basic objective was to determine whether all children in a locality had equal access to the same schools and the same curriculum, subsequent research led to the more complex issue of equality of the results of schooling. A major focus of recent research has been the relationship of social-class and minority-group characteristics to academic achievement.

MEASURING SOCIAL CLASS

Sociologists have identified various factors to be considered in determining social-class placement, but the most popular method was developed by W. Lloyd Warner and his associates in 1949. Their emphasis was on the status of community organizations, the social prestige of individuals in families and in social relationships, and the kinds of social-class groupings in a community. The procedure was for the investigators to move into a community, live there for some time, and analyze the social structure through the evaluation of social participation.

By intensive questioning of many individuals about the social standing of various organizations, occupations, and social groups, the investigators soon developed a general picture of how individuals within the community ranked one another in terms of status, or social class. As a result, they were able to place any individual on the social-class hierarchy through his activities and associations.

It is important to note that categorization of individuals by social class was made on the basis of reputation, regardless of objective, rational considerations. Thus, a member of an old, established family living on a meager inheritance might have higher social status than someone who had much more money but acquired it more recently.

Obviously, in very large urban areas such as Chicago, New York, Los Angeles, and St. Louis, it is not feasible to evaluate the social structure of the community in terms of how people perceive others around them. In these cases sociologists tend to resort to such socioeconomic indices as the occupation of individuals, their level of education, and the source and amount of their income. From these community studies a conception of the American social-class structure has developed.

Kahl (1957) has identified the major dimensions of social class as follows:

1. *Prestige.* Some members of the community are accorded greater respect and deference than others.
2. *Occupation.* Some occupations have higher status than others because they appear to be more important to the welfare of the com-

munity, they require special talents and qualifications, or they pay higher rewards.

3. *Possessions, wealth, or income.*

4. *Social interaction.* People tend to mix with others of their "own kind," and some of these social groups are higher in status than others.

5. *Class consciousness.* This refers to the extent to which individuals regard themselves as part of a distinctive social grouping—"working class," "managerial," "professional," and so on.

6. *Value orientation.* Individuals place different values on different sets of attitudes or value systems.

7. *Power,* or the degree of control over other people. This is not easily determined, but there is social status in being a member of a "power structure" of one kind or another.

All these dimensions interact to form the basis of the social-class structure. When an individual tends to be high (or low) on most or all of these dimensions, his social-class status tends to be correspondingly high (or low).

For public-school purposes, however, it is often difficult to get all the necessary information to determine social class. A convenient measure widely used in school and community research is the father's occupational level, which usually reveals his educational attainment and economic situation. In fact, if one wants to estimate the social class of a particular child and is unable to get access to all the information in his cumulative folder, his father's occupation would provide a fairly accurate indicator.

CHARACTERISTICS OF LOW SOCIAL CLASS

In terms of their cultural and economic status, individuals can be classified roughly into three categories: privileged (high), average (middle), and low (disadvantaged). By most indices, the majority of Americans were traditionally in the low or lower-middle class. In the past several decades, the middle-class rank has expanded. It may some day constitute the largest segment of our society. But the greatest number of people in both urban and rural areas are still in the low-social-class category.

The low social class tends to be concentrated in urban areas, generally in rundown, dingy neighborhoods. Here its members attempt to survive in substandard, deteriorated housing. The population of these depressed areas tends to group by similarities in background—e.g.,

Spanish-speaking people from Puerto Rico or Mexico, blacks from the South, and whites of various ethnic backgrounds.

Substandard housing is also characteristic of the rural poor, but rural slums are much more scattered and hence less visible, have more yard space, and have a lower incidence of crime, violence, and gangism. These advantages are offset to some extent by their isolation. Except in this respect, urban and rural disadvantaged children tend to be alike in educational, cultural, and experiential impoverishment.

According to Crow, Murray, and Smythe (1964), low social class can be characterized by low annual income, high rate of unemployment, underutilization of human resources, poor housing, large families, inadequate living space, poor sanitary conditions, widespread reliance on welfare, inadequate education, and attitudes of alienation and hopelessness. In an extensive survey of research, Kohn (1968) reported that the conditions of lower-social-class life are more conducive to serious mental illness (schizophrenia) than are those of other social classes.

It has been established that nearly 75 per cent of all black Americans are in the lowest socio-economic stratum. In absolute numbers, however, low-class whites exceed low-class blacks (Erickson, Bryan, and Walker, 1972).

ALIENATION

Low socio-economic circumstances often result in an alienation from the larger society. Charnofsky (1971) states that this alienation among the socially disadvantaged can be traced in large part to their lack of future orientation; hostility toward those who have "made it"; suspicion and resentment of outside interference; a tendency to rely on "chance," "luck," or "fate"; apathy in approaching problems; a sense of futility; and a childlike dependence on those who are gifted or capable or affluent or powerful. The alienated youth feels "out of it" in the sense that he believes whatever he does has little effect on the environment about him. He is invisible as far as others are concerned. He may accept this role as a "nonperson," or he may learn some form of compensatory behavior as he attempts to meet his natural needs for recognition and involvement. This is a condition that often shows itself quite early. Many low-class children feel "out of it" even before they begin first grade.

Studies have found that even in infancy there is alienation behavior, a sort of growing noninvolvement where one would normally expect the individual to want more—not less—interaction. This conception of alienation is one of several theories that have been advanced to account for the dynamics of mother-infant interaction, which in the middle class focus on developing in the child a generalized expectancy, based on his growing belief that his behavior can affect his environment.

Provence and Lipton (1962), for example, found that institutionalized infants differed from infants reared in emotionally supportive homes, not in their acquisition of skills, but in their motivation to *use* the skills. The maturational sequence was unfolding at the same rate for both groups, but the institutionalized infants showed no desire to practice what they learned—the beginning of alienation.

CHILD-REARING PRACTICES

Although individuals offer many exceptions to the usual patterns of class behavior, research evidence clearly shows that a person's position on one side or the other of the line that divides manual from non-manual workers has profound consequences for how he rears his children and for the probability of their success in school.

Gordon (1965, p. 378) has summarized research on the child-rearing practices of disadvantaged homes as follows:

1. Socially disadvantaged children have "closed and rigid relationships" with their parents as compared with middle-class families.
2. Socially disadvantaged children were found to exhibit a greater fear of parental authority and greater dependence on siblings and peers than middle-class children.
3. Overprotection of girls and inadequate discipline of boys were more likely to be the rule in lower-class than in middle-class homes.
4. While the middle-class mother expected the father to be as supportive of the child as she was, and saw his role as disciplinarian as secondary, working-class mothers wanted their husbands to be more directive in relationships with the child and considered his major responsibility to be imposing restraints.
5. Lower-class families tend to train their children by means of immediate punishments and rewards, while middle-class parents tend to stress the future, with punishment and reward often deferred.

Disadvantaged children seem to have little sustained contact with adults. They rarely participate in shared family activities. At mealtimes, these children often eat alone or in the company of their brothers and sisters. Frequently the children are not supported solely by the earnings of their fathers, whereas fully nine-tenths of the white children have fathers who assume the traditional role of breadwinner.

Lower-social-class teen-agers, especially blacks, tend to have a perception of authority figures different from that of teen-agers of higher socio-economic status, in part because they are more likely to come from a fatherless home. In a study of high-school-senior boys, McKinley (1964) asked subjects from five social-class levels: "Whom do you most admire in your family or among your relatives?" This question was intended to provide some measure of the boys' identification. All upper-class boys chose their father or a male relative as "most admired"; in the working and lower classes, only 58 per cent picked their father or a male relative, the others choosing females.

Even in those black households headed by a male, too often the parents were themselves unsuccessful in school and have substandard verbal skills, few intellectual interests, and a fear of and distaste for activities and authority figures that cause them frustrations and humiliations in the past. In educational attainment, too, white families are advantaged. A study by Keller (1962) of white and black children attending school in a poor neighborhood of New York City found that the fathers of white children had an average of one more year of schooling than the black fathers.

The poor throughout history have always been at the lash-end of relationships with authorities, and one of the ways in which they have learned to cope with the situation is by adopting a sullen, uncooperative stance. But authoritarianism often begets authoritarianism; an odd characteristic of low socio-economic life is that those same people who are so often at the receiving end of authority tend to treat their own families in a similar way. Working-class parents want their children to conform to external authority because the parents themselves are forced to accord respect to authority in return for security and respectability. It is possible that as a consequence socially disadvantaged children may develop the need to defy school authorities and adults in general. They frequently come from homes where they have to knuckle under to get along. "Good" children are those who behave themselves and keep quiet. Such treatment is likely to build a strong wish to defy authority. The school represents authority away from home.

ATTITUDES TOWARD EDUCATION

Neale and Proshek (1967) measured the attitudes of elementary-school children in Minneapolis toward school and school-related activities. Disadvantaged children were compared with children from a middle socio-economic school by means of a semantic-differential instrument. The researchers found that disadvantaged children regard school perhaps as something difficult to attain and perhaps as a place where unpleasant things may occur, but nevertheless believe that it is important. However, the findings of the study suggest a systematic change in attitudes toward school as a function of grade level. Disadvantaged children express increasingly negative views of school activities as they grow older. Interestingly, they also indicate increasingly negative views of self as they get older.

By adolescence, lower-class children, both boys and girls, express more selective perceptions of school. They all tend to like useful courses—typing, industrial arts, and sewing are among the popular high-school subjects. Girls place a high value on courses that can lead to the so-called hospitality careers—airline stewardess, receptionist, hotel desk clerk. Both boys and girls recognize, too, that the school functions as the primary "farm system" for nonacademic fields such as entertainment and athletics. Disadvantaged adolescents view academic subjects, however, with something less than enthusiasm, for they associate these courses with low grades and failure. These youth often lack the cultural background important for success in the tool subjects such as reading and mathematics.

With advancing age, disadvantaged adolescents reveal a growing dilemma with respect to their attitudes toward school and education. They usually acknowledge that the school is probably the only channel for improving their lot. They continue to affirm in general the need for an education, but at the same time they express increasingly negative feelings about the educational process itself. Many school officials have noted that disadvantaged children, early in their school careers, are eager to please their teachers, responsive to recognition and affection from the teachers, and happy to take on school activities and tasks. But for many, this initial eagerness and alertness are destroyed by continual failure. Teachers need to find ways to maintain and strengthen the initial drive and motivation so characteristic of lower-social-class children by providing an environment for learning based on success rather than failure.

THE EFFECTS OF LOW SOCIAL CLASS IN THE CLASSROOM

Social class poses a problem in American education because the attitudes and values that children of various backgrounds bring to school may or may not fit into the dominant middle-class culture of the school. It should be pointed out that "culturally disadvantaged" children do not lack a "culture." Spanish-speaking children, for example, have a culture of tremendous vitality, artistry, and a colorful tradition that goes back centuries; so do black, Mexican, and Oriental children. However, working-class groups, especially, foster values and attitudes that conflict with the goals of the public school in that they are less appropriate in our contemporary society than in the milieu in which they originated. For example, early in the twentieth century, the sturdy, active, outdoor-loving boy from a working-class family was certainly not culturally deprived in any way, regardless of his social class or the recent-immigrant status of his family. He probably was able to cope quite effectively with his world. Physical strength and vitality were definite advantages in America's growing cities, when so much of the work was manual. Today, an active, outdoorsy boy who likes to do things with his hands and wants to experience life directly rather than vicariously is likely to find school too slow and passive an experience for his taste. Unfortunately, he has little choice but to come to terms with school subjects, for survival in the urban arena requires technological skills. The need for manual labor has leveled off while the demand for semiskilled and skilled labor increases at a rapid pace.

Further, the experiences the child has at home—the attitudes and values he has internalized toward education and the school as an institution—affect his performance in the classroom. People in very limited economic circumstances, who live in poor housing, and whose existence revolves primarily around the attainment of the basic needs of food, shelter, and so forth, have an outlook on life that is colored by the day-to-day struggle for survival. This outlook influences the way their children talk, think, and act in the presence of authority figures as well as the way they feel about themselves and their future. The slum child's way of life also affects the development of his language skills— a crucial tool for success in the classroom.

Perhaps the single most crucial handicap of the disadvantaged minority-group child is in language. Many blacks, Puerto Ricans, American Indians, Mexican-Americans, recent immigrants, and poor whites as well speak a language that differs markedly from standard American English. Most of these children are limited in their language development by a system of closely shared nonverbal identifications, which serves as the basic substance of their communication. The form of the social relationship acts selectively on this language potential. It is not so much a question of specific vocabulary; it is a matter of the ways in which language is organized and used in a particular kind of social relationship.

Furthermore, for the black child especially, dialect is an identity label; it is a reflection of his culture. Teachers often reject black dialect as an illegitimate or inferior form of English; in so doing they reject the identity of the person who speaks it. But black children enter the classroom learning situation with a complete language system of their own. It may be unintelligible to the teacher, but to the children it has structure, coherence, and meaning. Nor is the black child using a substandard or backward language pattern. This long-held belief has no support in linguistic research and certainly should have no place in the teaching of language skills.

As a result of extensive research, Frazier (1964) suggested that there are three kinds of underdeveloped language found among disadvantaged children with learning disabilities. (1) Some have true verbal destitution—that is, actually less language; (2) some have full but nonstandard language development—that is, language that is highly developed but deviates markedly from standard English; and (3) some have underdeveloped language skills as a result of a paucity of fully conceptualized experiences. For this last group of children, there may have been no occasion to verbalize meanings for some of the experiences valued by the school. Each type of disability requires a distinctive approach in the classroom.

The school, as we have noted, is largely an extension of the middle-class home, not only in its culture but also in its social organization. The school's attempt to help the child bridge the gap between his world and the adult world is therefore most likely to succeed with middle-class children, who have already acquired the social skills and background experiences necessary to meet the expectations of teachers. A child is likely to be "culturally disadvantaged" to the extent that he lacks that background or comes from a cultural environment different from that of the school.

Bloom (1964) has estimated that the long-term effect of living in a culturally deprived environment is likely to be an IQ as much as 20 points lower than the child's potential—an enormous difference in terms of society's and the school's expectations. Recently, however, Jerome Kagan (1973) has presented important evidence that early retardation resulting from an inadequate environment is reversible, and that cognitive development is sufficiently plastic to permit children to make up early deficits later. On the basis of extensive studies of infants and children living in isolated subsistence-farming villages in Guatemala, Kagan asserts that environmental factors can slow down or speed up the emergence of basic intellectual competencies, but that the capacities for symbolism, inference, and memory eventually emerge in "sturdy form" in all children who grow up in a natural, stimulating environment.

The message for American education is that the schools give up too soon on disadvantaged children, taking their failure for granted. Kagan believes that programs that instill self-confidence and self-esteem would help these children to master the basic skills, and that the best teachers should be assigned to teach them.

PARENTAL INFLUENCES

Research has identified factors of the home environment that appear to be significant in affecting a child's school performance. According to White (1969), the relative advantages of upper- and middle-class children in the use of words and the development of concepts can be traced to three sources: (1) Upper- and middle-class parents reinforce the verbal achievement of their children much more frequently; (2) they are generally more adequate models for acceptable speech patterns; and (3) they have more positive attitudes toward books, school, and communication skills. For the most part, it is the adults in the home who stimulate the child's intellectual development (Hunt, 1961).

Parental expectations of a child's school performance are also largely a product of social class. Expectations that are similar to the values of the school more often result in adaptive and successful school performance. Even if the school is restrictive, uninteresting, or downright boring, the "good" child is likely to conform anyway. The "deviant" student, however, is not likely to be passive in his attitude toward school practices and requirements.

In a study of 118 eight-year-old English children, Kent and Davis (1957) found that children of "unconcerned" parents had significantly lower scores on the *Stanford-Binet* and *Wechsler Intelligence Scale for Children* than did children from "normal" or demanding homes. Parents defined as unconcerned had few ambitions for their children, were indifferent to their success or failure, and gave them little encouragement or guidance. Children who obtained the highest IQs were from *demanding* homes, with parents who were ambitious for their children and expected them to conform to a somewhat inflexible model of behavior. (Since these evaluations of the home were made at about the time the children were tested, there is no way of knowing whether the inflexible model might have an inhibiting effect later.) In a more recent study, McCarthy (1969) found that culturally disadvantaged preschool children whose parents participated in an individualized home-visit program gained more significantly in language abilities than did children whose parents did not participate.

Interestingly, several studies on the origins of children's attitudes show that youngsters are more likely to acquire the attitudes and beliefs of their parents when the parents are strict rather than permissive (Argyle, 1958). Yet, when parents become too authoritarian in their attempts to control adolescent sons and daughters, these youths often become disaffected and estranged (Maccoby, Mathews, and Morton, 1954).

Douvan (1956) investigated the extent to which middle-class parents impose on their children earlier and more persistent demands for personal achievement than lower-class parents. Included in the experiment were 336 high-school seniors identified as either middle or lower class. When the two groups competed in a test situation with a monetary reward for those who made a certain score or better, there were no differences between middle- and lower-class subjects. But when the groups competed without the monetary incentive, the motivation of the middle-class subjects remained high while that of the lower-class students declined.

Most parents of disadvantaged children appreciate the value of an education, but they lack the intellectual skills and the self-confidence usually required to help their children in the specifics of schooling. Parent-teacher meetings in both middle-class and lower-class communities tend to attract the more sophisticated, knowledgeable parents. Unfortunately, too often the parents who most need to learn how to help their children are the ones most likely to avoid school meetings because they feel like outsiders. This problem is aggravated somewhat by teachers who cannot relate or communicate to the parents of disadvantaged students.

TEACHERS' PERCEPTIONS

We have discussed some forces of cultural deprivation that appear to influence the school achievement of children. But these are only part of the problem. There is evidence that the so-called culturally deprived child is in double jeopardy. First, he experiences a debilitating home environment; then he experiences a subtle form of discrimination by often well-meaning teachers. There is a growing belief that the attitudes and values of teachers and administrators have a telling effect on the child's capacity to deal with the situations that confront him in school. Rist (1970) reports that much of the difficulty culturally different pupils encounter in schools may be attributed to how the teacher views the pupil, what he expects of the pupil, and how he deals with the pupil.

Deutsch (1967) asks what happens if:

—the teacher assumes that the children have limited ability
—the principal is unhappy about his assignment to a depressed area school
—it is assumed that all children know what museums, farms, orchestras, and zoos are all about
—it is assumed that if children do not understand what goes on in a classroom they will ask questions
—it is assumed that where there is a lack of reading material, pictures, and other things in the home, the teacher cannot be successful in teaching reading
—it is assumed that because the children spend a good part of their after school lives playing in dirty, crowded, violent streets there is no alternative to being tough and heavy-handed in dealing with them— or, the opposite, that the children only need love and informal learning atmosphere
—the teachers do not understand the background and home life of the children but are uneasy and fearful.

The importance of teachers' feelings toward children was underscored in a study by Davidson and Lang (1960) of fourth-, fifth-, and sixth-graders in New York City. These researchers found that positive perceptions of the teachers' feelings were significantly related to the children's academic achievement and "more desirable classroom behavior," as rated by the teachers. The findings of the study also showed significant social-class differences in perceptions of teachers' feelings; upper- and middle-class subjects felt that their teachers perceived them more favorably than lower-class subjects felt that their teachers perceived them.

Black children and white children also differ in their notions of how their teachers perceive them. The difference is suggestive not only of the black child's insecurity and uncomfortable feelings in school but also of teachers' actual perceptions of black and other socially disadvantaged children.

In the black culture the relationship between a child and an adult differs from that in the dominant culture. The black child is not expected to carry on a discussion with an adult as if he or she were an equal, or an almost equal, with the adult. A teacher from the dominant culture expects a conversational skill from the black child that is simply outside of his life-cycle. The teacher then often judges the child dull purely because he lacks a knowledge of the child's culture [Johnson and Simons, 1972].

Current educational writing identifies a lack of trust as the most pervasive attitude of disadvantaged children in school. Inner-city youth frequently state their feeling that teachers and school administrators do not respect them as fellow human beings. Their experiences with parents and other adults have conditioned them to expect manipulation and personal rejection. For these individuals, violence and its expression often become acceptable means of resolving conflict situations.

Yet, many inner-city children enter school with very positive beliefs about teachers and school. Inner-city school personnel have noted that many young children have strong, implicit trust that the teachers will lead them to success. There appears to be considerable variability among children in the matter of trust. It is unfortunate that *any* child should perceive the school with anything less than hope and confidence.

TEACHING THE DISADVANTAGED

Teaching socially disadvantaged learners must be based upon the premise that they can learn and the expectation that among the disadvantaged there is a wide range of aptitudes and abilities. Unconsciously or consciously, many teachers have operated on the premise that certain children are mentally inferior—especially blacks and unsophisticated children from very poor homes. Most teachers are educated to the professional goal of attempting to teach each child, but in practice they may tend to give up a little sooner with certain children. Even for the best-intentioned teacher, the pressures and workload of a typical day too often result in the feeling that there just isn't enough time to deal adequately with every child, let alone the reluctant or slow learner.

The major goal of all teachers at all grade levels should be to help the disadvantaged child build his self-concept, to instill the belief that he *can* achieve something, that he is an able and worthwhile person. Praise and other forms of external reward from the teacher can help to bring this about.

The immediacy of reward, sometimes referred to by psychologists as the gradient of reinforcement, is a significant concept for teachers of disadvantaged youth. Children, especially, work hardest for goals that are most attainable by them. Usually, the farther the child is from attainment of a goal, the less will be his interest in reaching it. But there are wide differences among children in the degree to which this principle holds. Some children learn quite early in life to work diligently for goals that are not immediate; others appear to work on an hour-to-hour basis.

This principle varies also from social class to social class. In fact, part of the meaning of "cultural deprivation" is the conditioned desire for a word of praise *now* rather than the hope for a good grade quite far in the future. Zigler and Kanzer (1962) discovered that, for lower-social-class children, some tangible reward or praise was the most effective reinforcement, while middle-class children needed only to know that their responses were correct in order to be reinforced in their learning.

In addition, different children seem to have different strengths. A better understanding of the life-style and specific abilities of the disadvantaged child should be reflected in how he is taught. For example, disadvantaged children need an appropriate balance between physical and mental activity. They tend to be predisposed toward the physical and the practical as contrasted with the abstract and the theoretical. Many inner-city schools have recognized this need by alternating the active with the more passive, abstract school subjects.

A PUPIL-CENTERED CURRICULUM

It is usually helpful for teachers to diagnose the pupil's strengths and weaknesses as soon as possible after he enters the school, and the process should be repeated throughout each school year. In order to plan appropriate classroom activities, the teacher has to know something about the child's developmental and family history, his language skills and ability, his physical development, and his emotional stability.

The educational program should be designed on the basis of the competencies in which the student needs to progress. The emphasis, above all, should be on success. Constant failure without achievement in one or more subjects is hardly a healthy school diet.

Although there is much debate on this, the prevailing view seems to be that the disadvantaged child should not be expected to follow the same curriculum that has been designed for middle-class children. This does not imply that a watered-down curriculum should be provided; rather, it argues that the basic skills should be presented within a content framework as close as possible to the lives of disadvantaged children.

But such a pupil-centered curriculum can lead to a serious dilemma in teaching the disadvantaged (or any reluctant or handicapped learner). The teacher will probably want to begin teaching the child "where he is at." That is, with success as his primary objective, the teacher does not want to teach over the child's head but will instead begin as close as possible to what he thinks the child can realistically accomplish. On the face of it, this seems like good teaching practice, but in actual classroom situations it often results in instruction that is too simple, low-level, and perhaps downright insulting to the student. If the attitude is, "These kids are so slow in learning, *anything* that is accomplished with them can be regarded as a gain," the result may be little better than babysitting. Of course, few teachers of the disadvantaged would acknowledge this intention, but to the impartial observer, the custodial atmosphere of the classroom is often very apparent.

Perhaps this dilemma can be resolved if the teacher is clever in planning classroom activities. For example, since all elementary children must learn to read, the perceptive teacher might begin by diagnosing each child's level of verbal development and then individualize the reading assignments—preferably tapping the children's interests. This will require the teacher to do some "listening with the third ear." Commercial curriculum guides provide valuable clues to the reading interests of the "typical" child of a given socio-economic level but cannot provide much help for the individual child. This is one of the reasons for taking time throughout the day to socialize with some of the children. Young ones, especially, love to tell teachers all kinds of things. Too often, teachers feel that they are too busy to take time for free-wheeling discussions. But these "rapping" contacts are necessary for the disadvantaged as for the middle-class child—perhaps more necessary. The ghetto child needs much speech practice, with gentle correction of grammar and pronunciation. A child's speech habits can be corrected with the least damage to his ego when he is so busy telling the teacher and other children about something that happened to him that he is not likely to resent some tactful prodding to speak clearly and grammatically. Disadvantaged children need fewer formal, passive learning activities and more "seminar" sessions, where they can speak and act out in a spontaneous environment the real-life events of their own existence. From these encounters, the teacher can encourage children to develop their own reading and instructional materials and to choose study topics from their own experiences.

Needless to say, all this is time-consuming and fatiguing for the teacher. Perhaps the increased use of teacher aides would facilitate this process. Unfortunately, teacher aides often make it easier for teachers to plan even *more* formal, textbook-oriented assignments by providing help in grading and evaluating student performance. It might be more beneficial for the children if the teacher utilized aides for the formal instructional activities and spent more of his own time in personal interaction with small groups or individual children.

PRESCHOOL AND ELEMENTARY SCHOOL

A widespread response to the intellectual deficits incurred by ghetto children has been the proliferation of nurseries or preschools. These schools appear to fall into two general categories: The first assumes that the observed differences between deprived and privileged children are more superficial than fundamental and that they are quantitative rather than qualitative. What the children need are largely supplementary experiences and learning materials of the kind that middle-class children already are familiar with. This may include school-related objects such as pencils, books, crayons, and games, experiences in following directions, and practice in social skills.

The other assumption is that the ghetto child lives in a culture that is fundamentally different from (but not necessarily inferior to) the dominant culture in language and thought pattern. There is increasing support for the belief that "black English" is a distinct, highly consistent language with fixed grammatical rules that differ from the rules governing the language used by most white Americans (Labov, 1972; Marwit, Marwit, and Boswell, 1972; Butters, 1972). This approach demands a more complex teaching strategy, utilizing nonstandard English forms as a medium or as the first step toward the development of language and conceptual skills. In the primary grades this may mean books in which the child reads his own dialect and the standard English version side by side. According to this linguistic approach, the child is reached by his own dialect but is motivated to build on the contrast between it and standard English (Baratz, 1973). (See Fig. 11.1.) Also, placing his language on an equal plane with standard English is intended to increase his feelings of respect for his own culture (Raspberry, 1970).

The method of teaching English "as a second language" (i.e., by means of another language) is especially popular among experts in curriculum for urban, Spanish-speaking youth. Thus far, it has not been very successful, but admittedly it hasn't been used widely enough to warrant firm conclusions (Wright, 1973). Its proponents point to successful examples, such as in Montreal, where many children are taught both language and mathematics entirely in French and have little

LESSON 14: STORIES FOR PRACTICE IN
GOING FROM EVERYDAY TALK TO SCHOOL TALK

The stories are to be used to give the child practice in going from his
dialect to the standard dialect so that the standard dialect becomes
meaningful and increasingly comfortable for him. The emphasis is on
aural-oral learning. The child is to be helped to hear the difference
between the EVERYDAY TALK and the SCHOOL TALK.

Read each story aloud in its entirety so that the children can understand
the theme of the story and can absorb the flavor of the speech patterns.

Ask the children if the story is in EVERYDAY TALK or SCHOOL TALK.

Read the story again, stopping after each sentence to—

    1. ask if the sentence is EVERYDAY TALK or SCHOOL TALK.

    2. invite changes by the children.

Read the entire story again, this time in SCHOOL TALK.

Story 1

I know a bad boy. He don't do like he should. He don't do like we do.
He do bad things. He don't behave. He got a friend who bad, too. They
don't play nice. They mean.

Story 2

I got a big brother. He nice. He don't bother me none. He do lots of
good things. He play baseball with his friends. They don't let us play
much, but sometimes they be nice and we play, too. Then we do just like
the big boys.

Story 3

Sometimes we got to clean up the house. I do the floors. My brother, he
do the windows and my sister, she do the dusting. They do good work. We
all do good work. Then my mama say, "Do you think you through? Come on
back here and get through. That mop, it don't move by itself."

Fig. 11.1 Instructional procedure for using dialect ("Everyday Talk") as a
basis for transition to standard English ("School Talk"). (From *Psycholinguistics Oral Language Program: A Bi-Dialectical Approach,* Chicago Board
of Education, 1968, p. 139.)

trouble transferring what they have learned from French to English. It is believed that a factor in this succ sful transfer is that the two cultures have equal status. According to Cazden (1973), the lack of success American children have had in transfe ing from Spanish to English may reflect the disparity between the nondominant and dominant cultures rather than deficits in the children themselves.

EARLY TRAINING

A research and demonstration project by McConnell, Horton, and Smith (1969) reflects a philosophy that differs from that of the traditional school. The major premise was that the period in which language development occurs is crucial; thus emphasis was placed on instruction in the early preschool years. Five teacher clinicians provided daily instruction to 228 children (111 black and 117 Caucasian) ranging in age from 2 years 8 months to 5 years 11 months. The instruction, designed to stimulate and enhance the development of linguistic skills, affected the children's performance positively in a number of areas. Not only did linguistic functioning improve, but intellectual and visual-perceptive functioning also showed significant gains.

Khatena (1971) taught disadvantaged preschool children to think creatively with pictures. According to his findings, children as young as five or six have the cognitive development to handle nonverbal material more creatively than verbal material. He stresses the point that disadvantaged children need early creative and intellectual experiences to provide them with the strength to combat and overcome the negative forces they inevitably face as they progress to higher grade levels in school.

COMPENSATORY EDUCATION

The U.S. Office of Education's Head Start program was the first massive attempt to alleviate the condition of the socially and culturally disadvantaged child. Educational research had already pointed out that children from poor economic and social environments were preconditioned to failure in school. Head Start was designed to provide such children formally with what the middle-class child already had—language skills; familiarity with books, toys, and games; and positive feelings about school and teachers.

The original Head Start programs were brief, intensive summer sessions. In the belief that the preschool years are by far the most crucial, the focus was on three- to five-year-olds. It was expected that intensive enrichment experiences in this preschool period should suffice to carry a child through the grades. However, follow-up studies of the summer programs (and of later full-year programs) revealed that gains in IQ and achievement, though apparently significant in the short ter ., did not hold up well through first and second grades (Jensen, 1969). In the words of Harold Howe, U.S. Commissioner of Education during the Johnson administration: "If the preschool experience was not bolstered by superlative education in the primary grades, it could do more harm than good." This evaluation led to an expanded "compensatory education" program featuring small classes, enriched curricula, and parental involvement through the third grade. Until recently, educational theory as well as lack of funds made the third grade the upper limit of the Head Start program, but a follow-through program has now been initiated for the intermediate and upper elementary grades.

A project undertaken in Milwaukee, Wisconsin, in 1964 developed research evidence that, while early environment has a powerful impact on a child's intellectual growth, a slum environment does not necessarily form a lifetime trap for the disadvantaged child (Strickland, 1971). The area selected for the study was the residential section of Milwaukee, which, according to Census data, had the lowest median family income, the greatest population density per housing unit, and the most dilapidated housing in the city. It was, in short, a "classic urban slum." In the first stage, it was discovered that the lower the mother's IQ, the greater the likelihood of the child's scoring low on intelligence tests. Using mother's IQ as a guide, the investigators selected a group of children from birth to four years of age who appeared to be close to mental retardation. Two-thirds of these children were placed in an experimental group and one-third in the control group. The experimental children received intensive enrichment experiences under the tutelage of highly competent teachers, chosen especially for their capacity for sensitive interaction with infants and small children and their ability to work within a system of special instruction that was both structured and flexible, requiring both discipline and initiative. The children in the control group followed the normal educational route.

Over a period of four years, the experimental group made gains in many aspects of social, emotional, and intellectual development. "At 42 months of age, the children in the active-stimulation program measured an average of 33 IQ points higher than the children in the control group, with some of them registering IQ's as high as 135." Many children who were classified as potentially retarded eventually came to learn and behave like normal, intelligent children. Equally remarkable is the fact that the children in the experimental program were learning at a rate faster than the national norm for their age peers (Strickland, 1971). Although the children became somewhat "testwise," and research findings from the project require further analysis, there appears to be little question that the enrichment activities greatly improved the children's performance. This study is consistent with others in supporting the conclusion that preschool enrichment programs often have the effect of revealing real talent and motivation among seemingly bland and backward children. What is not clearly known is how to guarantee continuance of this intellectual and social growth over a period of years.

Although the trend is running strongly in favor of preschool "intervention" strategies—especially for the socially disadvantaged—there is some opposition to the concept. In a comprehensive summary of research, Moore, Moon, and Moore (1972) argue not only that the costs of early schooling are formidable but that the results can be damaging to the children. Their conclusions are based on three types of research: (1) studies comparing early and later school entrants; (2) neurophysiological research, including brain changes that affect vision, hearing, cognition, etc.; and (3) maternal-deprivation studies. The authors suggest that cultural enrichment should be provided for very young children through parental education and the development of home schools rather than in school settings away from the home.

SECONDARY SCHOOL

Within the classroom, there must be increased emphasis on communication skills. English courses, for example, should concentrate more on developing students' abilities in speaking, writing, and listening and give less emphasis to traditional literature. Speech courses should provide the skills and practice to enable the disadvantaged teenager to "sell himself," for the deprived child needs a positive self-concept and social adroitness in order to function effectively in the larger world of business and industry.

There should be increased emphasis not only on programs to correct reading deficiencies but also on developmental reading (increasing speed and study skills) for those children who already have a basic grasp of reading. By building on his natural interests—even at the cost of including some "sensational" material—the teacher should make every effort to get him "hooked on books." Small groups of adolescents can read certain books together and then have seminar-type discussions of what they have read. The emphasis should be placed on contemporary issues, events, and ideas.

More "human relations" courses should be offered at the high-school level, especially to socially disadvantaged adolescents, who are dropout-prone. Frequent opportunities should be provided within the classroom context for youngsters to discuss and evaluate the meaning of school and the curriculum, of the rules and regulations, and of various trends of modern life—without censure from the teacher. One of the characteristics of middle-class-oriented teachers is that they interpret the complaints of a middle-class student as "critical thinking" but the gripes of a disadvantaged kid as "hostility."

More courses should be provided on a pass-fail basis to give the socially disadvantaged youth some experiences in a noncompetitive situation. He should be involved in setting some of the goals and in deciding what learning activities are appropriate for him, so that the responsibility for meeting the objectives are also his.

Emphasis should be placed on learning activities that stress action and physical involvement, such as role playing.

Tape-recording devices should be used so that children can hear their own speech patterns and vocabulary and can work at speech improvement independently.

The socially disadvantaged youth needs greater exposure to museums, zoos, music, and other "cultural" experiences, with heavy emphasis on their relevance to contemporary life from the point of view of the disadvantaged themselves.

Students should be used as tutors whenever possible. A youngster with learning difficulties who nevertheless has some achievement can be valuable in teaching others, at the same time building his own self-image as a person of worth and importance.

Finally, bright, talented, curious youth from the culturally deprived classes should be identified and nurtured, for teachers run the risk of viewing *all* disadvantaged children as slow learners.

EXPLORING THE POSITIVE VALUES
OF LOW-SEC CHILDREN

Children from lower-social-class families bring positive values and attitudes to school. If these values can be integrated into the curriculum and activities of the classroom, they can contribute to the educational enrichment of all the children in the school.

Most disadvantaged youth are forced to develop responsible, adaptive behavior in practical, day-to-day circumstances. A disadvantaged boy may know a great deal about the internal-combustion engine because he has to keep the family car going as long as possible. A girl from a deprived background may be a competent and understanding guardian of younger children because she has had to assume the responsibility for younger siblings. Furthermore, these youth know something about the hard realities of economic and social institutions. They may know something about illegitimacy. They may know what it is like to be evicted or to be suddenly out of work. They are often acquainted with social-security provisions and unemployment-insurance regulations, with workingmen's compensation, welfare practices, and the services and sorrows of large hospitals. Through the pain and ugliness, the cruelty and compassion he might have seen, the disadvantaged child may have acquired patience and a resolute courage—values of inestimable worth. He exists in an environmental classroom where the chief subjects are "people psychology" and street-corner economics.

Many disadvantaged children early in life develop a sense of self-sufficiency, often as a result of their less firmly structured family life, the absence of reliable father figures, and the autonomous nature of many youthful peer associations. It is not uncommon for such youth—boys, especially—to leave the house in the morning and wander blocks and even miles from home, whereas middle-class children tend to be under close surveillance by their parents. This sense of self-direction and independence often leads to conflict when school authorities attempt to control, supervise, and direct youthful willfulness.

Lower-class youth are often ingenious in solving and manipulating practical problems. Many of them are money-wise, frugal, and enterprising—forever buying, selling, bargaining, and setting up informal business arrangements. They often know how to utilize materials at hand for their projects. They roam the alleys and industrial areas for utilizable wood, metal, machine parts, and so on.

Young people from a working-class environment tend to develop especially strong feelings of identification with their peers. Peer associations are in fact the core of the values and attitudes of culturally and socially disadvantaged youths. But peer-group loyalty can also be a source of hostility and resistance to the standards and authority of a school if the school fails to provide opportunities for expression, recognition, respect, and some measure of hope and success for the disadvantaged. School officials at the high-school level especially are often vexed because so many adolescents seem to have so little "school spirit." The "spirit" is there, of course, but not so much toward the school as toward other youths with whom the disadvantaged youngster shares values and attitudes. Perhaps perceptive teachers and administrators should concentrate on building constructive learning activities around these peer affiliations.

THE TEACHER-STUDENT RELATIONSHIP: THE CRITICAL MASS

There is no question that the "critical mass" essential to teaching disadvantaged children is the teacher himself. How the teacher teaches —his techniques, materials, measurement and evaluation procedures, and·so forth—is very important, of course. But the electricity, the vital force that ultimately reaches and changes these children, is the positive attitude that the teacher has toward his role and that he projects to the children. The teacher's expectations constitute a ı omnipresent and effective environmental network that affects the achievement of all pupils, but especially those for whom learning is difficult (Finn, 1972).

To become fully effective with socially and culturally disadvantaged children, the teacher must first come to terms with himself—his capacities, values, life-style, and perceptual biases—because when he enters the classroom he faces a moment of truth. He has to believe fervently and honestly that, although his influence on these hard-to-teach children may really be quite limited, nevertheless he is a positive force in their lives. He cannot fully or even partially solve the problems that disadvantaged children encounter. But he can provide hope and inspiration, which may lead many of them to develop better ways of learning and living.

The teacher must ask himself—honestly: "Is this where I *really* want to be?" Would he rather utilize his talents somewhere else— perhaps in a school whose children and social environment are closer to what he is familiar with and easier to handle? The prospective teacher should not feel guilty if he is drawn to more motivated students. But it should be clearly understood that anyone who chooses to teach disadvantaged children just to hold a job, as a temporary step to something else, from curiosity, or what have you, will inevitably be a poor teacher—and a profoundly frustrated, dissatisfied human being. In many subtle ways, "playing the role" of a sincere and dedicated teacher will stand revealed as a façade only. In no other teaching situation is coming to grips with one's self so essential as in the teaching of disadvantaged, minority-group children.

REFERENCES

American Education, 1973. July, 9(6), 33.
ARGYLE, M. 1958. *Religious behavior*. London: Routledge & Kegan Paul.
BARATZ, J. C. 1973. Educational considerations for teaching standard

English to Negro children. In T. W. Hipple (ed.), *Readings for teaching English in secondary schools.* New York: Macmillan.

BAZELI, F. P. 1971. Educating teachers for the inner city. In P. A. Dionisopoulos (ed.), *Racism in America.* De Kalb, Ill.: Northern Illinois University Press.

BLOOM, B. S. 1964. *Stability and change in human characteristics.* New York: Wiley.

BUTTERS, R. R. 1972. A linguistic view of Negro intelligence. *The Clearing House, 46,* 259–63.

CAZDEN, C. B. 1973. Problems for education: Language as curriculum content and learning environment. *Daedalus, 102*(3), 135–48.

CHARNOFSKY, S. 1971. *Educating the powerless.* Belmont, Calif.: Wadsworth.

CROW, L. D., W. I. MURRAY, and H. H. SMYTHE. 1966. *Educating the culturally deprived.* New York: David McKay.

DAVIDSON, H. H., and G. LANG. 1960. Children's perceptions of teachers' feelings toward them. *Journal of Experimental Education, 20,* 107–18.

DEUTSCH, C. P. 1967. Learning in the disadvantaged. In M. Deutsch *et al., The disadvantaged child.* New York: Basic Books.

DOUVAN, E. 1956. Social status and success strivings. *Journal of Abnormal and Social Psychology, 52,* 219–23.

ERICKSON, E. L., C. E. BRYAN, and L. WALKER. 1972. The educability of dominant groups. *Phi Delta Kappan, 53,* 319–21.

FINN, J. D. 1972. Expectations and the educational environment. *Review of Educational Research, 42,* 387–410.

FRAZIER, A. 1964. A research proposal to develop the language skills of children with poor backgrounds. In A. Jeweh, J. Mersand, and D. V. Gunduson (eds.), *Improving English skills of culturally different youth in large cities.* U.S. Department of Health, Education, and Welfare Bulletin No. 5. Washington, D.C.: U.S. Government Printing Office, 69–79.

GORDON, E. W. 1965. Characteristics of socially disadvantaged children. *Review of Educational Research,* December, 35(5), 377–88.

HOLLINGSHEAD, A. B., and F. C. REDLICH. 1958. *Social class and mental illness.* New York: Wiley & Sons.

HUNT, J. McV. 1961. *Intelligence and experience.* New York: Ronald Press.

JENSEN, A. R. 1969. How much can we boost I.Q. and scholastic achievement? *Harvard Educational Review,* Winter, 39(1), 1–123.

JOHNSON, K. R., and H. D. SIMONS. 1972. Black children and reading: What teachers need to know. *Phi Delta Kappan, 53,* 288–90.

KAGAN, J. 1973. Speech presented before the annual meeting of the American Association for the Advancement of Science, Washington, D.C., January.

KAHL, J. A. 1957. *The American class structure.* New York: Holt, Rinehart & Winston.

KELLER, S. 1962. The social world of the urban slum child: Some early findings. *American Journal of Orthopsychiatry, 33,* 27–34.

KENT, N., and D. R. DAVIS. 1957. Discipline in the home and intellectual development. *British Journal of Medical Psychology*, 30, 27–34.

KHATENA, J. 1971. Teaching disadvantaged preschool children to think creatively with pictures. *Journal of Educational Psychology*, 62, 384–86.

KOHN, M. L. 1968. Social class and schizophrenia: A critical review. *Psychiatric Research*, 6, 155–73.

LABOV, W. 1972. Academic ignorance and Black intelligence. *Atlantic Monthly*, 229, 59–67.

McCARTHY, J. L. G. 1969. Changing parent attitudes and improving language and intellectual abilities of culturally disadvantaged four-year-old children through parent involvement. *Contemporary Education*, 40(3), 166–68.

MACCOBY, E. E., R. E. MATHEWS, and A. S. MORTON. 1954. Youth and political change. *Public Opinion Quarterly*, 18, 23–99.

McCONNELL, F., K. B. HORTON, and B. R. SMITH. 1969. Language development and cultural disadvantagement. *Exceptional Children*, 35, 597–606.

McKINLEY, D. G. 1964. *Social class and family life*. New York: Free Press, 152–66.

MARWIT, S. J., K. L. MARWIT, and J. J. BOSWELL. 1972. Negro children's use of nonstandard grammar. *Journal of Educational Psychology*, 63, 218–24.

MOORE, R. S., R. D. MOON, and D. R. MOORE. 1972. The California report: Early schooling for all? *Phi Delta Kappan*, June, 53(10), 615–21.

NEALE, D. C., and J. M. PROSHEK. 1967. School-related attitudes of culturally disadvantaged elementary school children. *Journal of Educational Psychology*, 58, 238–44.

PROVENCE, S., and R. C. LIPTON. 1962. *Infants in institutions*. New York: International University Press.

RASPBERRY, W. 1970. Should ghettoese be accepted? *Educational Leadership*, 59, 30–31, 61–62.

RIST, R. C. 1970. Student social class and teacher expectations: The self-fulfilling prophecy in ghetto education. *Harvard Educational Review*, August, 411–49.

STRICKLAND, S. P. 1971. Can slum children learn? *American Education*, 7(6), 3–7.

WAGNER, A. E. 1909. Retardation and elimination in the schools of Mauch Chunk township. *Psychological Clinic*, 3, 164.

WARNER, W. L., M. MEEKER, and K. EELLS. 1949. *Social class in America*. Chicago: Science Research Associates.

WHITE, W. F. 1969. *Psychosocial principles applied to the classroom*. New York: McGraw-Hill.

WRIGHT, L. 1973. The bilingual education movement at the crossroads. *Phi Delta Kappan*, 55 (3), 183–86.

ZIGLER, E., and P. KANZER. 1962. The effectiveness of two classes of verbal reinforcers on the performance of middle- and lower-class children. *Journal of Personality*, 30, 157–63.

Bibliographies

Chapter One

AUSUBEL, D. P., *Educational Psychology: A Cognitive View*. Holt, Rinehart & Winston, 1965.
CRONBACH, L. J., *Educational Psychology*. Hart-Davis, 2nd ed., 1968.
HEBB, D. O. *A Text-book of Psychology*. Saunders, 2nd ed., 1966.
LOVELL, K., *Educational Psychology and Children*. Univ. of London Press, 10th ed., 1970.
O'CONNELL, B., *Aspects of Learning*. Allen & Unwin, UEB Series, 1973.
OESER, O., *Teacher, Pupil and Task*. Tavistock Publications, 1966.
PEEL, E. A., *The Psychological Basis of Education*. Oliver & Boyd, 2nd ed., 1962.
STONES, E., *Introduction to Educational Psychology*. Methuen, 1966.
WALL, W. D. and VARMA, V. P. (eds), *Advances in Educational Psychology*. Univ. of London Press, 1972.

Chapter Two

BIGGE, M. L., *Learning Theories for Teachers*. Harper & Row, 1964.
BORGER, R. & SEABORNE, A. E. M., *Psychology of Learning*. Penguin, 1966.
DE BONO, E., *Children Solve Problems*. Allen Lane, 1972.
ELLIS, H., *The Transfer of Learning*. Macmillan, 1965.
GAGNE, R. M., *Conditions of Learning*. Holt-Blond, 2nd ed., 1970.
HEBB, D. O., *The Organization of Behaviour*. Free Press, Collier-Macmillan, 1965.
HILGARD, E. R., *Theories of Learning*. Methuen, 1958.
HUNTER, I. M. L., *Memory: Facts and Fallacies*. Penguin, 1957.
JAMES, D. E., *Introduction to Psychology*. Panther, 1970.
LAYCOCK, S. R. and MUNRO, B. C., *Educational Psychology*. Pitman, 1968.

303

LINDGREN, H. C., *Educational Psychology in the Classroom*. J. Wiley, 3rd ed., 1967.

MCFARLAND, H. S. N., *Psychological Theory and Educational Practice*. Routledge, 1971.

O'CONNELL, B., *Aspects of Learning*. Allen & Unwin, UEB Series, 1973.

PINSENT, A., *The Principles of Teaching-Method*. Harrap, 3rd ed, 1969. Chapter 9, 'Transfer of the Effects of Training'.

PITTINGER, O. and GOODING, C., *Learning Theories in Educational Practice*. J. Wiley, 1971.

SLAMECKA, N. J. (ed.), *Human Learning and Memory*. O.U.P., 1967.

THOMSON, R., *Psychology and Thinking*. Penguin, 1958.

THYNE, J. M., *Psychology of Learning and Techniques of Teaching*. Univ. of London Press, 2nd ed., 1966.

VALENTINE, C. W., *Latin: Its Place and Value in Education*. Univ. of London Press, 1935.

Chapter Three

BALDWIN, L. A., *Theories of Child Development*. J. Wiley, 1967.

BEARD, Ruth M., *An Outline of Piaget's Developmental Psychology*. Routledge, 1969.

BREARLEY, M. and HITCHFIELD, E. *A Teacher's Guide to Reading Piaget*. Routledge, 1966.

BRUNER, J. S., *The Process of Education*. Harvard Univ. Press, 1960.

BRUNER, J. S., *The Relevance of Education*. Allen & Unwin, 1972.

FLAVELL, J. H., *The Developmental Psychology of Jean Piaget*. Van Nostrand, 1963.

FURTH, H. G., *Piaget for Teachers*. Prentice-Hall, 1970.

GESELL, A., *The First Five Years of Life*. Harper, 1940.

GESELL, A. et al., *The Child from Five to Ten*. Hamish Hamilton, 1946.

GESELL, A. et al., *Youth: The Years from Ten to Sixteen*. Hamish Hamilton, 1956.

HADFIELD, J. A., *Childhood and Adolescence*. Penguin, 1962.

HURLOCK, E. B., *Child Development*. McGraw-Hill, 1964.

KATZ, D., *Gestalt Psychology*. Methuen, 1951.

KOFFKA, K., *Principles of Gestalt Psychology*. Routledge, 1935.

LUNZER, E. A., *Recent Studies in Britain Based on the Work of Jean Piaget*. N.F.E.R., 1960.

LUNZER, E. A., *Development in Learning: The Regulation of Behaviour*. Staples Press, 1968.

MCFARLAND, H. S. N., *Human Learning: A Developmental Analysis*. Routledge, 1969.

MUSSEN, P., *The Psychological Development of the Child*. Prentice-Hall, 1965.

O'CONNELL, B., *Aspects of Learning*. Allen & Unwin, UEB Series, 1973.

RICHMOND, P. G., *Introduction to Piaget*. Routledge, 1970.

SANDSTRÖM, C. I., *The Psychology of Childhood and Adolescence*. Penguin, 1968.

SIGEL, I. E. and HOOPER, F. H., *Logical Thinking in Children*. Holt, Rinehart & Winston, 1970.

VALENTINE, C. W., *The Normal Child*. Penguin, 1956.

WERTHEIMER, M., *Productive Thinking*. Tavistock Publications, 1961.

Chapter Four

BARNES, D. *et al.*, *Language, the Learner and the School*. Penguin, revised ed., 1971.
BEREITER, C. *et al.*, *Teaching Disadvantaged Children in the Pre-School*. Prentice-Hall, 1966.
BERNSTEIN, B., *Class, Codes and Control: Vol. 1*. Routledge, 1971.
BERNSTEIN, B. (ed.), *Class, Codes and Control: Vol. 2*. Routledge, 1973.
BRANDIS, W. and HENDERSON, D. (eds), *Social Class, Language and Communication*. Routledge, 1969.
BRITTON, J. N., *Language and Learning*. Allen Lane, Penguin Press, 1970.
BRUNER, J. S., *The Relevance of Education*. Allen & Unwin, 1972. Chapter 9, 'Poverty and Childhood'.
CARROLL, J. B. (ed.), *Language, Thought and Reality: Selected Writings of B. L. Whorf*. J. Wiley, 1956.
CASHDAN, A. *et al.*, *Language in Education: A Source Book*. Routledge & The Open University, 1972.
CHURCH, J., *Language and the Discovery of Reality*. Random House, 1961.
CLARK, Margaret M., *Reading Difficulties in Schools*. Penguin, 1970.
CRYSTAL, D., *Linguistics*. Penguin, 1971.
DEUTSCH, M. *et al.*, *The Disadvantaged Child*. Basic Books, 1967.
DEUTSCH, M. *et al.* (eds), *Social Class, Race and Psychological Development*. Holt, 1968.
DOWNING, J. A., *The i.t.a. Reading Experiment*. Evans, 1964.
DOWNING, J. A. *et al.*, *Reading Readiness*. Univ. of London Press, 1971.
FANTINI, M. D. and WEINSTEIN, G., *The Disadvantaged: Challenge to Education*. Harper & Row, 1968.
FRIES, C. C., *Linguistics and Reading*. Holt, Rinehart & Winston, 1962.
GIGLIOLI, P. P. (ed.), *Language and Social Context*. Penguin, 1972.
HALLIDAY, M. A. K. *et al.*, *The Linguistic Sciences and Language Teaching*. Longmans, 1964.
HASLAM, K. R., *Learning in the Primary School*. Allen & Unwin, UEB Series, 1971. Chapter 4.
LAWTON, D., *Social Class, Language and Education*. Routledge, 1968.
LEFEVRE, C. A., *Linguistics and the Teaching of Reading*. McGraw-Hill, 1964.
LEWIS, M. M., *Language, Thought and Personality in Infancy and Childhood*. Harrap, 1963.
LEWIS, M. M., *Language and the Child*. N.F.E.R., 1969.
LURIA, A. R. and YUDOVICH, F. J., *Speech and the Development of Mental Processes in the Child*. Staples Press, 1959.
LYONS, J., *New Horizons in Linguistics*. Penguin, 1970.
MOYLE, D., *The Teaching of Reading*. Ward Lock Educational, 2nd ed., 1970.
OLDFIELD, R. C. and MARSHALL, J. C. (eds), *Language*. Penguin, 1968.
ROBERTS, G. R., *Reading in Primary Schools*. Routledge, 1969.
TANSLEY, A. E., *Reading and Remedial Reading*. Routledge, 1967.
TAYLOR, Joy, *Reading and Writing in the First School*. Allen & Unwin, UEB Series, 1973.
TOUGH, Joan, *Focus on Meaning*. Allen & Unwin, UEB Series, 1973.
VERNON, M. D., *Reading and its Difficulties*. C.U.P., 1971.
VYGOTSKY, V., *Thought and Language*. M.I.T. Press, 1962.

Chapter Five

ALLPORT, F. H., *Theories of Perception and the Concept of Structure*. J. Wiley, 1961.

BLAKE, R. R. and RAMSEY, G. V. (eds), *Perception: an Approach to Personality*. Ronald Press, 1951.

BRUNER, J. S., *The Process of Education*. Harvard Univ. Press, 1960.

BRUNER, J. S., *The Relevance of Education*. Allen & Unwin, 1972.

ERIKSON, E. H., 'The Problem of Ego Identity'. *Journal of the American Psychoanalytic Association*, Vol. 4, 1956, pp. 56–121.

FISKE, D. W. and MADDI, S. R., *Functions of Early Experience*. Dorsey Press, 1961.

GOFFMAN, E., *Stigma*. Penguin, 1968.

GOFFMAN, E., *The Presentation of Self in Everyday Life*. Allen Lane, Penguin Press, 1969.

HOLDEN, A., *Teachers as Counsellors*. Constable, 1971.

HUGHES, P. M., *Guidance and Counselling in Schools*. Pergamon, 1971.

LEWIN, K., *A Dynamic Theory of Personality*. McGraw-Hill, 1935.

MACMURRAY, J., *The Self as Agent*. Faber, 1957.

MEAD, G. H., *Mind, Self and Society*. Univ. of Chicago Press, 1934.

MERLEAU-PONTY, M., *The Phenomenology of Perception*. Routledge, 1962.

MILLER, C. H., *Foundations of Guidance*, Harper & Row, 2nd ed., 1971.

MOORE, B. M., *Guidance in Comprehensive Schools: Study of Five Systems*. N.F.E.R.

O'CONNELL, B., *Aspects of Learning*. Allen & Unwin, UEB Series, 1973. Chapter 3, 'Insightful Learning'.

PIAGET, J., *The Construction of Reality in the Child*. Routledge, 1955.

ROLPH, C., *Personal Identity*. M. Joseph, 1957.

ROSENBERG, M., *Society and the Adolescent Self-Image*. Princeton Univ. Press, 1965.

ROWE, A., *School as a Guidance Community*. Ward Lock Educational, 1972.

SOLLEY, C. M. and MURPHY, G., *Development of the Perceptual World*. Basic Books, 1960.

STORR, A., *The Integrity of the Personality*. Penguin, 1963.

TAGUIRI, R. and PETRULLO, L., *Person Perception and Interpersonal Behaviour*. Stanford Univ. Press, 1958.

VERNON, M. D., *A Further Study of Visual Perception*. C.U.P., 1954.

VERNON, M. D., *The Psychology of Perception*. Penguin, 1968.

Chapter Six

ANDERSON, H. H. (ed.), *Creativity and its Cultivation*. Harper & Row, 1959.

BURT, C. L., *Mental and Scholastic Tests*. Staples Press, 1947.

BUTCHER, H. J., *Human Intelligence, Its Nature and Assessment*. Methuen, 1967.

CATTELL, R. B. and BUTCHER, H. J., *The Prediction of Achievement and Creativity*. Bobbs-Merrill, 1968.

CROPLEY, A. J., *Creativity*. Longman, 1967.

EELLS, K. *et al.*, *Intelligence and Cultural Differences*. Univ. of Chicago Press, 1951.

EYSENCK, H. J., *Dimensions of Personality*. Routledge, 1947.

EYSENCK, H. J., *The Structure of Human Personality*. Methuen, 1960.

EYSENCK, H. J., *The Biological Basis of Personality*. C. C. Thomas, 1967.

FOSTER, J., *Creativity and the Teacher*. Macmillan, 1972.

GHISELIN, B., *The Creative Process: A Symposium*. Mentor Books, 1955.

GORDON, W. J. J., *Synectics: The Development of Creative Capacity*. Harper, 1961.

GOWAN, J. C. *et al.* (eds), *Creativity, its Educational Implications*. J. Wiley, 1967.

GRUBER, H. E. *et al.* (eds), *Contemporary Approaches to Creative Thinking*. Atherton Press, 1962.

GUILFORD, J. P., *Personality*. McGraw-Hill, 1959.

HUDSON, L., *Contrary Imaginations*. Penguin, 1967.

HUNT, J. McV., *Intelligence and Experience*. Ronald Press, 1961.

JONES, T. P., *Creative Learning in Perspective*. Univ. of London Press, 1972.

LYTTON, H., *Creativity and Education*. Routledge, 1971.

MEADE, J. E. and PARKES, A. S., *Genetic and Environmental Factors in Human Ability*. Oliver & Boyd, 1966.

MOONEY, R. L. and RAZIK, T. A. (eds), *Explorations in Creativity*. Harper & Row, 1967.

OSBORN, A. F., *Applied Imagination: Principles and Procedures of Creative Thinking*. Scribner, 1953.

PIAGET, J., *The Psychology of Intelligence*. Routledge, 1950.

RIESMAN, Z., *The Culturally Deprived Child*. Harper & Row, 1962.

SCHOFIELD, H., *Assessment and Testing: An Introduction*. Allen & Unwin, UEB Series, 1972. Chapters 4 and 5.

SHUEY, A. M., *The Testing of Negro Intelligence*. Social Science Press, 2nd ed., 1966.

STEIN, M. I. and HEINZE, S. J. ,*Creativity and the Individual*. Free Press, 1960.

TAYLOR, C. W., *Creativity: Progress and Potentiality*. McGraw-Hill, 1964.

TAYLOR, C. W. (ed.), *Widening Horizons in Creativity*. J. Wiley, 1964.

TAYLOR, C. W. and BARRON, F. (eds), *Scientific Creativity: Its Recognition and Development*. J. Wiley, 1963.

THOMSON, G. H., *Factorial Analysis of Human Ability*. Univ. of London Press, 1950.

THURSTONE, L. L., *Multiple Factor Analysis*. Univ. of Chicago Press, 1947.

TORRANCE, E. P., *Guiding Creative Talent*. Prentice-Hall, 1962.

TORRANCE, E. P., *Rewarding Creative Behaviour*. Prentice-Hall, 1965.

VERNON, P. E., *The Structure of Human Abilities*. Methuen, 1950.

VERNON, P. E., *Intelligence and Attainment Tests*. Univ. of London Press, 1960.

VERNON, P. E. (ed.), *Creativity*. Penguin, 1970.

WALLACH, M. A. and KOGAN, N., *Modes of Thinking in Young Children: A Study of the Creativity-Intelligence Distinction*. Holt, Rinehart & Winston, 1965.

WISEMAN, S., *Education and Environment*. Manchester Univ. Press, 1964.

WISEMAN, S. (ed.), *Intelligence and Ability*. Penguin, 2nd ed., 1967.

Chapter Seven

BANDURA, A. *et al.*, *Adolescent Aggression*. Ronald Press, 1959.

BROOKS, R., *Bright Delinquents*. N.F.E.R., 1972.

BUSH, R. N., *The Teacher-Pupil Relationship*. Prentice-Hall, 1954.

CARTWRIGHT, D. (ed.), *Group Dynamics*. Tavistock Publications, 1955.

CUTTS, N. E. *et al.*, *Teaching the Disorderly Pupil*. Longmans, 1957.

DOLLARD, J. and MILLER, N. E., *Personality and Psychotherapy*. McGraw-Hill, 1950.

EGGLESTON, S. J., *The Social Context of the School*. Routledge, 1967.

ERIKSON, E. H., *Childhood and Society*. Penguin, 1965.

FANTINI, M. D. and WEINSTEIN, G., *The Disadvantaged: Challenge to Education*. Harper & Row, 1968.

FLEMING, C. M., *Adolescence: Its Social Psychology*. Routledge, 2nd ed., 1962.

FREUD, Anna, *The Ego and the Mechanisms of Defence*. International Universities Press, 1946.

FYVEL, T. R., *The Insecure Offenders*. Penguin, 1963.

HADFIELD, J. A., *Psychology and Mental Health*. Allen & Unwin, 1950.

HARGREAVES, D. H., *Social Relations in a Secondary School*. Routledge, 1967.

HORNEY, Karen, *The Neurotic Personality of Our Time*. Routledge, 1937.

LEWIN, K., *A Dynamic Theory of Personality*. McGraw-Hill, 1935.

LOVELL, K., *Educational Psychology and Children*. Univ. of London Press, 10th ed, 1970.

MAHL, G. F., *Psychological Conflict and Defence*. Harcourt Brace, 1961.

MARCH, J. G. (ed.), *Handbook of School Organization*. Rand McNally, 1965.

MAYS, J. B., *On the Threshold of Delinquency*. Liverpool Univ. Press, 2nd ed., 1964.

MORRISH, I., *The Sociology of Education: An Introduction*. Allen & Unwin, UEB Series, 1972.

MUSGRAVE, P. W., *The School as an Organization*. Macmillan, 1968.

MUSGROVE, F., *Youth and the Social Order*. Routledge, 1964.

OESER, O. (ed.), *Pupil, Teacher and Task*. Tavistock Publications, 1955.

PRINGLE, W. L. KELLMER, *Deprivation and Education*. Longmans, 1965.

QUAY, H. C., *Children's Behaviour Disorders*. Van Nostrand, 1968.

REISSMAN, F., *Culturally Deprived Children*. Harper & Row, 1962.

ROUCEK, J. (ed.), *Slow-Learner*. P. Owen, 1970.

SEGAL, S. S., *Teaching Backward Pupils*. Evans Bros., 1963.

SEGAL, S. S., *No Child is Ineducable*. Pergamon, 1967.

SHIPMAN, M. D., *Sociology of the School*. Longmans, 1968.

TANSLEY, A. E. and GULLIFQRD, R., *Education of Slow Learning Children*. Routledge, 1960.

VALENTINE, C. W., *The Difficult Child and the Problem of Discipline*. Methuen, 1950.

WALLER, W., *The Sociology of Teaching*. J. Wiley, 1932.

WILLIAMS, A. A., *Basic Studies for the Slow Learner*. Methuen Educational, 1970.

Chapter Eight

ATKINSON, J. W. *et al.*, *The Achievement Motive*. Appleton-Century-Crofts, 1953.

ATKINSON, J. W. (ed.), *Motives in Fantasy, Action and Society*. Van Nostrand, 1958.

BINDRA, D., *Motivation: A Systematic Reinterpretation*. Ronald Press, 1959.

BINDRA, D. and STEWART, J. (eds), *Motivation: Selected Readings.* Penguin, 2nd ed., 1971.

BROWN, J. S., *The Motivation of Behaviour.* McGraw-Hill, 1961.

BRUNER, J. S., *The Process of Education.* Harvard Univ. Press, 1960. Chapter 5, 'Motives for Learning'.

CATTELL, R. B., *Personality and Motivation Structure and Measurement.* Harrap, 1958.

HILGARD, E. R., Human Motives and the Concept of the Self. *American Psychologist*, Vol. 4, 1949, pp. 374–82.

JAMES, D. E., *Introduction to Psychology.* Panther, 1970. Chapter 6, 'The Forces which Produce Behaviour'.

MCCLELLAND, D. C., *Studies in Motivation.* Appleton-Century-Crofts, 1955.

MCDOUGALL, W., *The Energies of Men.* Methuen, 1932.

MCDOUGALL, W. *An Introduction to Social Psychology.* Methuen, 1950.

MASLOW, A. H., *Motivation and Personality.* Harper, 1954.

MURRAY, E. J., *Motivation and Emotion.* Prentice-Hall, 1964.

O'CONNELL, B., *Aspects of Learning.* Allen & Unwin, UEB Series, 1973. Chapter 6, 'Motivation, Emotion and Learning'.

PETERS, R. S., *The Concept of Motivation.* Routledge, 2nd ed., 1965.

PINSENT, A., *The Principles of Teaching-Method.* Harrap, 3rd ed., 1969. Section II, 'Motivation and Interest', pp. 77–154.

SARNOFF, I., *Personality Dynamics and Development.* J. Wiley, 1962.

SKINNER, B. F., *Science and Human Behaviour.* Free Press, 1965.

TEEVAN, R. C. and BIRNEY, R. C. (eds), *Theories of Motivation and Learning.* Van Nostrand, 1964.

TOLMAN, E. C., *Purposive Behaviour in Animals and Men.* Appleton-Century-Crofts, 1932.

VERNON, M. D., *Human Motivation.* C.U.P., 1969.

YOUNG, P. T., *Motivation and Emotion.* J. Wiley, 1961.

Chapter Nine

ANDERSON, R. C. *et al.* (eds), *Readings in the Psychology of Cognition.* Holt, Rinehart & Winston, 1965.

BIGGE, M. L., *Learning Theories for Teachers.* Harper, 1964.

BRUNER, J. S., *Toward a Theory of Instruction.* Harvard Univ. Press, 1966.

CALLENDER, P., *Programmed Learning: Its Development and Structure.* Longmans, 1969.

DAVIS, R. A., *Learning in the Schools.* Wadsworth, 1968.

FERSTER, C. B. and SKINNER, B. F., *Schedules of Reinforcement.* Appleton-Century-Crofts, 1957.

GAGNE, R. M., *Conditions of Learning.* Holt-Blond, 2nd ed., 1970.

GERARD, R. W. (ed.), *Computers and Education.* McGraw-Hill, 1967.

GOODMAN, R., *Programmed Learning and Teaching Machines.* English Universities Press, 3rd ed., 1967.

HASLAM, K. R., *Learning in the Primary School.* Allen & Unwin, UEB Series, 1971.

HILL, W., *Learning, a Survey of Psychological Interpretations.* Methuen, 2nd ed., 1972.

HOLT, J., *How Children Fail.* Penguin, 1964.

HOLT, J., *How Children Learn*. Penguin, 1967.

JACKSON, B., *Streaming, an Education System in Miniature*. Routledge, 1964.

JAMES, D. E., *Introduction to Psychology*. Panther, 1970. Chapter 7, 'The Processes through which Behaviour Changes'.

JENSEN, A. R., *Educability and Group Differences*. Methuen, 1973.

KLAUSMEIER, H. J. and GOODWIN, W. L., *Learning and Human Abilities*. Harper & Row, 3rd ed., 1971.

O'CONNELL, B., *Aspects of Learning*. Allen & Unwin, UEB Series, 1973. Chapter 2, 'Operant Conditioning and Programmed Learning'.

PINSENT, A., *The Principles of Teaching-Method*. Harrap, 3rd ed., 1969. Section III, 'Transfer of the Effects of Training', pp. 258–417.

RICHARDSON, J. E., *The Environment of Learning*. Nelson, 1967.

RICHMOND, W. K., *Concept of Educational Technology*. Weidenfeld & Nicolson, 1970.

SKINNER, B. F., *Cumulative Record*. Methuen, 1959.

SLUCKIN, W., *Imprinting and Early Learning*. Methuen, 1964.

SMITH, K. U. *et al.*, *Cybernetic Principles of Learning and Educational Design*. Holt-Bond, 1966.

STEPHENS, J. M., *Psychology of Classroom Learning*. Holt-Blond, 1965.

STONES, E. (ed.), *Readings in Educational Psychology: Learning and Teaching*. Methuen, 1970.

TANSLEY, A. E. and GULLIFORD, R., *The Education of Slow-Learning Children*. Routledge, 1960.

TAYLOR, Joy, *Organising and Integrating the Infant Day*. Allen & Unwin, UEB Series, 1971.

TAYLOR, Joy, *Reading and Writing in the First School*. Allen & Unwin, UEB Series, 1973.

THYNE, J. M., *Psychology of Learning and Techniques of Teaching*. Univ. of London Press, 2nd ed., 1966.

UNWIN, D. and LEEDHAM, J., *Aspects of Educational Technology*. Methuen 1967.

Chapter Ten

CATTELL, R. B., *The Scientific Analysis of Personality*. Penguin, 1965.

CRONBACH, L. J., *Essentials of Psychological Testing*. Harper & Row, 2nd ed., 1964.

FREEMAN, F. S., *Theory and Practice of Psychological Testing*. H. Holt, 1956.

GRONLUND, N. E., *Measurement and Evaluation in Teaching*. Collier-Macmillan, 1971.

GUILFORD, J. P., *Fundamental Statistics in Psychology and Education*. McGraw-Hill, 1950.

KNIGHT, R., *Intelligence and Intelligence Tests*. Methuen, 4th ed,, 1948.

LEWIS, D. G., *Statistical Methods in Education*. Univ. of London Press, 1967.

RAPAPORT, D. *et al.*, *Diagnostic Psychological Testing*. Univ. of London Press, 1971.

REMMERS, H. H. *et al.*, *A Practical Introduction to Measurement and Evaluation*. Harper & Row, 1966.

SCHOFIELD, H., *Assessment and Testing*. Allen & Unwin, UEB Series, 1972.

VERNON, P. E., *Personality Tests and Assessments*. Methuen, 1953.
VERNON, P. E., *Intelligence and Attainment Tests*. Univ. of London Press, 1960.
VERNON, P. E., *Personality Assessment: A Critical Survey*. Methuen, 1964.
VERNON, P. E., *The Structure of Human Abilities*. Methuen, 2nd ed., 1965.

Chapter Eleven

BARKER LUNN, Joan C., *Social Class, Attitudes and Achievement*. N.F.E.R., 1971.
BLYTH, W. A. L., *English Primary Education*. Vols 1 and 2. Routledge, 1965.
BRANDIS, W. and HENDERSON, D., *Social Class, Language and Communication*. Routledge, 1969.
CLEGG, A., *Children in Distress*. Penguin, 1968.
CROWE, Brenda, *The Playground Movement*. Allen & Unwin, 1973.
DAVIS, A., *Social Class Influences on Learning*. Harvard Univ. Press, 1948.
DOUGLAS, J. W. B., *The Home and the School*. Panther, 1967.
ERIKSON, E. H., *Childhood and Society*. Penguin, 1965.
FLOUD, J. E. *et al.*, *Social Class and Educational Opportunity*. Heinemann, 1956.
FORD, Julienne, *Social Class and the Comprehensive School*. Routledge, 1969.
GREEN, L., *Parents and Teachers*. Allen & Unwin, 1968.
JACKSON, B. *et al.*, *Education and the Working Class*. Penguin, 1966.
KOHL, H., *36 Children*. Penguin, 1971.
LAWTON, D., *Social Class, Language and Education*. Routledge, 1968.
MAYS, J. B., *Education and the Urban Child*. Liverpool Univ. Press, 1962.
MORRISH, I., *The Sociology of Education: An Introduction*. Allen & Unwin, UEB Series, 1972.
MORRISON, A. and McINTYRE, D., *Schools and Socialization*. Penguin, 1971.
NEWSON, J. and E., *Patterns of Infant Care in an Urban Community*. Penguin, 1965.
PRINGLE, W. L. KELLMER, *Able Misfits*. Longmans, 1970.
RIBICH, T. I., *Education and Poverty*. Allen & Unwin, 1968.
SHIPMAN, M. D., *Sociology of the School*. Longmans, 1968.
SHIPMAN, M. D., *Childhood: A Sociological Perspective*. N.F.E.R., 1972.
WALLER, W., *Sociology of Teaching*. J. Wiley, 1939.

Index

56; steps in, 36–37
Criterion-referenced testing, 263
Cronbach, L. J., 12, 41
Crow, L. D., 280, 300
Cues, 18, 62
Cultural deprivation (*see* Disadvantaged children)
Culture-fair tests, 148–49
Cureton, E. E., 145, 156
Curiosity, 56
Curriculum (*see* Instructional programs)
Curry, R. L., 204, 217
Cybernetics, and the brain, 194

Dallmann, M., 60, 91
D'Andrade, R. D., 204, 218
Davidson, H. H., 288, 300
Davis, A., 148, 156
Davis, D. R., 286, 301
Davis, J. K., 231, 239
Davis, R. A., 240
Davis-Eells Games, 149
Day, L. M., 12, 41
DeBoer, J. J., 60, 91
Decaroli, J., 229, 240
Decoding concept of reading, 60
Defense mechanisms, 169–73; types of, 170–71
Definition, operational, 100
Della-Piana, G. M., 76, 91
Denotative meaning, 85
Dependence (*see* Independence and self-concept)
Derived scores (*see* Norm scores)
Deutsch, C. P., 288, 300
Deutsch, M., 82, 91
Developmental psychology, 46–57, 70–73, 110–14, 162–64, 197–200
Deviation score, 251
Dewey, John, 37, 41
Differentiation, 104
Differentiation hypothesis of cognitive development, 129–30
Directed-discovery teaching, 228
Disadvantaged children: alienation in, 280–81; attitudes of, 280–83, 286–87; and authority, 282; cognitive development of, 285–86, 294; culture of, 276, 283–86, 292–94, 297–98; instructional programs for, 276–99; intelligence of, 131, 147–49; language development of, 81–84, 284–85, 292–94; *vs.* middle-class culture, 277, 283–84; parents of, 286–87; positive values of, 297–98; in preschool, 292–

96; and reading, 81–84; in secondary school, 296–97; teachers and, 276, 287–89, 299; teaching, 81–84, 289–99
Discipline, classroom, 182–83, 226
Discovery learning (*see* Exploratory learning)
Disjunctive concept, 86
Divergent thinking, 129
Dollard, J., 18, 20, 41, 62, 91, 203, 218
Doman, G., 72, 91
Douglass, H. R., 34, 41
Douvan, E., 287, 300
Driscoll, F. G., 184–85
Drives, 18, 61, 195–97; and needs, 197; physiological and psychological, 195; primary and secondary, 196–97
Dropping out, 162
Duncan, C. P., 31, 41
Durkin, D., 71–72, 91
Dykstra, R., 76, 90

Education, U.S.A., 237, 240
Education (*see* Schools)
Educational goals (*see* Instructional objectives)
Educational Policies Commission, 220
Educational psychology, 3–90; behaviorism in, 8–9, 12–40, 61–63, 66–68; cognitive development, 43–58; language development, 54, 59–90; origins of, 3–5; as science, 4–5; and teachers, 8–11, 23–24; trends in, 57–58
Eells, K., 301
Effect, law of, 13
Eischens, R., 234, 240
Ellena, W. J., 10–11
Elliott, A., 202, 217
Ellison, Ralph, 89
Emotional development, 159–85; *vs.* cognitive development, 179–80; and intelligence, 146–47; and language development, 80–81; problems in, 173–79; schools and, 161–62, 166–67, 179–83; teachers and, 176–81; transcendental meditation and, 183–85
Encyclopedia of Educational Research, 23, 41, 60, 91, 152, 156, 208, 217
Endo, G. T., 76, 91
English, nonstandard, 284–85, 292–94
Ennis, P. H., 81, 91
Enrichment (*see* Compensatory education)
Environment (*see also* Experience), 131–33

319 / *Index*

Staats, A. W., 15, 42 62–63, 67, 93
Staats, C. K., 15, 42 62–63, 67
Stages of development (*see* Developmental psychology)
Stains, J. W., 119, 125
Stallings, W. M., 271, 274
Stanchfield, J. M., 72, 93
Standard deviation, 247–48, 252–53
Standard error of measurement (SEM), 247–48
Standardized achievement tests, 263–64
Stanford-Binet Individual Intelligence Scale, 129
Stanford-Binet Intelligence Test, 135–38
Stanines, 261
Stansberry, S. T., 229, 240
Starr, R. J., 229, 241
Statistics, 248–62
Stauffer, R. G., 85, 93
Stedman, J. M., 161, 187
Steiner, G. A., 202, 210, 217
Stern, Wilhelm, 136
Stimulation, deprivation of, 209–10
Stimulus, 14–15; stimulus generalization, 15–16
Stone, L. J., 113, 125
Stouffer, G. A., 175, 177, 187
Strang, R., 78, 93
Stress, responses to, 165–68
Strickland, S. P., 295–96, 301
Stroud, J. B., 61–62, 84, 93
Student involvement, 230–31
Students: academic performance of, 149–52, 162, 213, 215, 233–34; cognitive style of, 313–19; emotional development of, 162; and relevance, 120–21, and teachers, 10, 215–16, 224–25, 230–31, 233–34, 287–89, 299
Subject matter, relevance of, 120–21
Subjectivity (*see* Objectivity)
Success, cumulative nature of, 212–15
Suicide, 161–62
Suitability test, 248, 268–69
Super, D. E., 115–16, 125
Supervision (*see* Discipline, classroom)
Suppes, P., 233, 241
Sutton, H., 71, 93
Systems, homeostasis in, 194–95
Szasz, T. S., 178, 187

Tachistoscope, 79
Tanner, L. N., 187
Teacher aides, 291–92
Teacher-made tests, 264–69
Teachers: and behavior modification, 23–24; and behaviorism, 8–9, 23–24;

and disadvantaged children, 276, 287–89, 299; educational requirements of, 8–9; and emotional development, 176–81; and instructional objectives, 221–22, 224–25; and motivation, 203–4, 215–16; and perceptualism, 9–11; role of, 8–11, 180–81; and self-concept, 119, 181; and students, 10, 215–16, 224–25, 230–31, 233–34, 287–89, 299; teaching style, 10–11, 215–16, 226, 230–31
Teaching machines, 24–26
Tedeschi, J. T., 210–11, 218
Terman, L. M., 131, 136, 146–48, 157
Terminal behavior, 222–23
Test report, 140–43
Tests, 262–74; construction of, 265–69; grading of, 245, 266, 271–74; reliability of, 247–48, 256–58, 266–67; standardized achievement tests, 263–64; suitability of, 248, 268–69; teacher-made tests, 264–69; validity of, 245–47, 257–58, 265–66
Theory, scientific, 4–5
Thomas, W. I., 197, 218
Thompson, R., 12, 42
Thoresen, C. E., 27, 42
Thorndike, E. L., 3, 13–14, 35, 42–44, 86, 205, 218
Thorndike, R. L., 265, 267, 275
Thought (*see* Concept formation)
Thurstone, L. L., 128–29, 157
Thurstone, T. G., 129, 157
Tinker, M. A., 59, 73, 78, 80, 90
Tolor, A., 176, 187
Torrance, E. P., 180, 187, 209, 218
Total immersion (*see* Massed practice)
Tracy, W., 149, 157
Transcendental meditation(TM),183–85
Transfer of training, 33–36, 229–30
Travers, R. M. W., 27, 42
Trial-and-error learning, 13–14
True score, 247–48
Trust, 110, 288–89
Tyler, L. E., 146, 157

Uhl, N. P., 83, 93
Unconditioned response, 14–15
Unconditioned stimulus, 14
Underachievers, 150–52, 215

Valdes, A. L., 238, 241
Validity test: of standardized achievement tests, 263–64; of teacher-made tests, 265; types of, 245–47; validity coefficient, 257–58